FUTURE IMPERFECT

Future Imperfect describes and discusses a variety of technological revolutions that might happen over the next few decades, their implications, and how to deal with them. Topics range from encryption and surveillance through biotechnology and nanotechnology to life extension, mind drugs, virtual reality, and artificial intelligence. One theme of the book is that the future is radically uncertain. Technological changes already begun could lead to more or less privacy than we have ever known; freedom or slavery; effective immortality or the elimination of our species; radical changes in life, marriage, law, medicine, work, and play. We do not know which future will arrive, but it is unlikely to be much like the past. It is worth starting to think about it now.

David D. Friedman is Professor of Law at Santa Clara University, California. After receiving a Ph.D. in theoretical physics at the University of Chicago, he switched fields to economics and taught at Virginia Polytechnic University, the University of California at Irvine, the University of California at Los Angeles, Tulane University, the University of Chicago, and Santa Clara University. A professional interest in the economic analysis of law led to positions at the law schools of the University of Chicago and Cornell and thereafter to his present position, where he developed the course on legal issues of the twenty-first century that led to his writing *Future Imperfect.*

Professor Friedman's first book, *The Machinery of Freedom: Guide to a Radical Capitalism,* was published in 1973, remains in print, and is considered a libertarian classic. He wrote *Price Theory: An Intermediate Text* (1986), *Hidden Order: The Economics of Everyday Life* (1996), and *Law's Order: An Economic Account* (2000). His first work of fiction, *Harald,* was published in 2006.

Professor Friedman's scientific interest in the future is long-standing. The Cypherpunks, an online group responsible for much early thinking about the implications of encryption, included *The Machinery of Freedom* on their list of recommended readings. Professor Friedman's web page, www.davidfriedman.com, averages more than 3,000 visitors a day and his blog, *Ideas,* at http://daviddfriedman.blogspot.com receives about 400 daily visits.

Future Imperfect

Technology and Freedom in an Uncertain World

DAVID D. FRIEDMAN

CAMBRIDGE
UNIVERSITY PRESS

CAMBRIDGE UNIVERSITY PRESS
Cambridge, New York, Melbourne, Madrid, Cape Town, Singapore, São Paulo, Delhi

Cambridge University Press
32 Avenue of the Americas, New York, NY 10013-2473, USA

www.cambridge.org
Information on this title: www.cambridge.org/9780521877329

First published 2008

Printed in the United States of America

A catalog record for this publication is available from the British Library.

Library of Congress Cataloging in Publication Data
Friedman, David D.
Future imperfect : technology and freedom in an uncertain world / David D. Friedman.
p.   cm.
Includes bibliographical references and index.
ISBN 978-0-521-87732-9 (hardback)
1. Technological forecasting.   2. Technology – Social aspects.   I. Title.
T174.F75   2008
303.48′3–dc22   2008000515

ISBN   978-0-521-87732-9 hardback

Contents

PART ONE

PROLOGUE

ONE

Introduction

A few years ago I attended an event where the guest speaker was a Cabinet member. In conversation afterwards, the subject of long-term petroleum supplies came up. He warned that at some point, perhaps a century or so in the future, someone would put his key in his car's ignition, turn it, and nothing would happen – because there would be no gasoline.

What shocked me was not his ignorance of the economics of depletable resources – if we ever run out of gasoline it will be a long, slow process of steadily rising prices, not a sudden surprise – but the astonishing conservatism of his view of the future. It was as if a similar official, 100 years earlier, had warned that by the year 2000 the streets would be so clogged with horse manure as to be impassable. I do not know what the world will be like a century hence. But it is not likely to be a place where the process of getting from here to there begins by putting a key in an ignition, turning it, and starting an internal combustion engine burning gasoline.

This book grew out of a seminar on future technologies that I taught for a number of years at the law school of Santa Clara University. Each Thursday we discussed a technology that I was willing to argue, at least for a week, could revolutionize the world. On Sunday, students emailed me legal issues that that revolution would raise, to be put on the class web page for other students to read. Tuesday, we discussed the issues and how to deal with them. Next Thursday a new technology and a new revolution.

The idea for the course started with two then obscure technologies: public key encryption and nanotechnology. As the course developed I found myself exploring a considerable range of others, with one feature in common: Each might change the world within my lifetime. What you are reading is an exploration of those technologies, the futures each might generate, and how we might deal with them. This chapter briefly surveys the technologies; the next discusses the problem of adjusting our lives and institutions to their consequences.

At the moment, the fashionable focus for worries about the future is global warming. It is probably a real problem and perhaps something should at some point be done about it. But, despite all the public furor and images of flooded cities, on current evidence it is not a very large problem. The latest estimates from the United Nations International Panel on Climate Change (IPCC) predict, if nothing is done, a sea level rise of a foot or two by the end of the century, an increase in average temperature of a few degrees, and perhaps a small increase in the frequency and force of hurricanes. It is possible that those predictions will turn out to be far too modest, but they are what we currently have to work with.

At least three of the technologies I discuss in this book – nanotech, biotech, and artificial intelligence (AI) – have the potential to wipe out our species well before the end of the century. They also have the potential to create a future sufficiently rich and technologically advanced to make global warming a problem that can be solved at the cost of the spare cash of a few philanthropists. Other technologies might create futures strikingly different from the present in a wide variety of ways: a radically more, or radically less, free society than we now live in, more privacy than humans have ever known or less, humans living like gods or like slaves. Their consequences will affect not only law but marriage, parenting, political institutions, businesses, life, death, and much else.

I am not a prophet; any one of the technologies I discuss may turn out to be a wet firecracker. It only takes one that does not to remake the world. Looking at some candidates will make us a little better prepared if one of those revolutions turns out to be real. Perhaps more important, after we have thought about how to adapt to any of ten possible revolutions, we will at least have a head start when the eleventh drops on us out of the blue. The conclusion I want readers to draw from this book is not that any one of the futures I sketch is going to happen. The conclusion I want them to draw is that the future is radically uncertain. In interesting ways.

And that it is worth starting to think about the possibilities, and how to deal with them, now.

POSSIBLE FUTURES

We start with three technologies relevant to privacy – one that radically increases it, two that radically decrease it.

Privacy x 3 or

Now You Have It, Now You Don't
Public key encryption makes possible untraceable communications intelligible only to the intended recipient. My digital signature demonstrates that I am the same online persona you dealt with yesterday and your colleague dealt with last year, with no need for either of you to know such irrelevant details as age, sex, or what continent I am living on. The combination of computer networking and public key encryption makes possible a level of privacy humans have never known, an online world where people have both identity and anonymity – simultaneously. One implication is free speech protected by the laws of mathematics, arguably more reliable and certainly with broader jurisdiction than the Supreme Court. Another is the possibility of criminal enterprises with brand-name reputation – online pirate archives selling other people's intellectual property for a penny on the dollar, temp agencies renting out the services of forgers and hit men.

On the Other Hand . . .
In the not-too-distant future you may be able to buy an inexpensive video camera with the size and aerodynamic characteristics of a mosquito. Even earlier, we will see – are already seeing – the proliferation of cameras on lampposts designed to deter crime. Ultimately, this could lead to a society where nothing is private. Science fiction writer David Brin has argued that the best solution available will be not privacy but universal transparency – a world where everyone can watch everyone else. The police are watching you – but someone is watching them.

It used to be that a city was more private than a village, not because nobody could see what you were doing but because nobody could keep track of what everybody was doing. That sort of privacy cannot survive modern data processing. The computer on which I am writing these words has sufficient storage capacity to hold at least a modest amount of information about every human being in the United States and enough processing power to quickly locate any one of those by name or characteristics. From that fact arises the issue of who has what rights with regard to information about me currently in the hands, and minds, of other people.

Put all of these technologies together and we may end up with a world where your realspace identity is entirely public, with everything about you known and readily accessible, while your cyberspace activities, and information about them, are entirely private – with you in control of the link between your cyberspace persona and your realspace identity.

Commerce in Cyberspace

The world that encryption and networking create requires a way of making payments – ideally without having to reveal the identity of payer or payee. The solution, already worked out in theory but not yet fully implemented, is ecash – electronic money, privately produced, potentially untraceable. One minor implication is that money laundering laws become unenforceable, since large sums can be transferred by simply sending the recipient an email.

A world of strong privacy requires some way of enforcing agreements; how do you sue someone for breach of contract when you have no idea who, where, or what he, she, or it is? That and related problems lead us to a legal technology in which legal rules are privately created and enforced by reputational sanctions. It is an ancient technology, going back at least to the privately enforced *Lex Mercatoria* from which modern commercial law evolved.[1] But for most modern readers, including most lawyers and law professors, it will be new.

Property online is largely intellectual property, which raises the problem of how to protect it in a world where copyright law is becoming unenforceable. One possibility is to substitute technological for legal protection. A program or database comes inside a piece of software – Intertrust called it a digibox – that regulates its use. To run the program or query the database costs ten cents of ecash, instantly transmitted over the net to the copyright owner.

Finally and perhaps most radically, a world of fast, cheap communication greatly facilitates decentralized approaches to production. One possible result is to shift substantial amounts of human effort out of the context of hierarchically organized corporations into some mix of marketplace coordination of individuals or small firms and the sort of voluntary cooperation, without explicit markets, of which open source software development is a recent and striking example.

Crime, Cops, and Computers

Some technologies make the job of law enforcement harder. Others make it easier – even too easy. A few years ago, when the digital wiretap bill was going through Congress, critics pointed out that the capacity the FBI was demanding the phone companies provide them added up to the ability to tap more than a million telephones – simultaneously.

We still do not know if they intend to do it, but it is becoming increasingly clear that if they want to, they can. The major cost of a wiretap is labor. As software designed to let people dictate to their computers gets better, that someone can be a computer converting conversation to text, searching the text for keywords or phrases, and reporting the occasional hit to a human being. Computers work cheap.

In addition to providing police new tools for enforcing the law, computers raise numerous problems for both defining and preventing crimes. Consider the question of how the law should classify a "computer break-in" – which consists, not of anyone actually breaking into anything, but of one computer sending messages to another and getting messages in reply. Or consider the potential for applying the classical salami technique – stealing a very small amount of money from each of a very large number of people – in a world where tens of millions of people linked to the Internet have software on their computers designed to pay bills online.

Designer Kids, Long Life, and Corpsicles

The technologies in our next cluster are biological. Two – paternity testing and in vitro fertilization – have already abolished several of the facts on which the past 1,000 years of family law are based. It is no longer only a wise child who knows his own father – any child can, given access to tissue samples and a decent lab. And it is no longer the case that the woman from whose body an infant is born is necessarily its mother. The law has begun to adjust. One interesting question that remains is to what degree we will restructure our mating patterns to take advantage of changes in the technology of producing babies.

A little further into the future are technologies to give us control over our children's genetic heritage. My favorite is the libertarian eugenics sketched decades ago by science fiction author Robert Heinlein – technologies that permit each couple to choose, from among the children they might have, which ones they do have, selecting the egg that does not carry the mother's tendency to nearsightedness to combine with the sperm that does not carry the father's heritage of a bad heart. Run that process through five or ten generations with a fair fraction of the population participating and you get a substantial change in the human gene pool. Alternatively, if we learn enough to do cut-and-paste genetic engineering, parents can forget about the wait and do the whole job in one generation.

Skip next from the beginning of life to the end. Given the rate of progress in biological knowledge over the past century, there is no reason to assume that the problem of aging will remain insoluble. Because the payoff not only is enormously large but goes most immediately to the currently old, some of whom are also rich and powerful, if it can be solved it is likely that it will be.

In one sense it already has been. There are currently more than 100 people whose bodies are not growing older because they are frozen, held at the temperature of liquid nitrogen. All are legally dead. But their hope in arranging their current status was that it would not be permanent, that with sufficient medical progress it will someday be possible to revive them. If it begins to look as though they are going to win their bet we will have to think seriously about adapting laws and institutions to a world where there is an intermediate state between alive and dead and quite a lot of people are in it.

The Real Science Fiction

Finally, we come to three technologies whose effects, if they occur, are sufficiently extreme that all bets are off, with both the extinction and the radical alteration of our species real possibilities within the life span of most of the people reading this book.

One such technology is nanotechnology – the ability to engineer objects at the atomic scale, to build machines whose parts are single atoms. That is the way living things are engineered: A DNA strand or an enzyme is a molecular machine. If we get good enough at working with very small objects to do it ourselves, possibilities range from microscopic cell repair machines that go through a human body fixing everything that is wrong to microscopic self-replicating creatures dedicated to turning the entire world into copies of themselves – known in nanocircles as the "gray goo" scenario.

Artificial intelligence might beat nanotech in the annihilation stakes – or in making heaven on earth. Raymond Kurzweil, a well-informed computer insider, estimates that in about thirty years there will be programmed computers with human-level intelligence. At first glance this suggests a world of science fiction robots – if we are lucky, obeying us and doing the dirty work. But if in thirty years computers are as smart as we are and if current rates of improvement – for computers but not for humans – continue, that means that in forty years we will be sharing the planet with beings at least as much smarter than we are as we are smarter than chimpanzees. Kurzweil's solution is for us to get smarter too – to learn to do part of our thinking in silicon. That could give us a very strange world – populated by humans, human/machine combinations, machines programmed with the contents of a human mind that think they are that human, machines that have evolved their own intelligence, and much else.

The final technology is virtual reality (VR). Present versions use the brute-force approach: feed images through goggles and headphones to eyes and ears. But if we can crack the dreaming problem, figure out how our nervous system encodes the data that reach our minds as sensory perceptions, goggles and headphones will no longer be necessary. Plug a cable into a socket at the back of your neck for full sense perception of a reality observed by mechanical sensors, generated by a computer, or recorded from another brain.

The immediate payoff is that the blind will see – through video cameras – and the deaf hear. The longer run consequence may be a world where most of the important stuff consists of signals moving from one brain to another over a network, with physical acts by physical bodies playing only a minor role. To visit a friend in England there is no need to move either his body or mine – being there is as easy as dialing the phone. That is one of many reasons why I do not expect gasoline-powered automobiles to play a major role in transportation a century from now.

A few pages back we were considering a world where realspace was entirely public, cyberspace entirely private. As things currently are, that would be a very public world, since most of us live most of our lives in realspace. But if deep VR gives us a world where all the interesting stuff happens in cyberspace and realspace activity consists of little more than keeping our bodies alive, it could be a very private world.

Having labeled the section science fiction, I could not resist adding a chapter on ways in which current and near future technologies may make possible the old science fiction dream: space travel, space habitats, and perhaps, in time, the stars.

Alternatives

Any of the futures I have just sketched might happen, but not all. If nanotech turns the world into gray goo in 2030, it will also turn into gray goo the computers on which artificial super intelligences would have been developed in 2040. If nanotech bogs down and AI does not, the programmed computers that rule the world of 2040 may be more interested in their own views of how the human species should evolve than in our view of what sort of children we want to have. And, closer to home, if strong private encryption is built into our communication systems, with the encryption and decryption under the control not of the network but of the individuals communicating with each other – the National Security Agency's nightmare for the past twenty years or so – it won't matter how many telephone lines the FBI can tap.

That is one reason this book is not prophecy. I expect parts of what I describe to happen but I do not know which parts. My purpose is not to predict which future we will get but to use possible futures to think about how technological change will affect us and how we can and should change our lives and institutions to adapt to it.

That is also one reason that, with a few exceptions, I have limited my discussion of the future to the next thirty years or so. That is roughly the point at which both AI and nanotech begin to matter. It is also long enough to permit technologies that have not yet attracted my attention to start to play an important role. Beyond that my crystal ball, badly blurred at best, becomes useless; the further future dissolves into mist.

TWO

Living with Change

New technologies change what we can do. Sometimes they make what we want to do easier. After writing a book with a word processor, one wonders how it was ever done without one. Sometimes they make what someone else is doing easier – and make it harder for us to prevent him from doing it. Enforcing copyright law became more difficult when photo typesetting made the cost of producing a pirated edition lower than the cost of the authorized edition it competed with, and more difficult again when inexpensive copying put the tools of piracy in the hands of any college professor in search of reading material for his students. As microphones and video cameras become smaller and cheaper, preventing other people from spying on me becomes harder.

The obvious response is to try to keep doing what we have been doing. If that is easier, good. If it is harder, too bad. The world must go on, the law must be enforced. Let justice be done, though the sky fall.

Obvious – and wrong. The laws we have, the ways we do things, are not handed down from heaven on tablets of stone. They are human contrivances, solutions to particular problems, ways of accomplishing particular ends. If technological change makes a law hard to enforce, the best solution is sometimes to stop enforcing it. There may be other ways of accomplishing the same end – including some enabled by the same technological change. The question is not how to continue to do what we have been doing but how best to achieve our objectives under new circumstances.

Insofar as this book has a theme, that is it.

A SIMPLE EXAMPLE: THE DEATH OF COPYRIGHT

Copyright law gives the author of a copyrightable work the right to control who copies it. If copying a book requires an expensive printing plant operating on a large scale, that right is reasonably easy to enforce. If every reader owns equipment that can make a perfect copy of a book at negligible cost, enforcing the law becomes very nearly impossible.

So far as printed material is concerned, copyright law has become less enforceable over the past century but not yet unenforceable. The copying machines most of us have access to can reproduce a book, but the cost is comparable to the cost of buying the book and the quality worse. Copyright law in printed works can still be enforced, even if less easily than in the past.

The same is not true for intellectual property in digital form. Anyone with a CD-R drive can copy a $400 program onto a one-dollar CD. Anyone with a reasonably fast Internet connection can copy anything available online, anywhere in the world, to his hard drive.

Under those circumstances enforcing copyright law against individual users is very nearly impossible. If my university decides to save on its software budget by buying one copy of Microsoft Office and making lots of copies, a discontented employee with Bill Gates' email address could get us in a lot of trouble. But if I choose to provide copies to my wife and children – which under Microsoft's license I am not permitted to do – or even to a dozen of my friends, there is in practice little that Microsoft can do about it.

That could be changed. If we wanted to enforce present law badly enough, we could do it. Every computer in the country would be subject to random search. Anyone found with an unlicensed copy of software would go straight to jail. Silicon Valley would empty and the prisons would fill with geeks, teenagers, and children.

Nobody regards that as a tolerable solution to the problem. Although there has been some shift recently in the direction of expanded criminal liability for copyright infringement, software companies for the most part take it for granted that they cannot use the law to prevent individual copying of their programs and so have fallen back on other ways of getting rewarded for their efforts.

Holders of music copyrights face similar problems. As ownership of tape recorders became common, piracy became easier. Shifting to CDs temporarily restored the balance, since they provided higher quality than tape and were expensive to copy – but then cheap CD recorders and digital audio tape came along. Most recently, as computer networks have gotten faster, storage cheaper, and digital compression more efficient, the threat has been from online distribution of MP3 files encoding copyrighted songs.

Faced with the inability to enforce copyright law against individuals, what are copyright holders to do? There are at least three answers.

1. Substitute technological protection for legal protection.

In the early days of home computers, some companies sold their programs on disks designed to be uncopyable. Consumers found this inconvenient, either because they wanted to make copies for their friends or because they wanted to make backup copies for themselves. So other software companies sold programs designed to copy the copy-protected disks. One company produced a program (SuperUtility Plus) designed to do a variety of useful things, including copying other companies' protected disks. It was itself copy-protected. So another company produced a program (SuperDuper) whose sole function in life was to make copies of SuperUtility Plus.

Technological protection continues in a variety of forms. All face a common problem. It is fairly easy to provide protection sufficient to keep the average user from using software in ways that the producer does not want him to use it. It is very hard to provide protection adequate against an expert. And one of the things experts can do is to make their expertise available to the average user in the form of software designed to defeat protection schemes.

This suggests a possible solution: technological protection backed up by legal protection against software designed to defeat it. In the early years, providers of copy protection tried that approach. They sued the makers of software designed to break the protection, arguing that they were guilty of contributory infringement (helping other people copy copyrighted material), direct infringement (copying and modifying the protection software in the process of learning how to defeat it), and violation of the licensing terms under which the protection software was sold. They lost.[1]

More recently, owners of intellectual property successfully supported new legislation – Section 1201 of the Digital Millennium Copyright Act – which reverses that result, making it illegal to produce or distribute software whose primary purpose is defeating technological protection. It remains to be seen whether or not that restriction will itself prove enforceable.

2. Control only large-scale copying.

Anyone with a video recorder, some additional hardware, and a little expertise can copy videos for his friends. Nonetheless, video rental stores remain in business. They inexpensively provide their customers with a much larger selection than they could get by copying their friends' cassettes. The stores themselves cannot safely violate copyright law, buying one cassette for 100 outlets, because they are large, visible organizations. So producers of movies continue to get revenue from videocassettes despite the ability of customers to copy them.

There is no practical way for music companies to prevent one teenager from making copies of a CD or a collection of MP3s for his friends, but consumers of music are willing to pay for the much wider range of choice available from a store. The reason Napster threatened the music industry was that it provided a similar range of choice at a much lower cost. The situation is similar for computer programs. As long as copyright law can be used to prevent large-scale piracy, customers are willing to pay for the convenience provided by a legal (hence large-scale and public) source for their software. In both cases, the ability of owners of intellectual property to make piracy inconvenient enough to keep themselves in business is threatened by the Internet, which offers the possibility of large-scale public distribution of pirated music and software.

3. Permit copying; get revenues in other ways.

Most successful lecturers will in whispered tones confide to you that there is no other journalistic or pedagogical activity more remunerative – a point made by Mark Twain and Winston Churchill.

William F. Buckley, Jr.[2]

A century ago, prominent authors got a good deal of their income from public lectures. Judging by the quotation from Buckley – and my own experience – some still do. This suggests that in a world without enforceable copyright, some authors could write books, provide them online to anyone who wanted them, and make their living selling services to their readers – public lectures, consulting services, or the like. This is not a purely conjectural possibility. Currently I provide the full text of four books and numerous articles on my web page, for free – and receive a wide range of benefits, monetary and nonmonetary, by doing so.

This is one example of a more general strategy: Give away the intellectual property and get your income from it indirectly. That is how both of the leading web browsers were at one time provided. Netscape gave away Navigator and sold the server software that Navigator interacted with; Microsoft followed a similar strategy. Apple provided a competing browser – which was (and is) available for free, but only ran on Apple computers. Currently a variety of other browsers are open source, an approach to creating software discussed in a later chapter. It is also how radio and television programs pay their bills; give away the program and get revenue from the ads.

As these examples show, the death of copyright does not mean the death of intellectual property. It does mean that producers of intellectual property must find other ways of getting paid for their work. The first step is recognizing that, in the long run, simply enforcing existing law is not going to be an option.

DEFAMATION ONLINE: A LESS SIMPLE EXAMPLE

A newspaper publishes an article asserting that I am a wanted criminal, having masterminded several notorious terrorist attacks. Colleagues find themselves otherwise engaged when I propose going out to dinner. My department chair assigns me to teach a course on Sunday mornings with an enrollment of one. I start getting anonymous phone calls. My recourse under current law is to sue the paper for libel, forcing them to retract their false claims and compensate me for damage done.

Implicit in the legal solution to defamation are two assumptions. One is that when someone makes a false statement to enough people to do scrious damage, the victim can identify either the person who made the statement or someone else responsible for his making it – the newspaper if not the author. The other is that at least one of the people identified as responsible will have enough assets to be worth suing.

Twenty years ago, both assumptions were usually true. The reporter who wrote a defamatory article might be too poor to be worth suing, but the newspaper that published it was not – and could reasonably be held responsible for what it printed. It was possible to libel someone by a mass mailing of anonymous letters, but a lot of trouble to do it on a large enough scale to matter to most victims.

Neither is true any longer. It is possible, with minimal ingenuity, to get access to the Internet without identifying yourself. With a little more technical expertise, it is possible to communicate online through inter-mediaries – anonymous remailers – in such a way that the message cannot be linked to the sender. Once online, there are ways to communicate with large numbers of people at near zero cost: mass email, posts on Usenet news, a page on the World Wide Web. And if you choose to abandon anonymity and spread lies under your own name, access to the Internet is so inexpensive that it is readily available to people without enough assets to be worth suing.

One possible response is that we must enforce the law whatever it takes. If the originator of the defamation is anonymous or poor, find someone else, somewhere in the chain of causation, who is neither. In practice, that probably means identifying the Internet service provider (ISP) through whom the message passed and holding him liable. A web page is hosted on some machine somewhere; someone owns it. An email came at some point from a mail server; someone owns that.

That solution makes no more sense than holding the U.S. Post Office liable for anonymous letters. The publisher of a newspaper can reasonably be expected to know what is appearing in his pages. But an ISP has no practical way to monitor the enormous flow of information that passes through its servers – and if it could, we wouldn't want it to. We can – in the context of copyright infringement we do – set up procedures under which an ISP can be required to take down webbed material. But that does no good against a Usenet post, mass email, webbed defamation hosted in places reluctant to enforce U.S. law, or defamers willing to go to the trouble of hosting their web pages on multiple servers, shifting from one to another as necessary. Defamation law is of very limited use for preventing online defamation.

There is – has always been – another solution to the problem. When people tell lies about me, I answer them. The technological developments that make defamation law unenforceable online also make possible superb tools for answering lies and thus provide a substitute, arguably a superior substitute, for legal protection.

My favorite example is Usenet News, a part of the Internet older and less well known than the Web. To the user it looks like a collection of online bulletin boards, each on a different topic: anarchy, short-wave radios, architecture, cooking history. When I post a message to a newsgroup, the message goes to a computer (a news server) provided by my ISP. The next time that news server talks to another they exchange messages – and mine spreads gradually across the world. In an hour, it may be answered by someone in Finland or Japan. The server I use hosts more than 100,000 groups. Each is a collection of conversations spread around the world – a tiny nongeographical community united, and often divided, by common interests.

Google, which hosts a popular web search engine, also provides a search engine for Usenet. Using it I can discover in less than a minute whether anyone has mentioned my name anywhere in the world any time in the last three days – or weeks, or years – in any of more than 100,000 newsgroups. If I get a hit, one click brings up the message. If I am the David Friedman mentioned (the process would be easier if my name were Myron Whirtzlburg), and if the message requires an answer, a few more clicks put my response in the same thread of the same newsgroup, where almost everyone who read the original post will see it. It is as if, when anyone slandered me anywhere in the world, the wind blew his words to me and my answer back to the ears of everyone who had heard them.

The protection Usenet offers against defamation is not perfect; a few people who read the original post may miss my reply and more may choose not to believe it. But the protection offered by the courts is imperfect too. Most damaging false statements are not important enough to justify the cost and trouble of a lawsuit. Many that are do not meet the legal requirements for liability. Given the choice, I prefer Usenet.

Suppose that instead of defaming me on a newsgroup you do it on a web page. Finding it is easy – Google provides a search engine for the Web too. The problem is how to answer it. I can put up a web page with my answer and hope that sufficiently interested readers will come across it, but that is all I can do. The links on your web page are put there by you, not by me – and you may be reluctant to add one to the page that proves you are lying.

There is a solution to this problem, a technological solution. Current web browsers show only forward links – links from the page being read to other pages. It would be possible to build a web browser, say Netscape Navigator 12.0, that automatically showed backlinks, letting the user see not only what pages the author of this page chose to link to but also what pages chose to link to it.[3] Once such browsers are in common use, I need only put up a page with a link to yours. Anyone browsing your page with the backlink option turned on will be led to my rebuttal.[4]

There is a problem with this solution – a legal problem. Your web page is covered by copyright, which gives you the right to forbid other people from making either copies or derivative works. A browser that displays your page as you intended is making a copy, but one to which you have given implicit authorization by putting your page on the Web. A browser that displays your page with backlinks added is creating a derivative work – one that you may not have intended and, arguably, did not authorize. To make sure your lies cannot be answered, you notify Netscape that they are not authorized to display your page with backlinks added.

The issue of when one web page is an unauthorized derivative work of another is currently being fought out in the context of "framing" – one web site presenting material from another along with its own advertising.[5] If my view of online defamation is correct, the outcome of that litigation may be important to an entirely different set of issues. The same legal rule (a strong reading of the right to prevent derivative works online) that would protect a site from other people free riding on its content would also provide protection to someone who wants to spread lies online.

UNSTEADY GROUND

My mother was a test tube, my father was a knife.

Friday, Robert A. Heinlein

Technological changes alter the cost of doing things. But they may also affect us in a more subtle way by making obsolete the categories we use to talk and think about the world around us.

Consider the category of "parent." It used to be that, although there might be some uncertainty about the identity of a child's father, there was no question what "father" and "mother" meant. Laws and social norms specifying the rights and obligations of fathers and mothers were unambiguous in meaning, if not always in application.

That is no longer the case. With current reproductive technology there are at least two biological meanings of "mother" and will soon be a third. A gestational mother is the woman in whose womb a fetus was incubated. An egg mother is the woman whose fertilized egg became the fetus. Once human cloning becomes an established technology, a mitochondrial mother will be the woman whose egg, with its nucleus replaced by the nucleus of the clone donor but with its own extranuclear mitochondrial DNA, developed into the fetus. And once genetic engineering becomes a mature technology, permitting us to produce offspring whose DNA is a patchwork from multiple donors, the concept of "a" biological mother (or father) will be very nearly meaningless.

The Child with Five Parents

A California couple wanted a child. The husband was sterile. His wife was doubly sterile – she could neither produce a fertile egg nor bring a fetus to term. They contracted with a sperm donor, an egg donor, and a gestational mother. The donated egg was impregnated with the donated sperm and implanted in the rented womb. Then, before the baby was born, their marriage broke up, leaving the courts with a puzzle: What person or persons had the legal rights and obligations of parenthood?

Under California law read literally, the answer was clear. The mother was the woman from whose body the child was born. The father was her husband. That was a sensible enough legal rule when the laws were written. But it made no sense at all in a world where neither that woman пот her husband either was related to the child or had intended to parent it.

The court that finally decided the issue held that the parents were the couple who had set the train of events in motion, intending at that time to rear the child as their own. They thus substituted for a biological definition that had become technologically obsolete a social definition – motherhood by neither egg nor womb but by intention.

This is a true story. If you don't believe me, go to a law library and look up *John A. B. v. Luanne H. B.* (72 Cal. Rptr. 2d 280 (Ct. App. 1998)).

The Living Dead

Consider someone whose body is preserved at the temperature of liquid nitrogen while awaiting the medical progress needed to revive and cure him. Legally he is dead; his wife is a widow, his heirs have his estate. But if he is in fact going to be revived, then in a very real sense he is not dead – merely sleeping very soundly. Our legal system, more generally our way of thinking about people, takes no account of the special status of such a person. There is a category of alive, a category of dead, and – outside of horror movies and computer games – nothing between them.

The absence of such a category matters. It may, quite literally, be a matter of life and death.

You are dying of a degenerative disease that will gradually destroy your brain. If you are cured today, you will be fine. If you are cured a year later, your body may survive but your mind will not. After considering the situation, you decide that you are more than willing to trade a year of dying for a chance of getting back your life. You call up the Alcor Life Extension Foundation and ask them to arrange to have your body frozen – tomorrow if possible.

They reply that while they agree with your decision they cannot help you. As long as you are legally alive, freezing you is legally murder. You will simply have to wait another year until you are declared legally dead and hope that somehow, some day, medical science will become capable of reconstructing you from what by that time is left.

This too is, allowing for a little poetic license, a true story. In *Donaldson v. Van de Kamp*, Thomas Donaldson went to court in an unsuccessful attempt to get permission to be frozen before, rather than after, his brain was destroyed by a cancerous tumor.

The issues raised by these cases – the meaning of parenthood and of death – will be discussed at greater length in later chapters. Their function here is to illustrate the way in which technological change alters the conceptual ground under our feet.

All of us deal with the world in terms of approximations. We describe someone as tall or short, kind or cruel, knowing that the former is a matter of degree and the latter both of degree and of multiple dimensions. We think of the weather report as true, although it is quite unlikely that it provides a perfectly accurate description of the weather, or even that such a description is possible. When the weatherman says the temperature is seventy degrees in the shade, just which square inch of shade is he referring to? We classify a novel as fiction and this book as nonfiction, although quite a lot of the statements in the former are true and some in the latter are false.

Dealing with the world in this way works because the world is not a random assemblage of objects; there is pattern to it. Temperature varies from one patch of shade to another, but not by very much. Although a statement about "the" temperature in the shade may not be precisely true, we rarely lose much by treating it as if it were. Similarly for the other useful simplifications of reality that make possible both thought and communication.

When the world changes enough, some simplifications cease to be useful. It was always true that there was a continuum between life and death; the exact point at which someone is declared legally dead is arbitrary. But, with rare exceptions, it was arbitrary to within seconds, perhaps minutes – which almost never mattered. When it is known that, for a large number of people, the ambiguity not only exists but will exist for decades, the simplification is no longer useful. It may, as could have happened in the case of Thomas Donaldson, become lethal.

IT'S NOT JUST LAW, IT'S LIFE

So far my examples have focused on how legal rules should respond to technological change. But similar issues arise for each of us in living his or her own life in a changing world. Consider, for a story now in part played out, the relations between men and women.

The Decline of Marriage

For a very long time, human societies have been based on variants of the sexual division of labor. All started with a common constraint: women bear and suckle children, men do not. For hunter-gatherers, that meant that the men were the hunters and the women, kept relatively close to camp by the need to care for their children, the gatherers. In more advanced societies that became, with many variations, a pattern where women specialized in household production and men in production outside the household.

A second constraint was the desire of men to spend their resources on their own children rather than on the children of other men – a desire rooted in the fact that Darwinian selection has designed organisms, including human males, to be good at passing down their own genes to future generations. Since the only way a man could be reasonably confident that he was the father of a particular child was for the child's mother not to have had sex with other men during the period when it was conceived, the usual arrangement of human societies, with a few exceptions, gave men sexual exclusivity. One man might under some circumstances sleep with more than one woman but one woman was supposed to, and most of the time did, sleep with only one man.

Over the past few centuries two things have sharply altered the facts that led to those institutions. One was the decline in infant mortality. In a world where producing two or three adult children required a woman to spend most of her fertile years bearing and nursing, the sexual division of labor was sharp – one profession, "mother," absorbed close to half the labor force. In today's world, a woman need bear only two babies in order to end up with two adult children.

A second change, the increased division of labor, has drastically reduced the importance of household production. You may still wash your own clothes, but most of the work was done by the people who built the washing machine. You may still cook your own dinner, but you are unlikely to cure your own ham or make your own soap. That change eliminated a good deal of what wives traditionally did, freeing women for other activities.[6]

As being a wife and mother went from a full- to a part-time job, human institutions adjusted. Market employment of women increased. Divorce became more common. The sexual division of labor, while it still exists, is much less sharp – many women do jobs that used to be done almost exclusively by men, some men do jobs that used to be done almost exclusively by women.

The Future of Marriage

One consequence of married women working largely outside of the home is to make the enforcement of sexual exclusivity, never easy,[7] very nearly impossible. Modern societies developed a social alternative: companionate marriage. A wife who is your best friend instead of your subordinate or slave is less likely to want to cheat on you, a good thing if you have no practical way of stopping her. Modern society also produced, somewhat later, a technological alternative: paternity testing. It is now possible for a husband to know whether his wife's children are his even if he is not confident that he is her only sexual partner.

This raises some interesting possibilities. We could have – are perhaps moving toward – a variant of conventional marriage institutions in which paternal obligations are determined by biology, not marital status. We could have a society with group marriages but individual parental responsibilities, since a woman would know which of her multiple husbands had fathered any particular child. We could have a society with casual sex but well-defined parental obligations – although that raises some practical problems. It is much easier for a couple to share parental duties if they are also living together, and the fact that two people enjoy sleeping together is inadequate evidence that they will enjoy living together.

All of these mating patterns exist already (for a partial sample, see the Usenet newsgroup alt.polyamory). Whether any become common will depend in large part on the nature of male sexual jealousy. Is it primarily a learned pattern, designed to satisfy an instinctual preference for one's own children? Or is it itself instinctual, hardwired by evolution as a way of improving the odds that the children a male supports carry his genes?[8] If the former, then once the existence of paternity testing makes jealousy obsolete we can expect its manifestations to vanish, permitting a variety of new mating patterns. If the latter, jealousy is still obsolete but, given the slow pace of evolutionary change, that fact will be irrelevant to behavior for a very long time, hence we can expect to continue with some variant of monogamy, or at least serial polygamy, as the norm.

The basic principle here is the same as in earlier examples of adjustment to technological change. Our objective is not to save marriage. It is to accomplish the purposes that marriage evolved to serve. One way is to continue the old pattern even though it has become more difficult – as exemplified by the movement for giving couples the option of covenant marriage, marriage on something more like the old terms of "till death do us part." Another is to take advantage of technological change to accomplish the old objective – producing and bringing up children – in new ways.

Doing Business Online

Technology affects law and love. Also business. Consider the problem of contract enforcement.

Litigation has always been a clumsy and costly way of enforcing contractual obligations. It is possible to sue someone in another state, even another country – but the more distant the jurisdiction, the harder it is. If online commerce eventually dispenses with not only geography but real-world identity, so that much of it occurs between parties linked only to an identity defined by a digital signature, enforcing contracts in the courts becomes harder still. It is difficult to sue someone if you do not know who he is.

There is an old solution – reputation. Just as in the case of defamation, the same technology that makes litigation less practical makes the private substitute more practical.

eBay provides a low-tech example. When you win an auction and take delivery of the goods, you are given an opportunity to report on the result – did the seller deliver when and as scheduled, were the goods as described? The reports on all past auctions by a given seller are available, both in full and in summary form, to anyone who might want to bid on that seller's present auctions. In a later chapter we will consider more elaborate mechanisms, suitable for higher stakes transactions, by which modern information technology can use reputational enforcement to substitute for legal enforcement.

BRAKES? WHAT BRAKES?

When considering the downside of technologies – Murder Incorporated in a world of strong privacy or some future James Bond villain using nanotechnology to convert the entire world to gray goo – your reaction may be "Stop the train, I want to get off!" In most cases, that is not an option. This particular train is not equipped with brakes.

Most of the technologies we are discussing can be developed locally and used globally. Once one country has a functional nanotechnology, permitting it to build products vastly superior to those made with old technologies, there will be enormous pressure on other countries to follow suit. It is hard to sell glass windshields when the competition is using structural diamond. It is even harder to persuade cancer patients to be satisfied with radiation therapy when they know that, elsewhere in the world, microscopic cell repair machines are available that simply go through your body and fix whatever is wrong.

For an example already played out, consider surrogacy contracts – agreements by which a woman bears a child, either from her own or another woman's egg, for another couple to rear as their own. The Baby M case established that such contracts are not enforceable, at least in New Jersey. State legislation followed, with the result that in four states merely signing such a contract is a criminal act and in one, Michigan, arranging a surrogacy contract is a felony punishable by up to five years and $50,000.

None of this mattered very much. Someone who could afford the costs of hiring a surrogate mother, still more someone who could afford the cost necessary to arrange for one mother to incubate another's egg, could almost certainly afford the additional cost of doing it in a friendly state. As long as there was one state that approved of such arrangements, the disapproval of others had little effect. And even if the contracts were legally unenforceable, it was only a matter of time before people in the business of arranging them learned to identify and avoid potential surrogate mothers likely to change their mind after the child was born.[9]

Or consider research into the causes of aging. Many people believe (I think mistakenly) that the world suffers from serious problems of overpopulation. Others argue (somewhat more plausibly) that a world without aging would risk political gerontocracy and cultural stasis.[10] Many would – some do – argue that even if the problem of aging can be solved, it ought not to be.

That argument becomes less convincing the older you get. Old people control large resources, both economic and political. Although arguments against aging research may win out somewhere, they are unlikely to win out everywhere – and the cure only has to be found once.

For a more disturbing example, consider artificial intelligence – a technology that might well make human beings obsolete. At each stage, doing it a little better means being better able to design products, predict stock movements, win wars. That almost guarantees that at each stage, someone will take the next step.

Even if it is possible to block or restrict a potentially dangerous technology, as in a few cases it may be, it is not clear that we should do it. We might discover that we had missed the disease and banned the cure. If an international covenant backed by overwhelming military power succeeds in restricting nanotechnological development to government-approved labs, that might save us from catastrophe. But since government-approved labs are the ones most likely to be working on military applications of new technology, while private labs mostly try to produce what individual customers want, the effect might also be to prevent the private development of nanotechnological countermeasures to government-developed mass destruction. Or it might turn out that our restrictions had slowed the development of nanotechnology by enough to leave us unable to defend against the result of a different technology – a genetically engineered plague, for example.

There are legitimate arguments for trying to slow or prevent some of these technological developments. Those arguments will be made,[11] but not here. For my purposes, it is more interesting to assume that such

attempts, if made, will fail, and try to think through the consequences –
how new technologies will change things, how human beings will and
should adapt to those changes.

Technological progress means learning more about how to do things;
on the face of it, one would expect that to result in an improvement in
human life. So far, with few or no exceptions, it has. Despite a multitude of
dire prophecies over the past two centuries, human life almost everywhere
is better today than it was 50 years ago, better 50 years ago than 100 years
ago, and better 100 years ago than 200 years ago.[12]

Past experience is not always a reliable guide to the future. Despite
the progress of the past 200 years, quite a number of people continue
to predict future catastrophe from present progress – including a few
sufficiently well informed and competent to be worth taking seriously.
In my final chapter, I will return to the question of whether, how, and
under what circumstances they might be right.

PART TWO

PRIVACY AND TECHNOLOGY

THREE

A World of Strong Privacy

There has been a lot of concern in recent years about the end of privacy. As we will see in the next two chapters, there is reason for such fears; the development of improved technologies for surveillance and data processing does indeed threaten our ability to restrict other people's access to information about us. But a third and less familiar technology is working in precisely the opposite direction. If the arguments of this chapter are correct we will soon be experiencing in part of our lives – an increasingly important part – a level of privacy that human beings have never known before. It is a level of privacy that not only scares the FBI and the National Security Agency, two organizations whose routine business involves prying into other people's secrets; it sometimes even scares me.

We start with an old problem: how to communicate with someone without letting other people know what you are saying. There are a number of familiar solutions. If you are worried about eavesdroppers, check under the eaves before saying things you do not want the neighbors to hear. To be safer still, hold your private conversation in the middle of a large, open field or a boat in the middle of a lake. The fish are not interested and nobody else can hear.

That approach no longer works. Even the middle of a lake is within range of a shotgun mike. The eaves do not have to contain eavesdroppers – just a microphone and a transmitter. If you check for bugs, someone can still bounce a laser beam off your windowpane and use it to pick up the vibration from your voice. I am not sure that satellite observation is good enough yet to read lips from orbit – but if not, it soon will be.

Much of our communication is now indirect, over phone wires, airwaves, the Internet. Phone lines can be tapped; cordless or cell phone messages intercepted. An email bounces through multiple computers on its way to its destination – anyone controlling one of those computers can, in principle, save a copy.

A different set of old technologies was used for written messages. A letter sealed with the sender's signet ring could not protect the message but at least it let the recipient know if it had been opened – unless the spy was very good with a hot knife. A letter sent via a trusted messenger was safer still, provided he deserved the trust.

A more ingenious approach was to protect not the physical message but the information it contained, by scrambling the message and providing the intended recipient with the formula for unscrambling it. A simple version was a substitution cipher, in which each letter in the original message was replaced by a different letter. If we replace each letter with the next one in the alphabet, we get "mjlf uijt" from the words "like this."

"Mjlf uijt" does not look much like "like this," but it is not very hard, if you have a long message and patience, to deduce the substitution and decode the message. More sophisticated scrambling schemes rearrange the letters according to an elaborate formula, or convert letters into numbers and do complicated arithmetic with them to convert the message (plaintext) into its coded version (ciphertext). Such methods were used, with varying degrees of success, by both sides in World War II.

There were two problems with this way of keeping secrets. The first was that it was slow and difficult – it took a good deal of work to convert a message into its coded form or to reverse the process. It was worth doing if the message was the order telling your fleet when and where to attack, but not for casual conversations among ordinary people.

That problem has been solved. The computers most of us have on our desktops can scramble messages, using methods that are probably unbreakable even by the NSA, faster than we can type them. They can even scramble – and unscramble – the human voice as fast as we can speak. Encryption is now available not merely to the Joint Chiefs of Staff but to you and me for our ordinary conversation.

The other problem is that in order to read my scrambled message you need the key – the formula describing how to unscramble it. If I do not have a safe way of sending you messages, I may not have a safe way of sending you the key either. If I sent it by a trusted messenger but made a small mistake as to who was entitled to trust him, someone else now has a copy and can use it to decrypt my future messages to you. This may not be too much of a problem for governments, willing and able to send information back and forth in briefcases handcuffed to the wrists of military attachés, but for the ordinary purposes of ordinary people that is not a practical option.

About twenty-five years ago, this problem was solved. The solution was public key encryption, a new way of scrambling and unscrambling messages that does not require a secure communication channel for either the message or the key. The software to implement that solution is now widely available.

Public key encryption works by generating a pair of keys – call them A and B – each a long number that can be used to unscramble what the other has scrambled. If you encrypt a message with A, someone who possesses only A cannot decrypt it – that requires B. If you encrypt a message with B, you have to use A to decrypt it. If you send a friend key A (your public key) while keeping key B (your private key) secret, your friend can use A to encrypt messages to you and you can use B to decrypt them. If a spy gets a copy of key A, he can send you secret messages too. But he still cannot decrypt the messages from your friend. That requires key B, which never leaves your possession.

How can one have the information necessary to encrypt a message yet be unable to decrypt it? How can it be possible to produce two keys with the necessary relationship but not, starting with one key, to calculate the other? The answer to both questions depends on the fact that there are some mathematical processes that are much easier to do in one direction than another.

Most of us can multiply 293 by 751 reasonably quickly, using nothing more sophisticated than pencil and paper, and get 220,043. Starting with 220,043 and finding the only pair of three-digit numbers that can be multiplied together to give it takes a lot longer. The most widely used version of public key encryption depends on that asymmetry – between multiplying and factoring – using much larger numbers. Readers who are still puzzled may want to look at Appendix I of this chapter, where I describe a very simple form of public key encryption suited to a world where people know how to multiply but have not yet learned how to divide, or check one of the webbed descriptions of the mathematics of the El-Gamal and RSA algorithms, the most common forms of public key encryption.

When I say that encryption is unbreakable, what I mean is that it cannot be broken at a reasonable cost in time and effort. Almost all encryption schemes, including public key encryption, are breakable given an unlimited amount of time. If, for example, you have key A and a message 1,000 characters long encrypted with it, you can decrypt the message by having your computer create every possible 1,000-character message, encrypt each with A, and find the one that matches. Alternatively, if you know that key B is a number 100 digits long, you could try all possible 100-digit numbers, one after another, until you found one that correctly decrypted a message that you had encrypted with key A.

Both of these are what cryptographers describe as "brute-force" attacks. To implement the first of them, you should start by providing yourself with a good supply of candles – the number of possible 1,000-character sequences is so astronomically large that, using the fastest computers now available, the sun will have burned out long before you finish. The second is workable if key B is a sufficiently short number – which is why people who are serious about protecting their privacy use long keys, and why people who are serious about violating privacy try to pass laws restricting the length of the keys that encryption software uses.

ENCRYPTION CONCEALS . . .

Imagine that everyone has an Internet connection and suitable encryption software, and that everyone's public key is available to everyone else – published in the phone book, say. What follows?

What I Say

One obvious result is that we can have private conversations. If I want to send you a message that nobody else can read, I first encrypt it with your public key. When you respond, you encrypt your message with my public key. The FBI, or my nosy neighbor, is welcome to tap the line – everything he gets will be gibberish to anyone who does not have the corresponding private key.

To Whom

Even if the FBI does not know what I am saying, it can learn a good deal by watching who I am saying it to – known in the trade as *traffic analysis*. That problem too can be solved, using public key encryption and an anonymous remailer, a site on the Internet that forwards email. When I want to communicate with you I send the message to the remailer, along with your email address. The remailer sends it to you.

If that was all that happened, someone tapping the net could follow the message from me to the remailer and from the remailer to you. To prevent that, the message to the remailer, including your email address, is encrypted with the remailer's public key. When he receives it he uses his private key to strip off that layer of encryption, revealing your address, and forwards the decrypted message. Our hypothetical spy sees 1,000 messages go into the remailer and 1,000 come out, but he can neither read the email addresses on the incoming messages – they are hidden under a layer of encryption – nor match up incoming and outgoing message.

What if the remailer is a plant – a stooge for whoever is spying on me? There is a simple solution. The email address he forwards the message to is not actually yours – it is the email address of a second remailer. The message he forwards is your message plus your email address, the whole encrypted with the second remailer's public key. If I am sufficiently paranoid, I can bounce the message through ten different remailers before it finally gets to you. Unless all ten are working for the same spy, there is no way anyone can trace the message from me to you. (Readers who want a more detailed description of how remailers work will find it in Appendix II.)

We now have a way of corresponding that is doubly private – nobody can know what we are saying and nobody can find out whom we are saying it to. But there is still a problem.

Who I Am

When interacting with other people, it is helpful to be able to prove your identity – which can be a problem online. If I am leading a conspiracy to overthrow an oppressive government, I want my fellow conspirators to be able to tell which messages are coming from me and which from the secret police pretending to be me. If I am selling my consulting services online, I need to be able to prove my identity in order to profit from the reputation earned by past consulting projects and make sure that nobody else free rides on that reputation by masquerading as me.

That problem too can be solved by public key encryption. In order to digitally sign a message, I encrypt it using my private key instead of your public key. I then send it to you with a note telling you whom it is from. You decrypt it with my public key. The fact that what comes out is a message and not gibberish tells you that it was encrypted with the matching private key. Since I am the only one who has that private key, the message must be from me.

My digital signature not only demonstrates that I sent the signed message, it does so in a form that I cannot later disavow. If I try to deny having sent it, you point out that you have a copy of the message encrypted with my private key – something that nobody but I could have produced. Thus a digital signature makes it possible for people to sign contracts that they can be held to – and does so in a way much harder to forge than an ordinary signature.

And Whom I Pay

If we are going to do business online we need a way of paying for things. Checks and credit cards leave a paper trail. What we want is an online equivalent of currency – a way of making payments that cannot later be traced, either by the parties themselves or anyone else.

The solution, discussed in some detail in a later chapter, is anonymous ecash. Its essential feature is that it permits people to make payments to each other by sending a message, without either party having to know the identity of the other and without any third party having to know the identity of either of them. One of the many things it can be used for is to pay for the services of an anonymous remailer, or a string of anonymous remailers, thus solving the problem of how to keep remailers in business without sacrificing their customers' anonymity. Another, as we will see later, is to help us eliminate one of the chief minor nuisances of modern life – spam email.

Combine and Stir

Combine public key encryption, anonymous remailers, digital signatures, and ecash, and we have a world where individuals can talk and trade with reasonable confidence that no third party is observing them.

A less obvious implication is the ability to combine anonymity and reputation. You can do business online without revealing your real-world identity – your true name.[1] You prove you are the same person who did business yesterday, or last year, by digitally signing your messages. Your online persona is defined by its public key. Anyone who wants to communicate with you privately uses that key to encrypt his messages; anyone who wants to be sure that you are the person who sent a message uses it to check your digital signature.

With the exception of fully anonymous ecash, all of these technologies already exist, implemented in software that is currently available for free.[2] At present, however, they are mostly limited to the narrow bandwidth of email – sending private text messages back and forth. As computers and computer networks get faster, that will change.

Twice in the past month I traveled several hundred miles – once by car, once by air – in order to give a series of talks. With only mild improvements in current technology I could have given them from my office. Both my audience and I would have been wearing virtual reality goggles – glasses with the lenses replaced by tiny computer screens. My computer would be drawing the view of the lecture room as seen from the podium – including the faces of my audience – at sixty frames a second. Each person in the audience would have a similar view, from his seat, drawn by his computer. Earphones take care of sound. The result would be the illusion, for all of us, that we were present in the same room seeing and hearing each other.

Virtual reality not only keeps down travel costs, it has other advantages as well. Some lecture audiences expect a suit and tie – and not only do I not like wearing ties, all of the ones I own possess a magnetic attraction for foodstuffs in contrasting colors. To give a lecture in virtual reality I do not need a tie, or even a shirt. My computer can add both to the image it sends out over the net. It can also remove a few wrinkles, darken my hair, and cut a decade or so off my apparent age.

As computers get faster they can not only create and transmit virtual reality worlds, they can also encrypt them. That means that any human interaction involving only sight and sound can be moved to cyberspace and protected by strong privacy.

Handing Out the Keys: A Brief Digression

In order to send an encrypted message to a stranger or check the digital signature on a message from a stranger, I need his public key. Earlier in the chapter, I assumed that problem away by putting everyone's public key in the phone book. Although that is a possible solution, it is not a very good one.

A key published in the phone book is only as reliable as whoever is publishing it. If our hypothetical bad guy can arrange for his public key to be listed under my name, he can read messages intended for me and sign bogus messages from me with a digital signature that checks against my supposed key. A phone book is a centralized system, vulnerable to failures at the center, whether due to dishonesty or incompetence. There is, however, a simple decentralized solution; as you might guess, it too depends on public key encryption.

Consider some well-known organization, such as American Express, which many people know and trust. American Express arranges to make its public key very public – posted in the window of every American Express office, printed – and magnetically encoded – on every American Express credit card, included in the margin of every American Express ad. It then goes into the identity business.

To take advantage of its services, I use my software to create a public key/private key pair. I then go to an American Express office, bringing with me my passport, driver's license, and public key. After establishing my identity to their satisfaction, I hand them a copy of my public key and they create a message saying, in language a computer can understand, "The public key of David D. Friedman, born on 2/12/45 and employed by Santa Clara University, is 1001101100011011100101011000 1101000. . . . " They digitally sign the message using American Express's private key, copy the signed message to a flash disk, and give it to me.

To prove my identity to a stranger, I send him a copy of the digital certificate from American Express. He now knows my public key – allowing him to send encrypted messages that only David Friedman can read and check digital signatures to see if they are really from David Friedman. Someone with a copy of my digital certificate can use it to prove to people what my public key is but cannot use it to masquerade as me – because he does not possess the matching private key.

So far this system has the same vulnerability as the phone book; if American Express or one of its employees is working for the bad guy, they can create a bogus certificate identifying someone else's public key as mine. But nothing in a system of digital certificates requires trust in any one organization. I can email you a whole pack of digital certificates – one from American Express, one from the U.S. Post Office, one from the Catholic Church, one from my university, one from Microsoft, one from Apple, one from AOL – and you can have your computer check all of them and make sure they all agree. It is unlikely that a single bad guy has infiltrated all of them.[3]

So far I have been assuming that real-world identities are unique – each individual has only one. But each of us has, in a very real sense, multiple identities – different things about us are relevant identifiers to different people. What my students need to know is that a message really came from the professor teaching the course they are taking. What my daughter needs to know is that it really came from her father. One can imagine circumstances where it is important to keep multiple real-world identities separate – to conceal from some of the people you are interacting with identifying features that you want to be able to reveal to others. A system of multiple certifying authorities makes that possible, provided you remember which certificates to send to which correspondent. Sending your superior in the criminal organization you are infiltrating the certificate identifying you as a police officer might be hazardous.

A WORLD OF STRONG PRIVACY

One of the attractive features of the world created by these technologies is free speech. If I communicate online under my own name using encryption, I can be betrayed only by the person I am communicating with. If I do it using an online persona, with reputation but with no link to my realspace identity, not even the people I communicate with can betray me. Thus strong privacy creates a world that is, in important ways, safer than the one we now live in – a world where you can say things other people disapprove of without the risk of punishment, legal or otherwise.

This brings me to another digression – one directed especially at my friends on the right wing of the political spectrum.

The Virtual Second Amendment

The Second Amendment to the U.S. Constitution guarantees Americans the right to bear arms. A plausible interpretation of its history views it as a solution to a problem of considerable concern to eighteenth-century thinkers – the problem of standing armies. Everyone knew that professional armies beat amateur armies. Everyone also knew – with Cromwell's dictatorship still fairly recent history – that a professional army posed a serious risk of military takeover.

The Second Amendment embodied an ingenious solution to that problem. Combine a small professional army under the control of the Federal government with an enormous citizen militia – every able-bodied adult man. Let the Federal government provide sufficient standardization so that militia units from different states could work together but let the states appoint the officers – thus making sure that the states and their citizens maintained control over the militia. In case of foreign invasion, the militia would provide a large, if imperfectly trained and disciplined, force to supplement the small regular army. In case of an attempted coup by the Federal government, the Federal army would find itself outgunned a hundred to one.

The beauty of this solution is that it depends not on making a military takeover illegal but on making it impossible. In order for that takeover to occur, it would first be necessary to disarm the militia. But until the takeover had occurred the Second Amendment prevented the militia from being disarmed, since any such attempt would be seen as a violation of the Constitution and resisted with force.

It was an elegant solution 200 years ago, but I am less optimistic than some of my friends about its relevance today. The United States has a much larger professional military, relative to its population, than it did then; the states are much less independent of the Federal government than they were; and the gap between civilian and military weaponry has increased enormously.

Other things have changed as well over 200 years. In a world of broad-based democracy and network television, conflicts between the U.S. government and its citizens are likely to involve information warfare, not guns. A government that wants to do bad things to its citizens will do them by controlling the flow of information in order to make them look like good things.

In that world, widely available strong encryption functions as a virtual Second Amendment. As long as it exists, the government cannot control the flow of information. And once it does exist, eliminating it, like disarming an armed citizenry, is extraordinarily difficult – especially for a government that cannot control the flow of information to its citizens about what it is doing.

If You Work for the IRS, Stop Here

Freedom of speech is something most people, at least in this country, favor. But strong privacy will also reduce the power of government in less obviously desirable ways. Activities that occur entirely in cyberspace will be invisible to outsiders – including ones working for the Federal government. It is hard to tax or regulate things you cannot see.

If I earn money selling services in cyberspace and spend it buying goods in realspace, the government can tax my spending. If I earn money selling goods in realspace and spend it buying services in cyberspace, they can tax my income. But if I earn money in cyberspace and spend it in cyberspace they cannot observe either income or expenditure and so will have nothing to tax.

Similarly for regulation. I am, currently, a law professor but not a member of the State Bar of California, making it illegal for me to sell certain sorts of legal services in California. Suppose I wanted to do so anyway. If I do it as David D. Friedman I am likely to get in trouble. But if I do it as Legal Eagle Online, taking care to keep the true name – the real-world identity – of Legal Eagle a secret, there is not much the State Bar can do about it.

In order to sell my legal services I have to persuade someone to buy them. I cannot do that by pointing potential customers to my books and articles because they were all published under my own name. What I can do is to start by giving advice for free and then, when the recipients find that the advice is good – perhaps by checking it against the advice of their current lawyers – raise my price. Thus over time I establish an online reputation for an online identity guaranteed by my digital signature.

Legal advice is one example; the argument is a general one. Once strong privacy is well established, governmental regulation of information services can no longer be enforced. Governments may still attempt to maintain the quality of professional services by certifying professionals – providing information as to who they believe is competent. But it will no longer be possible to force customers to act on that information – to legally forbid them from using uncertified providers, as they currently are legally forbidden to use unlicensed doctors or lawyers who have not passed the Bar.

The Downside of Strong Privacy

Reducing the government's ability to collect taxes and regulate professions is in my view a good thing, although some will disagree. But the same logic also applies to government activities I approve of, such as preventing theft and murder. Online privacy will make it harder to keep people from sharing stolen credit card numbers or information on how to kill people or organizing plots to steal things or blow things up.

This is not a large change; the Internet and strong encryption merely make it somewhat easier for criminals to do things they are doing already. A more serious problem is that, by making it possible to combine anonymity and reputation, strong privacy makes possible criminal firms with brand-name reputation.

Suppose you very much want to have someone killed. The big problem is not the cost; so far as I can gather from public accounts, hiring a hit man costs less than buying a car, and most of us can afford a car. The big problem – assuming you have already resolved any moral qualms – is finding a reliable seller of the service you want to buy. That problem, in a world of widely distributed strong encryption, we can solve. Consider my four-step business plan for Murder Incorporated:

1. Arrange for mystery billboards on major highways. Each contains a single long number and the message "write this down." Display ads with the same message appear in major newspapers.
2. Put a full-page ad in the *New York Times*, apparently written in gibberish.
3. Arrange a multiple assassination with high-profile targets, such as film stars or major sports figures – perhaps a bomb at the Academy Awards.
4. Send a message to all major media outlets telling them that the number on all of those bulletin boards is a public key. If they use it to decrypt the *New York Times* ad they will get a description of the assassination, published the day before it happened.

You have now made sure that everyone in the world has, or can get, your public key – and knows that it belongs to an organization willing and able to kill people. Once you have taken steps to tell people how to post messages where you can read them, everyone in the world will know how to send you messages that nobody else can read and how to identify messages that can only have come from you. You are now in business as a middleman selling the services of hit men. Actual assassinations still have to take place in realspace, so being a hit man still has risks. But the problem of locating a hit man – when you are not yourself a regular participant in illegal markets – has been solved.

Murder Incorporated is a particularly dramatic example of the problem of criminal firms with brand-name reputations, operating openly in
cyberspace while keeping their realspace identity and location secret, but
there are many others. Consider "Trade Secrets Inc. – We Buy and Sell."
Or an online pirate archive, selling other people's intellectual property
in digital form, computer programs, music, and much else, for a penny
on the dollar, payable in anonymous digital cash.

Faced with such unattractive possibilities, it is tempting to conclude
that the only solution is to ban encryption. A more interesting approach
is to find ways of achieving our objectives – preventing murder, providing
incentives to produce computer programs – that are made easier by the
same technological changes that make the old ways harder.

Anonymity is the ultimate defense. Not even Murder Incorporated can
assassinate you if they do not know who you are. If you plan to do things
that might make people want to kill you – publish a book making fun of
the prophet Mohammed, say, or revealing the true crimes of Bill (Gates
or Clinton) – it might be prudent not to do it under a name linked to
your realspace identity. That is not a complete solution – the employer
of the hit man might, after all, be your wife, and it is hard to conduct a
marriage entirely in cyberspace – but it at least protects many potential
victims.

Similarly for the more common, if less dramatic, problem of protecting intellectual property online. Copyright law will become largely
unenforceable, but there are other ways of protecting property. One –
using encryption to provide the digital equivalent of a barbed wire fence
protecting your property – will be discussed at some length in Chapter 8.

Why It Will Not Be Stopped

For the past two decades powerful elements in the U.S. government, most
notably the National Security Agency and the FBI, have been arguing
for restrictions on encryption designed to maintain their ability to tap
phones, read seized records, and in a variety of other ways violate privacy
for what they regard as good purposes. After my description of the
downside of strong privacy, readers may think there is a good deal to be
said for the idea.

There are, however, practical problems. The most serious is that the cat is already out of the bag – has been for more than twenty-five years. The mathematical principles on which public key encryption is based are public knowledge. That means that any competent computer programmer with an interest in the subject can write encryption software. Quite a lot of such software has already been written and is widely available. And, given the nature of software, once you have a program you can make an unlimited number of copies. It follows that keeping encryption software out of the hands of spies, terrorists, and competent criminals is not a practical option. They probably have it already, and if they don't they can easily get it.

Banning the production and possession of encryption software is not a practical option, but what about banning or restricting its use? To enforce such a ban law enforcement agencies would randomly monitor a substantial fraction of all communications, taking advantage of the massive wiretapping capacity that current law requires the phone companies to provide them and expanding the legal requirements to apply to other communication providers as well. Any message that looked like gibberish and could not be shown to be the result of a legal form of encryption would lead to legal action against its author.

One practical problem is the enormous volume of information flowing over computer networks. A second problem is that while it is easy enough to tell whether a message consists of text written in English, it is much harder – in practice, impossible – to identify other sorts of content well enough to be sure that they do not consist of, or contain, encrypted messages.

Consider a three-million pixel digital photo. It is made up of three million colored dots, each described by three numbers – intensity of red, intensity of blue, intensity of green. Each of those numbers is, from the standpoint of the computer, a string of ones and zeros. Changing the rightmost digit – the "least significant bit" – from one to zero or zero to one will have only a tiny effect on the appearance of the dot, just as changing the rightmost digit in a long decimal number, say 9,319,413, has only a very small effect on its size.

To conceal a million-character-long encrypted message in my digital photo, I simply replace the least significant bit of each of the numbers in the photo with one bit of the message. The photo is now a marginally worse picture than it was – but there is no way an FBI agent, or a computer working for an FBI agent, can know precisely what the photo ought to look like. This is a simple example of *steganography* – concealing messages.

It is not practical for law enforcement to keep sophisticated criminals, spies, or terrorists from possessing and using strong encryption software. What is possible is to put limits on the encryption software publicly marketed and publicly used – to insist, for example, that if AOL or Microsoft builds encryption into their programs it must contain a back door permitting properly authorized persons – a law enforcement agent with a court order, say – to read the message without the key.

The problem with such an approach is that there is no way of giving law enforcement what it wants without imposing very high costs on the rest of us. In order to deal with crimes in progress, police have to be able to decrypt encrypted information they have obtained reasonably quickly; it does little good to read the intercepted message an hour after the bomb has gone off. The equivalent in realspace would be legal rules that let properly authorized law enforcement agents open any lock in the country in half an hour. That includes not only the lock on your front door but the locks protecting bank vaults, trade secrets, lawyers' records, lists of contributors to unpopular causes, and much else.

While access would be nominally limited to those properly authorized, it is hard to imagine any system flexible enough to do the job that was not vulnerable to misuse. If being a police officer gives you access to locks with millions of dollars behind them, in cash, diamonds, or information, some cops will become criminals and some criminals will become cops. Proper authorization presumably means a court order – but not all judges are honest, and half an hour is not long enough for even an honest judge to verify what the officer applying for the court order tells him.[4]

Encryption provides the locks for cyberspace. If nobody has strong encryption, everything in cyberspace is vulnerable to a sufficiently sophisticated private criminal. If people have strong encryption but it comes with a mandatory back door accessible in half an hour to any police officer with a court order, then everything in cyberspace is vulnerable to a private criminal with the right contacts. Those locks have billions of dollars' worth of stuff behind them – money in banks, trade secrets in computers.

One could imagine a system for accessing encrypted documents so rigorous that it required written permission from the President, Chief Justice, and Attorney General and only got used once every two or three years. Such a system would not seriously handicap online dealings. But it would also be of no real use to law enforcement, since there would be no way of knowing which one communication out of the billions crisscrossing the Internet each day they needed to crack.

In order for regulation to be useful, it has to either prevent the routine use of encryption or make it reasonably easy for law enforcement agents to access encrypted messages. Doing either will seriously handicap the ordinary use of the net. Not only will it handicap routine transactions, it will make computer crime easier by restricting the technology best suited to defend against it. And what we get in exchange is protection, not against the use of encryption by sophisticated criminals and terrorists – there is no way of providing that – but only against the use of encryption by ordinary people and unsophisticated criminals.

Readers who have followed the logic of the argument may point out that even if we cannot keep sophisticated criminals from using strong encryption, we may be able to prevent ordinary people from using it to deal with sophisticated criminals – and doing so would make my business plan for Murder Incorporated unworkable. While it would be a pity to seriously handicap the development of online commerce, some may think that price worth paying to avoid the undesirable consequences of strong privacy.

To explain why I do not expect that to happen requires a brief economic digression.

Property Rights and Myopia

You are thinking of going into the business of growing trees – hardwoods that mature slowly but produce valuable lumber. It will take forty years from planting to harvest. Should you do it? The obvious response is not unless you are confident of living at least another forty years.

Like many obvious responses, it is wrong. Twenty years from now you will be able to sell the land, covered with twenty-year-old trees, for a price that reflects what those trees will be worth in another twenty years. Following through the logic, it is straightforward to show that if what you expect the trees to sell for will more than repay your investment, including forty years of compound interest, you should do it.

This assumes a world of secure property rights. Suppose we assume instead that your trees are quite likely, at some point during the next forty years, to be stolen – legally via government confiscation or illegally by someone driving into the forest at night, cutting them down, and carrying them off. In that case you will only be willing to go into the hardwood business if the return from selling the trees is enough larger than the ordinary return on investments to compensate you for the risk.

Generalizing the argument, we can see that long-run planning depends on secure property rights. If you are confident that what you own today you will still own tomorrow – unless you choose to sell it – you can afford to give up benefits today in exchange for greater benefits tomorrow, or next year, or next decade. The greater the risk that what you now own will be taken out of your control at some point in the future, the greater the incentive to limit yourself to short-term projects.

Politicians in a democratic society have insecure property rights over their political assets; Bill Clinton could rent out the White House but he could not sell it. One consequence is that in such a system government policy is dominated by short-run considerations – most commonly the effect of current policy on the outcome of the next election. Very few politicians will accept political costs today in exchange for benefits ten or twenty or thirty years in the future, because they know that when the benefits arrive someone else will be in power to enjoy them.

Preventing the development of strong privacy means badly handicapping the current growth of online commerce. It means making it easier for criminals to hack into computers, intercept messages, defraud banks, steal credit cards. It is thus likely to be politically costly, not ten or twenty years from now but in the immediate future.

What do you get in exchange? The benefit of encryption regulation – the only substantial benefit, since it cannot prevent the use of encryption by competent criminals – is preventing the growth of strong privacy. From the standpoint of governments, and of people in a position to control governments, that may be a large benefit, since strong privacy threatens to seriously reduce government power, including the power to collect taxes. But it is a long-run threat, one that will not become serious for a decade or two. Defeating it requires the present generation of elected politicians to do things that are politically costly for them – in order to protect the power of whomever will hold their offices ten or twenty years from now.

The politics of encryption regulation so far fits the predictions of this analysis. Support for regulation has come almost entirely from long-lived bureaucracies such as the FBI and NSA. So far, at least, they have been unable to get elected politicians to do what they want when doing so involved any serious political cost.[5]

If this argument is right, it is unlikely that serious encryption regulation, sufficient to make things much easier for law enforcement and much harder for the rest of us, will come into existence, at least in the United States. So there is a reasonable chance that we will end up with something along the lines of the world of strong privacy described in this chapter.

In my view that is a good thing. The attraction of a cyberspace protected by encryption is that it is a world where all transactions are voluntary: You cannot get a bullet through a T1 line. It is a world where the technology of defense has finally beaten the technology of offense. In the world we now live in, our rights can be violated by force or fraud; in a cyberspace protected by strong privacy, only by fraud. Fraud is dangerous, but less dangerous than force. When someone offers you a deal too good to be true, you can refuse it. Force makes it possible to offer you deals you cannot refuse.

Truth to Tell

In several places in this chapter I have simplified the mechanics of encryption, describing how something could be done but not how it is done. Thus, for example, public key encryption is usually done not by encrypting the message with the recipient's public key but by encrypting the message with an old-fashioned single key encryption scheme, encrypting the single key with the recipient's public key, and sending both encrypted message and encrypted key. The recipient uses his private key to decrypt the encrypted key and uses that to decrypt the message. Although this is a little more complicated than the method I described, in which the message itself is encrypted with the public key, it is also significantly faster.

Similarly, a digital signature is actually calculated by using a one-way hash function to create a message digest of the original message and encrypting the digest with your private key, then sending both message and digest. The recipient decrypts the digest, creates a second digest from the message using the same hash function, and compares them to make sure they are identical, as they will be if the message has not been changed and the public and private keys match.

Such complications make describing the mechanics of encryption more difficult and are almost entirely irrelevant to the issues discussed here, so I ignored them.

A second set of complications, also ignored but more important, concerns indirect ways in which cryptographically protected anonymity might be attacked. One example is textual analysis. A perceptive reader or sufficiently sophisticated software might recognize stylistic similarities between the books of David Friedman and the written legal advice of Legal Eagle. The odds that the same person has read work by both identities closely enough to identify them as the same may not be very high – but software designed for textual analysis could create a database linking a very large number of known authors to stylistic identifiers for their writing. A simple one for me would be the overuse of "hence."

Another problem is that most of what I have described depends on your having complete control over your computer – or at least over a smart card containing your private key and enough software to use it to encrypt and decrypt. If someone else can get at your private key by either a physical or virtual intrusion, all bets are off. If someone else can get control of your computer, even without access to your private key, he can use that control to mislead you in a variety of ways – for instance, by falsely reporting that a message has a valid digital signature. As Mark Miller puts it, "People don't sign, computers sign." And encrypt, decrypt, and check signatures. So a crucial element of strong privacy is the ability of individuals to control the computers they use. In practice, a secure system is likely to include provisions for publicly canceling private keys that may have fallen into the wrong hands.

An alternative approach is to memorize your private key. A 128-bit key can be represented as a string of 19 numbers, letters, and punctuation marks, which is not that difficult to memorize. Alternatively, key can be derived from a passphrase, a procedure that is less secure but easier for the user. In either case, you still have the problem of making sure that your computer can be trusted to forget the key as soon as it has used it.

APPENDIX I: PUBLIC KEY ENCRYPTION: A VERY ELEMENTARY EXAMPLE

Imagine a world in which people know how to multiply numbers but not how to divide them. Further imagine that there exists some mathematical procedure capable of generating pairs of numbers that are inverses of each other: X and 1/X. Finally, assume that the messages we wish to encrypt are simply numbers.

I generate a pair X, 1/X. To encrypt the number M using the key X, I multiply X times M. We might write

$$[M, X] = MX,$$

meaning "Message M encrypted using the key X is M times X."

Suppose someone has the encrypted message MX and the key X. Since he does not know how to divide, he cannot decrypt the message and find out what the number M is. If, however, he has the other key, 1/X, he can multiply it times the encrypted message to get back the original M:

$$MX(1/X) = M(X/X) = M$$

Alternatively, one could encrypt a message by multiplying it by the other key, 1/X, giving us

$$[M, 1/X] = M/X.$$

Someone who knows 1/X but does not know X has no way of decrypting the message and finding out what M is. But someone with X can multiply it times the encrypted message and get back M:

$$(M/X)X = M$$

So in this world, multiplication provides a primitive form of public key encryption: a message encrypted by multiplying it with one key can only be decrypted with the other.

Public key encryption in the real world depends on mathematical operations that, like multiplication and division in my example, are much easier to do in one direction than the other. The RSA algorithm, for example, at present the most widely used form of public key encryption, depends on the fact that it is easy to generate a large number by multiplying together several large primes but much harder to start with a large number and factor it to find the primes that can be multiplied together to give that number. The keys in such a system are not literally inverses of each other, like X and 1/X, but they are functional inverses, since either one can undo (decrypt) what the other does (encrypts).

APPENDIX II: CHAINING ANONYMOUS REMAILERS

M is my actual message; [M, K] means "message M encrypted using key K." K_r is the public key of the intended recipient of my message, E_r is his email address. I am using a total of three remailers; their public keys are K_1, K_2, K_3, and their email addresses are E_1, E_2, E_3. What I send to the first remailer is:

$$[([([([M, K_r] + E_r), K_3] + E_3), K_2] + E_2), K_1]$$

The first remailer uses his private key to strip off the top layer of encryption, leaving him with:

$$[([([M, K_r] + E_r), K_3] + E_3), K_2] + E_2$$

He can now read E_2, the email address of the second remailer, so he sends the rest of the message to that address. The second remailer receives:

$$[([([([M, K_r] + E_r), K_3] + E_3), K_2]$$

and uses his private key to strip off a layer of encryption, leaving him with:

$$[([M, K_r] + E_r), K_3] + E_3$$

He then sends to the third remailer:

$$[([M, K_r] + E_r), K_3]$$

The third remailer strips the third layer of encryption off, giving him:

$$[M, K_r] + E_r$$

and sends $[M, K_r]$ to the intended recipient at E_r – who then uses his private key to strip off the last level of encryption, giving him M, the original message.

FOUR

Information Processing: Threat or Menace?
Or
If Information Is Property, Who Owns It?

Some years ago I decided to set up my own web site. One question was how much of my life to include. Did I want someone looking at my academic work – perhaps a potential employer – to discover that I had put a good deal of time and energy into researching medieval recipes, a subject unrelated to either law or economics, thus (arguably) proving that I was a dilettante rather than a serious scholar? Did I want that same potential employer to discover that I held unfashionable political opinions, ranging from support for drug legalization to support for open immigration? And did I want someone who might be outraged at my political views to be able to find out what I and my family members looked like and where we lived?

I concluded that keeping my life in separate compartments was not a practical option. I could have set up separate sites for each part, with no links between them – but anyone with a little enterprise could have found them all with a search engine. And even without a web site, anyone who wanted to know about me could find vast amounts of information by a quick search of Usenet, where I have been an active poster for more than fifteen years. Keeping my virtual mouth shut was not a price I was willing to pay, and nothing much short of that would do the job.

This is not a new problem. Before the Internet existed, I still had to decide to what degree I wanted to live in multiple worlds – whether, for example, I should discuss my hobbies or my political views with professional colleagues. What has changed is the scale of the problem. In a large world where personal information was spread mostly by gossip and processed almost entirely by individual human brains, facts about me were to a considerable extent under my control – not because they were secret but because nobody had the time and energy to discover everything knowable about everyone else. Unless I was a major celebrity, I was the only one specializing in me.

That was not true everywhere. In the good old days – say most of the past 3,000 years – one reason to run away to the big city was to get a little privacy. In the villages in which most of the world lived, anyone's business was everyone's business. In Sumer or Rome or London the walls were no more opaque and you were no less visible than at home, but there was so much going on, so many people, that nobody could keep track of it all.

That form of privacy – privacy through obscurity – cannot survive modern data processing. No individual can keep track of it all but many of us have machines that can. The data of an individual life are not notably more complicated than they were 2,000 years ago. It is true that the number of lives has increased thirty- or fortyfold in the last 2,000 years, but our ability to handle data has increased a great deal more than that. Not only can we keep track of the personal data for a single city, we could, to at least a limited degree, keep track of the data for the whole world, assuming we had it and wanted to.

The implications of these technologies have become increasingly visible over the past ten or fifteen years. Many are highly desirable. The ability to gather and process vast amounts of information permits human activities that would once have been impossible; to a considerable extent it abolishes the constraints of geography on human interaction. Consider two examples.

Thirty some years ago, I spent several summers as a counselor at a camp for gifted children. Many of the children, and some of my fellow counselors, became my friends – only to vanish at the end of the summer. From time to time I wondered what had become of them.

I can now stop wondering, at least about some. A few years ago, someone who had been at the camp organized an email list for ex-campers and counselors; membership is currently over 200. That list exists because of technologies that make possible not only easy communication with people spread all over the country but also finding them in the first place – searching a very large haystack for a few hundred needles. Glancing down a page of Yahoo! Groups, I find almost 3,000 such lists, each for a different camp; the largest has more than 700 members.

For a second example, consider a Usenet Newsgroup that I stumbled across many years ago, dedicated to a technologically ingenious but now long obsolete video game machine of which I once owned two – one for my son and one for me. Reading the posts, I discovered that someone in the group had located Smith Engineering/Western Technologies, the firm that held the copyright on the Vectrex and its games, and written to ask permission to make copies of game cartridges. The response, pretty clearly from the person who designed the machine, was an enthusiastic yes. He was obviously delighted to discover that there were people still playing with his toy, his dream, his baby. Not only were they welcome to copy cartridges, if anyone wanted to write new games he would be happy to provide the necessary software. It was a striking, to me heartwarming, example of the ability of modern communications technology to bring together people with shared enthusiasms.

Vectrex had cheats back when they were still known as bugs.
— from an FAQ by Gregg Woodcock

THE MARKET FOR INFORMATION

My examples so far are small and noncommercial – people learning other people's secrets or getting together with old friends or strangers with shared interests. While such applications of informational technology are an increasingly important feature of the world we live in, they are not nearly as prominent or politically contentious as large-scale commercial uses of personal information. A first step in understanding such activities is to think about why some people would want to collect and use individual information about large numbers of strangers. Consider two examples.

You are planning to open a new grocery store in an existing chain – a multi-million-dollar gamble. Knowledge about the people who live in the neighborhood – how likely they are to shop at your store and how much they will buy – is crucial. How do you get it?

The first step is to find out what sort of people shop in your present stores and what they buy. To do that you offer customers a shopping card. The card is used to get discounts, so shoppers pass the card through a reader almost every time they go through the checkout, providing you lots of detailed information about their shopping patterns. One way you use that information is to improve the layout of existing stores; if people who buy spaghetti almost always buy spaghetti sauce at the same time, putting them in the same aisle will make your store more convenient, hence more attractive, hence more profitable.

Another way is to help you decide where to locate your new store. If you discover that old people on average do not buy very much of what you are selling, perhaps a retirement community is the wrong place. If couples with young children do all their shopping on the weekend when one parent can stay home with the kids, singles shop after work on weekdays (weekends are for parties), and retired people during the working day (shorter lines), then a location with a suitable mix of all three types will give you a more even flow of customers, higher utilization of the store, and greater profits. Combining information about your customers with information about the demography of alternative locations, provided free by the U.S. census or at a higher price by private firms, you can substantially improve the odds on your gamble.

For a higher tech application of information technology, consider advertising. When I read a magazine, I see the same ads as everyone else – mostly for things I have no interest in. But a web page can send a different response to every query, customizing the ads I see to fit my interests. No TV ads, since I do not own a television, lots of ads for high-tech gadgets.

In order to show me the right ads, the people managing the page need to know what I am interested in. Striking evidence that such information is already out there and being used appears in my mailbox on a regular basis – a flood of catalogs.

How did the companies sending out those catalogs identify me as a potential customer? If they could see me, it would be easy. Not only am I wearing a technophile ID bracelet (Casio calls it a databank watch), I am wearing the model that, in addition to providing a calculator, database, and appointment calendar, also checks in three times a day with the U.S. atomic clock to make sure it has exactly the right time. *Sharper Image, Techno-Scout, Innovations* et al. cannot see what is on my wrist – although if the next chapter's transparent society comes to pass that may change. They can, however, talk to each other. When I bought my *Casio Wave Captor Databank 150* (the name would have been longer but they ran out of room on the watch), that purchase provided the proprietors of the catalog I bought it from with a snippet of information about me. They no doubt resold that information to anyone willing to pay for it. Sellers of gadgets respond to the purchase of a Casio Wave Captor the way sharks respond to blood in the water.

As our technology gets better, it becomes possible to create and use such information at lower cost and in much more detail. A web page can keep track not only of what you buy but also of what you look at and for how long. Combining information from many sources, it becomes both possible and potentially profitable to create databases with detailed information on the behavior of a very large number of individuals, certainly including me, probably including you.

The advantages of that technology to individual customers are fairly obvious. If I am going to look at ads, I would prefer that they be ads for things I might want to buy. If I am going to have my dinner interrupted by a telephone call from a stranger, I would prefer it be someone offering to prune my aging apricot tree – last year's crop was a great disappointment – rather than someone offering to refinance my nonexistent mortgage.

As these examples suggest, there are advantages to individuals to having their personal information publicly available and easy to find. What are the disadvantages? Why are many people upset about the loss of privacy and the misuse of "their" private information? Why did Lotus, after announcing its plan to offer masses of such data on a CD, have to cancel it in response to massive public criticism? Why is the question of what information web sites are permitted to gather about their customers, what they may do with it, and what they must tell their customers about what they are doing with it, a live political and legal issue?

One gut-level answer is that many people feel strongly that information about them is theirs. They should be able to decide who gets it; if it is going to be sold, they should get the money.

The economist's response is that they already do get the money. The fact that selling me a gadget provides the seller with a snippet of information that he can then resell makes the transaction a little more profitable for the seller, attracts additional sellers, and ultimately drives down the price I must pay for the gadget. The effect is tiny – but so is the price I could get for the information if I somehow arranged to sell it myself. It is only the aggregation of large amounts of such information that is valuable enough to be worth the trouble of buying and selling it.

A different response, motivated by moral intuition rather than economics, is that the argument confuses information about me – located in someone else's mind or database – with information that belongs to me. How can I have a property right over the contents of your mind? If I am stingy or dishonest, do I have an inherent right to forbid those I treat badly from passing on the information? If not, why should I have a right to forbid them from passing on other information about me?

There is, however, a vaguer but more important reason that people are upset at the idea of a world where anyone willing to pay can learn almost everything about them. Many people value their privacy not because they want to be able to sell information about themselves but because they do not want other people to have it. While it is hard to come up with a clear explanation of why we feel that way – a subject discussed at greater length in the final chapter of this section – it is clear that we do. At some level, control over information about ourselves is seen as a form of self-protection. The less other people can find out about me, the less likely it is that they will use information about me either to injure me or to identify me as someone they wish to injure – which brings us back to some of the issues I considered when setting up my web page.

Toward Information as Property

Concerns with privacy apply to at least two sorts of personal information. One is information generated by voluntary transactions with some other party – what products I have bought and sold, what catalogs and magazines I subscribe to, what web pages I browse. Such information starts in the possession of both parties to the transaction – I know what I bought from you, you know what you sold to me. The other kind is information generated by actions I take that are publicly visible – court records, newspaper stories, gossip.

Ownership of the first sort of information can, at least in principle, be determined by contract. A magazine can, and some do, promise its subscribers that their names will not be sold. Software firms routinely offer people registering their programs the option of having their names made or not made available to other firms selling similar products. Web pages can, and many do, provide explicit privacy policies limiting what they will do with the information generated in the process of browsing their sites.

To understand the economics of the process, think of information as a produced good; like other such goods, who owns how much of it is determined by agreement among the parties who produce it. When I subscribe to a magazine, the publisher and I are jointly producing a piece of information about my tastes – the information that I like that kind of magazine. That information is of value to the magazine, which may want to resell it. It is of value to me, either because I might want to resell it or because I might want to keep it off the market in order to protect my privacy. The publisher can, by selling subscriptions at a lower price without a privacy guarantee than with, offer to pay me for control over the information. If the information is worth more to me than he is offering, I refuse; if it is worth less, I accept. Control over the information ends up with whoever most values it. If no mutually acceptable terms can be found, I do not subscribe and that bit of information does not get produced.

This seems to imply that default rules about privacy, rules specifying who starts out owning the information, should not matter. That would be true in a world where arranging contracts was costless – a world of zero transaction costs. In the world we now live in, it is not. Most of us, unless we care a great deal about our privacy, do not bother to read privacy policies. Even if I prefer that catalogs and mailing lists not resell information about me, it is too much trouble to check the small print on everything I might subscribe to. It would be still more trouble if every firm I dealt with offered two prices, one with and one without a guarantee of privacy, and more still if the firm offered a menu of levels of protection, each with its associated price.

The result is that most magazines and web sites, at least in my experience, offer only a single set of terms; if they allow the subscriber some choice, it is not linked to price, probably because the amounts involved are too small to be worth bargaining over. Hence default rules matter and we get political and legal conflicts over the question of who, absent any explicit contractual agreement, has what control over the personal information generated by transactions.

That may change. What may change it is technology – the technology of intelligent agents. It is possible in principle, and is becoming possible in practice, to program your web browser with information about your privacy preferences. Using that information, the browser can decide what different levels of privacy protection are or are not worth to you and select pages and terms accordingly. Browsers work cheap.

For this to happen we need a language of privacy – a way in which a web page can specify what it does or does not do with information generated by your interactions with it in a form your browser can understand. Once such a language exists and is in widespread use, the transaction costs of bargaining over privacy drop sharply. You tell your browser what you want and what it is worth to you, your browser interacts with a program on the web server hosting the page and configured by the page's owner. Between them they agree on mutually satisfactory terms – or they fail to do so, and you never see the page.

This is not a purely hypothetical idea. Its current incarnation is the Platform for Privacy Preferences (P3P), supported by several of the leading web browsers. Web pages provide information about their privacy policies, users provide information about what they are willing to accept, and the browser notifies the user if a site's policies are inconsistent with his requirements. Presumably a web site that misrepresented its policies could be held liable for doing so, although, as far as I know, no such case has yet reached the courts.

How Not to Protect Privacy

> Safe to tell a secret to one,
> Risky to two,
> To tell it to three is folly,
> Everyone else will know.
> *Hávamál,*
> c. ninth century

Suppose we solve the transaction cost problems, permitting a true market in personal information. There remains a second problem – enforcing the rights you have contracted for. You can check the contents of your safe deposit box to be sure they are still there, but it does no good to check the contents of a firm's database to make sure your information is still there. They can sell your information and still have it.

The problem of enforcing rights with regard to information is not limited to a future world of automated contracting – it exists today. As I like to put it when discussing current privacy law, there are only two ways of controlling information about you and one of them doesn't work.

The way that doesn't work is to let other people have information about you and then make rules about how they use it. That is the approach embodied in modern privacy law. If you disagree with my evaluation, I suggest a simple experiment. Start with $5,000, the name of a random neighbor, and the Yellow Pages for "Investigators." The objective is to end up with a credit report on your neighbor – something that, under the Federal Fair Credit Reporting Act, you are not allowed to have. If you are a competent con man or Internet guru, you can probably dispense with the money and the phone book.

That approach to protecting privacy works poorly when enforcing terms imposed by federal law. It should work somewhat better for enforcing terms agreed to in the marketplace, since in that case it is supported by reputational as well as legal sanctions – firms do not want the reputation of cheating their customers. But I would still not expect it to work terribly well. Once information is out there, it is very hard to keep track of who has it and what he has done with it. It is particularly hard when there are many uses of the information that you do not want to prevent – a central problem with the Fair Credit Reporting Act. Setting up rules that permit only people with a legitimate reason to look at your credit report is hard; enforcing them is harder.

The other way of protecting information, the way that does work, is not to let the information out in the first place. That is how the strong privacy of the previous chapter was protected. You do not have to trust your ISP or the operator of an anonymous remailer not to tell your secrets; you haven't given them any secrets to tell.

There are problems with applying that approach to transactional information. When you subscribe to a magazine, the publisher knows who you are, or at least where you live – it needs that information to get the magazine to you. When you buy something from me, I know that I have sold it to you. The information starts in the possession of both of us – short of controlled amnesia, how can it end in the possession of only one?

In our present world, that is a nearly insuperable problem. But in a world of strong privacy, you do not have to know whom you are selling to. If, at some point in the future, privacy is sufficiently important to people, online transactions can be structured to make each party anonymous to the other, with delivery either online via a remailer (for information transactions) or via the less convenient realspace equivalent of a physical forwarding system. In such a world, we are back with one of the oldest legal rules of all: possession. If I have not revealed the information to you, you do not have it, so I need not worry about what you are going to do with it.

Returning to something more like our present world, one can imagine institutions that would permit a considerably larger degree of individual control over the uses of personal information than now exists, modeled on arrangements now used to maintain firms' control over their valuable mailing lists. Individuals subscribing to a magazine would send the seller not their name and address but the name of the information intermediary they employed and the number by which that intermediary identified them. The magazine's publisher would ship the intermediary 4,000 copies and the numbers identifying 4,000 (anonymous) subscribers, the intermediary would put on the address labels and mail them out. The information would never leave the hands of the intermediary, a firm in the business of protecting privacy. To check its honesty, I establish an identity with my own address and the name "David Freidmann," subscribe to a magazine using that identity, and see if David Freidmann gets any junk mail.

Such institutions would be possible and, if widely used, not terribly expensive. My guess is that it will not happen. The reason is that most people either do not want to keep the relevant information secret (I don't, for example; I like gadget catalogs) or do not want to enough to go to any significant trouble. But it is still worth thinking about how they could get privacy if they wanted to, and those thoughts may become of more practical relevance if technological progress sharply reduces the cost.

TWO ROADS TO PROPERTY IN PERSONAL INFORMATION

These discussions suggest two different ways in which the technologies that help to create the problem could be used to solve it. Both are ways of making it possible for an individual to treat information about himself as his property. One is to use computer technologies, including encryption, to give me or my trusted agents direct control over the information, permitting others to use it only with my permission – for instance, to send me information about goods they think I might want to buy – without ever getting possession of it. The other is to treat information as we now treat real estate – to permit individuals to put restrictions on the use of property they own that are binding on subsequent purchasers. If, for example, I sell you an easement permitting you to cross my land in order to reach yours and I later sell the land, the easement is good against the buyer. Even if he did not know it existed, he now has no right to refuse to let you through.

That is not true for most other forms of property.[1] If I sell you a car with the restriction that you agree not to permit it to be driven on Sunday, I may be able to enforce the restriction against you; I may be able to sue you for damages if, contrary to our contract, you sell it to someone else without requiring him to abide by the agreement. But I have no way of enforcing the restriction on him.

One plausible explanation of the difference is that land ownership involves an elaborate system for recording title, including modifications such as easements, making it possible for the prospective purchaser to determine in advance what obligations run with the land. We have no such system for recording ownership, still less for recording complicated forms of ownership, for most other sorts of property.

At first glance, personal information seems even less suitable for the more elaborate form of property rights than pens, chairs, or computers. In most likely uses, the purchaser is buying information about a very large number of people. If my particular bit of information is only worth three cents to him, a legal regime that requires him to spend a dollar checking the restrictions on it before he uses it means that the information will never be used.

A possible solution is to take advantage of the same data-processing technologies that make it possible to aggregate and use information on that scale to maintain the record of complicated property rights in it. One could imagine a legal regime where every piece of personal information had to be accompanied by a unique identification number. Using that number, a computer could access information about the restrictions on use of that information in machine-readable form at negligible cost. Again, it does not seem likely in the near future, but might become a real possibility farther down the road.

FIVE

Surveillance Technology

The Universal Panopticon

The trend began in Britain a decade ago, in the city of King's Lynn, where sixty remote controlled video cameras were installed to scan known "trouble spots," reporting directly to police headquarters. The resulting reduction in street crime exceeded all predictions; in or near zones covered by surveillance, it dropped to one seventieth of the former amount. The savings in patrol costs alone paid for the equipment in a few months. Dozens of cities and towns soon followed the example of King's Lynn. Glasgow, Scotland reported a 68% drop in citywide crime, while police in Newcastle fingered over 1500 perpetrators with taped evidence. (All but seven pleaded guilty, and those seven were later convicted.) In May 1997, a thousand Newcastle soccer fans rampaged through downtown streets. Detectives studying the video reels picked out 152 faces and published eighty photos in local newspapers. In days, all were identified.
David Brin, *The Transparent Society*, chapter 1, p. 5

In the early nineteenth century, Jeremy Bentham, one of the oddest and most original of English thinkers, designed a prison where every prisoner could be watched at all times. He called it the Panopticon. Elements of his design were later implemented in real prisons in the hope of better controlling and reforming prisoners. If Brin is correct, it is now in the process of being implemented on a somewhat larger scale.

The case of video surveillance in Britain suggests one reason – according to British reports it provides an effective and inexpensive way of fighting crime. In the United States, cameras have long been used in department stores to discourage shoplifting. More recently they have begun to be used to apprehend drivers who run red lights. While there have been challenges on privacy grounds, it seems likely that the practice will spread.

Crime prevention is not the only benefit of surveillance. Consider the problem of controlling auto emissions. The current approach imposes a fixed maximum on all cars, requires all to be inspected, including new cars that are almost certain to pass, and provides no incentive for lowering emissions below the required level. It makes almost no attempt to selectively deter emissions at places and times when they are particularly damaging.

One could build a much better system using modern technology. Set up unmanned detectors that measure emissions by shining a beam of light through the exhaust plume of a passing automobile; identify the automobile by a snapshot of the license plate. Bill the owner by amount of emissions and, in a more sophisticated system, when and where they were emitted.[1]

Another application of large-scale surveillance already being experimented with takes advantage of the fact that cell phones continually emit positioning cues, untraced signals produced in the process of keeping track of what tower they should communicate with. By monitoring the signals from drivers' phones, it is possible to observe traffic flows. That is very useful information if you want to advise drivers to route around a traffic jam, or locate an accident by the resulting cluster of phones. Currently it is anonymous information, locating a phone but not identifying its owner. As technology evolves that may change.

None of these useful applications of technology poses, at first glance, a serious threat to privacy. Few would consider it objectionable to have a police officer wandering around a park or standing on a street corner, keeping an eye out for purse snatchers and the like. Video cameras on poles are merely a more convenient way of doing the same thing – comfortably and out of the wet. Cameras at red lights, or photometric monitoring of a car's exhaust plume, are cheaper and more effective substitutes for traffic cops and emission inspections. What's the problem?[2]

The problem comes when we combine this technology with others. A cop on the street corner may see you, he may even remember you, but he has no way of combining everything he sees with everything that every other cop sees and so reconstructing your daily life. A video camera produces a permanent record. It is now possible to program a computer to identify a person from a picture of his face. That means that the videotapes produced by surveillance cameras will be convertible into a record of where particular people were when. Add in the ability of modern data processing to keep track of enormous amounts of information and we have the possibility of a world where large fractions of your doings are an open book to anyone with access to the appropriate records. Add to that the ability of computers to identify suspicious patterns of behavior, something already being experimented with in several places, and those in control of the technology can not only look at everything but know where to look.

So far I have been discussing the legal use of surveillance technology, mostly by governments – already happening on a substantial scale and likely to increase in the near future. A related issue is the use of surveillance technology, legally or illegally, by private parties. Lots of people own video cameras and those cameras are getting steadily smaller; even more people own cell phones with cameras built in. One can imagine, a decade or two down the road, an inexpensive video camera with the size and aerodynamic characteristics of a mosquito. The owner of a few dozen of them could collect a lot of information about his neighbors – or anyone else.

Of course technological development, in this area as in others, is likely to improve defense as well as offense. Possible defenses against such spying range from jamming transmissions to automated dragon-flies programmed to hunt down and destroy video mosquitoes. Such technologies might make it possible, even in a world where all public activities were readily observable, to maintain a zone of privacy within one's own house.

Then again, they might not. We have already had court cases over whether it is or is not a search to deduce marijuana growing inside a house by using an infrared detector to measure its temperature from the outside. We already have technologies that make it possible to listen to a conversation by bouncing a laser beam off a window and reconstructing from the measured vibrations of the glass the sounds that cause them. Even if it is not possible to spy on private life directly, further developments along these lines may make it possible to achieve the same objective indirectly.

Assume, for the moment, that the offense wins out over the defense – that preventing other people from spying on you becomes impractical. What options remain?

Brin argues that privacy will no longer be one of them. More interestingly, he argues that that may be a good thing. He proposes as an alternative to privacy universal lack of privacy: the transparent society. The police can watch you – but someone is watching them. The entire system of video cameras, including cameras in every police station, is publicly accessible. Click on the proper web page – read, presumably, from a handheld wireless device – and you can see anything that is happening in any public place. Parents can keep an eye on their children, children on their parents, spouses on each other, employers on employees and vice versa, reporters on cops and politicians.

The Upside of Transparency

Many years ago I was a witness to a shooting; one result was the opportunity for a certain amount of casual conversation with police officers. One of them advised me that, if I ever happened to shoot a burglar, there were two things I should make sure of: that he ended up dead and that the body ended up inside my house.

The advice was well meant and perhaps sensible – under U.S. law a homeowner is in a much stronger legal position killing an intruder inside his house than outside, and a dead man cannot give his side of the story. But it was also, at least implicitly, advice to commit a felony. That incident, and a less friendly one in another jurisdiction where I was briefly under arrest for disturbing the peace (my actual offense was aiding and abetting someone else in asking a policeman for his badge number), convinced me that at least some law enforcers, even ones who are honestly trying to prevent crime, have an elastic view of the application of the law to themselves and their friends. The problem is old enough to be the subject of a Latin tag – *Qui custodes ipsos custodiet?* "Who shall guard the guardians?"

The transparent society offers a possible solution. Consider the Rodney King case. A group of policemen captured a suspect and beat him up – a perfectly ordinary sequence of events in many parts of the world, including some parts of the United States. Unfortunately for the police, a witness got the beating on videotape, with the result that several of the officers ended up in prison. There have been a number of similar cases since then. Law enforcement agents, in deciding just how far they can go beyond what the public might approve of, must take account of the possibility that somebody might have a video camera pointed their way. In Brin's world, every law enforcement agent knows that he is on candid camera all of the time and conducts himself accordingly.

It is an intriguing vision and it might happen. But there are problems.

Selective Transparency

The first is getting there. If transparency comes, as it is coming in England, in the form of cameras on poles installed and operated by the government, Brin's version does not seem likely. All of the information will be flowing through machinery controlled by some level of government. Whoever is in charge can plausibly argue that although much of that information can and should be made publicly accessible, there ought to be limits. And even if they do not argue for limits, they can still impose them. If police are setting up cameras in police stations, they can arrange for a few areas to be accidentally left uncovered. If the FBI is in charge of a national network it can, and on all past evidence will, make sure that some of the information generated is accessible only to those whom they trust not to misuse it – most of whom are working for the FBI.

The situation gets more interesting in a world where technological progress enables private surveillance on a wide scale, so that every location where interesting things might happen, including every police station, has flies on the wall watching what happens and reporting back to their owners. A private individual, even a large corporation, is unlikely to attempt the sort of universal surveillance that Brin imagines for his public system, so each individual will be getting information about only a small part of the world. But if that information is valuable to others, it can be shared. Governments might try to restrict such sharing. But in a world of strong privacy that will be hard to do, since in such a world information transactions will be invisible to outside parties. Combining ideas from several chapters of this section, one can imagine a future where Brin's transparent society is produced not by government but by private surveillance.

A universal spy network is likely to be an expensive proposition, especially if you include the cost of information processing – facial recognition of every image produced and analysis of the resulting data. No single individual, probably no single corporation, will find it in its interest to bear that cost to produce information for its own use, although a government might. The information will be produced privately only if the producer can both use it himself and sell it to others. So a key requirement for a privately generated transparent society is a well-organized market for information.[3]

The Downside of Transparency

Following Brin, I have presented the transparent society as a step into the future, enabled by video cameras and computers. One might instead view it as a step into the past. The privacy that most of us take for granted is to a considerable degree a novelty, a product of rising incomes in recent centuries. In a world where many people shared a single residence, where a bed at the inn was likely to be shared by two or three strangers, transparency did not require video cameras.

For a more extreme example, consider a primitive society such as Samoa. Multiple families share a single house – without walls. While there is no Internet to spread information, the community is small enough to make gossip an adequate substitute. Infants are trained early on not to make noise. Adults rarely express hostility.[4] Most of the time, someone may be watching – so you alter your behavior accordingly. If you do not want your neighbors to know what you are thinking or feeling, you avoid clearly expressing yourself in words or facial expression. You have adapted your life to a transparent society.

Ultimately this comes down to two strategies, both familiar to most of us in other contexts. One is not to let anyone know your secrets – to live as an island. The other is to communicate in code, to use words or expressions that your intimates will correctly interpret and others will not. For a milder version of the same approach, consider parents who talk to each other in a foreign language when they do not want their children to understand what they are saying, or a nineteenth-century translation of a Chinese novel I once came across, with the pornographic passages translated into Latin instead of English.

In Brin's future transparent society, many of us will become less willing to express our opinions of our boss, employees, ex-wife, or present husband in any public place. People will become less expressive and more self-contained, conversation bland or cryptic. If some spaces are still private, more of social life will shift to them. If every place is public, we have stepped back at least several centuries, arguably several millennia.

WHAT IS PRIVACY AND WHY DO WE WANT IT?

Think of "privacy" as shorthand for an individual's ability to control other people's access to information about him. If I have a legal right not to have you tap my phone but cannot enforce that right – the situation at present for those using cordless phones without encryption – then I have little privacy with regard to my phone calls. I have almost complete privacy with regard to my own thoughts, even though it is perfectly legal for other people to use the available technologies – listening to my voice and watching my facial expressions – to try to figure out what I am thinking. Privacy in this sense depends on a variety of things, including both law and technology. If someone invented an easy and accurate way of reading minds, privacy would be radically reduced even if there were no change in my legal rights.[5]

One reason to define privacy in this way is that I am interested in its consequences, in the ways in which my ability to control information about me benefits or harms myself and others – whatever the source of that ability may be. Another is that I am interested in the ways in which technology is likely to change the ability of an individual to control such information – hence in changes in privacy due to sources other than changes in my legal rights.

The Case Against Privacy[6]

Many people go to some trouble to reduce the amount others can find out about them. Many people, sometimes the same people, make an effort to get information about other people. This suggests an interesting question: On net, is an increase in privacy good or bad? Do I gain more from your being unable to find out things out about me than I lose from my being unable to find out things about you?

Most people seem to think that the answer is yes. It is common to see some new product, technology, or legal rule attacked as reducing privacy, rare to see anything attacked as increasing privacy. Why?

The reason I value my privacy is straightforward: Information about me in the hands of other people sometimes permits them to gain at my expense. They may do so by stealing my property – if, for example, they know when I will not be home. They may do so by getting more favorable terms in a voluntary transaction – if, for example, they know just how much I am willing to pay for the house they are selling. They may do so by preventing me from stealing their property – by, for example, not hiring me as company treasurer after discovering that I am a convicted embezzler.

Information about me in other people's hands may also benefit me – for example, the information that I am honest and competent. But privacy does not prevent that information from being available to them. If I have control over information about myself I can release it when, and only when, doing so is in my interest.[7]

My examples included one – where my privacy protects me from burglary – in which privacy produced a net benefit, since the gain to a burglar is normally less than the loss to his victim. It included one – where my privacy permitted me to steal from others – in which privacy produced a net loss. And it included one case – bargaining – where the net effect appeared to be a wash, since what I lost someone else gained.[8]

Looked at more carefully, that third case is probably a net gain. One of the risks of bargaining is bargaining breakdown when a seller over-estimates the price a buyer is willing to pay or a buyer makes the corresponding mistake the other way and the deal falls through, making both parties worse off than if they had each more accurately read the other. Privacy makes it harder to know things about other people – buyers and sellers are, after all, deliberately misrepresenting what they are willing to offer or accept in the hope of getting a better deal – making bargaining breakdown more likely. It looks as though privacy produces, on average, a net loss in situations where parties are seeking information about each other in order to improve the terms of a voluntary transaction, since it increases the risk of bargaining breakdown.⁹ In situations involving involuntary transactions, privacy produces a net gain if it is being used to protect other rights (assuming that those rights have been defined in a way that makes their protection desirable) and a net loss if it is being used to violate other rights (with the same assumption). There is no obvious reason that the former situation should be more common than the latter. So while it is clear why I am in favor of my having privacy, it is not clear why I should expect my gains from my having privacy to outweigh my losses from your having it, why people should regard privacy, generally speaking, as a good thing.

Privacy and Government

It would have been impossible to proportion with tolerable exactness the tax upon a shop to the extent of the trade carried on in it, without such an inquisition as would have been altogether insupportable in a free country.

> Adam Smith's explanation of why a sales tax is impractical
> (*Wealth of Nations* Bk V, Ch II, Pt 2, Art. II)

The state of a man's fortune varies from day to day, and without an inquisition more intolerable than any tax, and renewed at least once every year, can only be guessed at.

> Smith's explanation of why an income tax is impractical
> (*Wealth of Nations* Bk V, Ch II, Pt 2, Art. IV)

Although private parties occasionally engage in involuntary transactions such as burglary, most of our interactions with each other are voluntary ones. Governments engage in involuntary transactions on an enormously larger scale. And governments almost always have an overwhelming superiority of physical force over the individual citizen. While I can protect myself from my fellow citizens with locks and burglar alarms, I can protect myself from government actors only by keeping information about me out of their hands.¹⁰

The implications depend on one's view of government. If government is the modern equivalent of Plato's philosopher-king, individual privacy simply makes it harder for government to do good. If, on the other hand, a government is merely a particularly large and well-organized criminal gang, stealing as much as it can from the rest of us, individual privacy against government as an unambiguously good thing. Most Americans appear, judging by expressed views on privacy, to be close enough to the latter position to consider privacy against government as on the whole desirable, with an exception for cases where they believe that privacy might be used to conceal crimes substantially more serious than tax evasion.

Seen from this standpoint, one problem with Brin's transparent society is the enormous downside risk. Played out under less optimistic assumptions than his, the technology could enable a tyranny that Hitler or Stalin might envy. Even if we accept Brin's optimistic assumption that the citizens are as well informed about the police as the police are about the citizens, it is the police who have the guns. They know if we are doing or saying anything they disapprove of and respond accordingly, arresting, imprisoning, perhaps torturing or executing their opponents. We have the privilege of watching. Why should they object? Public executions are an old tradition, designed in part to discourage other people from doing things that might get them executed.

It does not follow that Brin's prescription is wrong. His argument, after all, is that privacy will simply not be an option, either because the visible benefits of surveillance are so large or because the technology will make it impossible to prevent it. If he is right, his transparent society may at least be better than the alternative – surveillance to which only those in power have access, a universal Panopticon with government as the prison guards.

SAY IT AIN'T SO

So far I have ignored one interesting problem with Brin's world – verification. Consider the following courtroom drama:

My wife is suing me for divorce on grounds of adultery. In support of her claim, she presents videotapes, taken by hidden cameras, that show me making love to three different women, none of them her.

My attorney asks for a postponement to investigate the new evidence. When the court reconvenes, he submits his own videotape. The jury observes my wife making love, consecutively, to Humphrey Bogart, Napoleon, her attorney, and the judge. When quiet is restored in the courtroom, my attorney presents the judge with the address of the video effects firm that produced the tape.

With modern technology I do not, or at least soon will not, need your cooperation to make a film of you doing things; a reasonable selection of photographs will suffice. As Hollywood demonstrated with *Roger Rabbit*, it is possible to combine real and cartoon characters in what looks like a single filmstrip. In the near future the equivalent, using convincing animations of real people, will be something that a competent amateur can produce on his desktop. We may finally get to see John F. Kennedy making love to Marilyn Monroe, whether or not it ever happened.

In that world, the distinction between what I know and what I can prove becomes critical. Our world may be filled with video mosquitoes, each reporting to its owner and each owner pouring the information into a common pool, but some of them might be lying. When I pull information out of the pool I have no way of knowing whether to believe it.

There are possible technological fixes – ways of using encryption technology to build a camera that digitally signs its output, demonstrating that that sequence was taken by that camera at a particular time. But it is hard to design a system that cannot be subverted by the camera's owner. Even if we can prove that a particular camera recorded a tape of me making love to six women, how do we know whether it did so while pointed at me or at a video screen displaying the work of an animation studio? The potential for forgery significantly weakens the ability of surveillance technology to produce verifiable information.

For many purposes, unverifiable information will do – if my wife wants to know about my infidelity but does not need to prove it. As long as the government running a surveillance system can trust its own people it can use that system to detect crimes or politically unpopular expressions of opinion. And video evidence will still be usable in trials, provided that it is accompanied by a sufficient evidence trail to prove where and when it was taken – and that it has not been improved since. It becomes more believable with redundancy – five video mosquitoes, belonging to five independent owners, showing the same thing happening.

SHOULD WE ABOLISH THE CRIMINAL LAW?

Modern societies have two different systems of legal rules – criminal law and tort law – that do essentially the same thing. Someone does something that injures others. He is charged, tried, and convicted, and something bad happens to him as a result, which gives other people an incentive not to do such things. In the criminal system prosecution is controlled and funded by the state, in the tort system by the victim. In the criminal system a compromise is called a plea bargain, in the tort system an out of court settlement. Criminal law provides a somewhat different range of punishments – it is not possible to execute someone for a tort, for example, although it was possible for something very much like a tort prosecution to lead to execution under English law a few centuries back – and operates under somewhat different legal rules.[11] But in their general outlines, the two systems are no more than slightly different ways of doing the same thing.

This raises an obvious question – is there any good reason to have both? Would we, for example, be better off abolishing criminal law entirely and instead having the victims of crimes sue the criminals?

One argument against such a pure tort system is that some offenses are hard to detect. A victim may conclude that catching and prosecuting the offender costs more than it is worth, especially if the offender turns out not to have enough assets to pay substantial damages. Hence some categories of offense may routinely go unpunished.

In Brin's world that problem vanishes. Every mugging is on tape. If the mugger chooses to wear a mask while committing his crime we can trace him backwards or forwards through the record until he takes it off. While a sufficiently ingenious criminal might find a way around that problem, most of the offenses that our criminal law now deals with would be cases where most of the facts are known and only their legal implications remain to be determined. The normal crime becomes very much like the normal tort – an auto accident, say, where (except in the case of hit and run, which is a crime) the identity of the party and many of the relevant facts are public information. In that world it might make sense to abolish criminal law and shift everything to the decentralized, privately controlled alternative. If someone steals your car you check the video record to identify the thief, then sue for the car plus a reasonable payment for your time and trouble recovering it.

Like many radical ideas, this one looks less radical if one is familiar with the relevant history. Legal systems in which something similar to tort law dealt with what we think of as crimes – in which if you killed someone his kinsmen sued you – are common in the historical record.[12] Even as late as the eighteenth century, while the English legal system distinguished between torts and crimes, both were in practice privately prosecuted, usually by the victim.[13] One possible explanation for the shift to a modern, publicly prosecuted system of criminal law is that it was a response to the increasing anonymity that accompanied the shift to a more urban society in the late eighteenth and early nineteenth century.[14] Technologies that reverse that shift may justify a reversal of the accompanying legal changes.

WHERE WORLDS COLLIDE

In Chapter 4 I described a cyberspace with more privacy than we have today. In this chapter I have described a realspace with less. What happens if we get both?

It does no good to use strong encryption for my email if a video mosquito is sitting on the wall watching me type. So strong privacy in a transparent society requires some way of guarding the interface between my realspace body and cyberspace. This is no big problem in the version where the walls of my house are still opaque.[15] It is a serious problem in the version in which every place is, in fact if not in law, public. A low-tech solution is to type under a hood. A high-tech solution is some link between mind and machine that does not go through the fingers – or anything else visible to an outside observer.[16]

The conflict between realspace transparency and cyberspace privacy goes in the other direction as well. If we are sufficiently worried about other people hearing what we say, one solution is to encrypt face-to-face conversation. With suitable wireless gadgets, I talk into a throat mike or type on a virtual keyboard (keeping my hands in my pockets). My pocket computer encrypts my message with your public key and transmits it to your pocket computer, which decrypts the message and displays it through your VR glasses. To make sure nothing is reading the glasses over your shoulder, the goggles get the image to you not by displaying it on a screen but by using a tiny laser to write it on your retina. With any luck, the inside of your eyeball is still private space.

We could end up in a world where physical actions are entirely public, information transactions entirely private. It has some attractive features. Private citizens will still be able to take advantage of strong privacy to locate a hit man, but hiring him may cost more than they are willing to pay, since in a sufficiently transparent world all murders are detected. Each hit man executes one commission and then goes directly to jail.

What about the interaction between these technologies and data processing? On the one hand, it is modern data processing that makes the transparent society such a threat – without that, it would not much matter if you videotaped everything that happened in the world, since nobody could ever find the particular six inches of videotape he wanted in the millions of miles produced each day. On the other hand, the technologies that support strong privacy provide the possibility of reestablishing privacy, even in a world with modern data processing, by keeping information about your transactions from ever getting to anyone but you. That is a subject we will return to in a later chapter when we discuss digital cash – an idea dreamed up in part as a way of restoring transactional privacy.

PART THREE

DOING BUSINESS ONLINE

SIX

Ecash

I pay for things in one of three different ways – credit card, check, or cash. The first two let me make large payments without having to carry large amounts of money. What are the advantages of the third?

One is that a seller does not have to know anything about me in order to accept cash. That makes money a better medium for transactions with strangers, especially strangers from far away. It also makes it a better medium for small transactions, since using cash avoids the fixed costs of checking up on someone to make sure that there is really money in his checking account or that his credit is good. It also means that money leaves no paper trail, which is useful not only for criminals but for anyone who wants to protect his privacy – an increasingly important issue in a world where data processing threatens to make every detail of our lives public.

The advantage of money is greater in cyberspace, since transactions with strangers, including strangers far away, are more likely on the Internet than in my realspace neighborhood. The disadvantage is less, since my ecash would be stored inside my computer, which is usually inside my house, and hence less vulnerable to theft than my wallet.

Despite its potential usefulness, there is as yet no equivalent of cash available online, although there have been unsuccessful attempts to create one and successful attempts to create something close. The reason is not technological; those problems have been solved. The reason is in part the hostility of governments to competition in the money business, and in part the difficulty of getting standards, in this case private monetary standards, established. I expect both problems to be solved sometime in the next decade or two.

Before discussing how a system of electronic currency, private or governmental, might work, it is worth first giving at least one example of why it would be useful – for something more important than allowing men to look at pornography online without their wives or employers finding out.

SLICING SPAM

My email contains much of interest. It also contains READY FOR A SMOOTH WAY OUT OF DEBT?, A Personal Invitation from make_real_money@BIGFOOT.COM, You've Been Selected.... from friend@localhost.net, and a variety of similar messages, of which my favorite offers "the answer to all your questions." The Internet has brought many things of value, but for most of us unsolicited commercial email, better known as *spam*, is not one of them.

There is a simple solution to this problem – so simple that I am surprised it is not yet in common use. The solution is to put a price on your mailbox. Give your email program a list of the people you wish to receive mail from. Mail from anyone not on the list is returned with a note explaining that you charge five cents to read mail from strangers – and the URL of the stamp machine. Five cents is a trivial cost to anyone with something to say that you are likely to want to read, but five cents times ten million recipients is quite a substantial cost to someone sending out bulk email on the chance that one recipient in ten thousand may respond.

The stamp machine is located on a web page. The stamps are digital cash. Pay $10 from your credit card and you get in exchange 200 five-cent stamps – each a morsel of encrypted information that you can transfer to someone else who can in turn transfer it.

A virtual stamp, unlike a real stamp, can be reused; it is paying not for the cost of transmitting my mail but for my time and trouble reading it, so the payment goes to me, not the post office. I can use it the next time I want to send a message to a stranger. If lots of strangers choose to send me messages, I can accumulate a surplus of stamps to be eventually changed back into cash.

How much I charge is up to me. If I hate reading messages from strangers, I can make the price $1, or $10, or $100 – and get very few of them. If I enjoy junk email, I can set a low price. Once such a system is established, the same people who currently create and rent out the mailing lists used to send spam will add another service – a database keeping track of what each potential target charges to receive it.

What is in it for the stamp machine – why would someone maintain such a system? Part of the answer is seigniorage – the profit from coining money. After selling a hundred million five-cent stamps, you have five million dollars of money. If your stamps are popular, many of them may stay in circulation for a long time – leaving the money that bought them in your bank account accumulating interest.

In addition to the free use of other people's money, there is a second advantage. If you own the stamp machine, you also own the wall behind it – the web page people visit to buy stamps. Advertisements on that wall will be seen by a lot of people.

One reason this solution to spam requires ecash is that it involves a large number of very small payments. It would be a great deal clumsier if we used credit cards – every time you received a message with a five-cent stamp, you would have to check with the sender's bank before reading it to make sure the payment was good. A second reason is privacy. Many of us would prefer not to leave a complete record of our correspondence with a third party – which we would be doing if we used credit cards or something similar. What we want is not merely ecash but anonymous ecash – some way of making payments that provides no information to third parties about who has paid what to whom.

CONSTRUCTING ECASH

Suppose a bank wants to create a system of ecash. The first and easiest problem is how to provide people with virtual banknotes that cannot be counterfeited.

The solution is a digital signature. The bank creates a banknote that says "First Bank of Cyberspace: Pay the bearer one dollar in U.S. currency." It digitally signs the note, using its private key. It makes the matching public key widely available. When you come into the bank with a dollar, it gives you a banknote in the form of a file on a flash drive. You transfer the file to your hard disk, which now has a one-dollar bill with which to buy something from someone else online. When he receives the file he checks the digital signature against the bank's public key.

The Double Spending Problem

There is a problem – a big problem. What you have gotten for your dollar is not a single dollar bill but an unlimited number of them. Sending a copy of the file in payment for one transaction does not erase it from your computer, so you can send it again to someone else to buy something else. And again. That is going to be a problem for the bank, when twenty people come in to claim your original dollar bill.

One solution is for the bank to give each dollar its own identification number and keep track of which ones have been spent. When a merchant receives your file he sends it to the bank, which deposits the corresponding dollar in his account and adds its number to a list of banknotes that are no longer valid. When you try to spend a second copy of the note, the merchant who receives it tries to deposit it, is informed that it is no longer valid, and doesn't send you your goods.

This solves the problem of double spending, but it also eliminates most of the advantages of ecash over credit cards. The bank knows that it issued banknote 94602 . . . to Alice, and it knows that it came back from Bill, so it knows that Alice bought something from Bill, just as it would if she had used a credit card.

The solution to this problem uses what David Chaum, the Dutch cryptographer who is responsible for many of the ideas underlying ecash, calls *blind signatures*. It is a way in which Alice, having rolled up a random identification number for a dollar bill, can get the bank to sign that number (in exchange for paying the bank a dollar) without having to tell the bank what the number they are signing is. Even though the bank does not know the serial number it signed, both it and the merchant who receives the note can check that the signature is valid. Once the dollar bill is spent, the merchant has the serial number, which he reports to the bank, which can add it to the list of serial numbers that are now invalid. The bank knows it provided a dollar to Alice, and it knows it received back a dollar from Bill, but it does not know that they are the same dollar.

So it does not know that Alice bought something from Bill. The seller has to check with the bank and know that the bank is trustworthy, but it does not have to know anything about the purchaser.

Curious readers will want to know how it is possible for a bank to sign a serial number without knowing what it is. I cannot tell them without first explaining the mathematics of public key encryption, which requires more math than I am willing to assume my average reader has. Those who are curious can find the answers via the virtual footnotes (www.daviddfriedman.com/Future_Imperfect.html), which point to webbed explanations of both public key encryption and blind signatures.

So far I have been assuming that people who receive digital cash can communicate with the bank that issues it while the transaction is taking place – that they and the bank are connected to the Internet or something similar. That is not a serious constraint if the transaction is occurring online. But digital cash could also be useful for realspace transactions, and the cabby or hotdog vendor may not yet have an Internet connection.

The solution is another clever trick (Chaum specializes in clever tricks). It is a form of ecash that contains information about the person it was issued to but only reveals that information if the same dollar bill is spent twice. For an explanation of how it works, you must again go to the virtual footnotes.

Skeptical readers should at this point be growing increasingly unhappy at being told that everything about ecash is done by mathematics that I am unwilling to explain – which they may reasonably enough translate as "smoke and mirrors." For their benefit I have invented my own form of ecash – one that has all of the features of the real thing and can be understood with no mathematics beyond the ability to recognize numbers. It is a good deal less convenient than Chaum's version but a lot easier to explain, and so provides at least a possibility proof for the real thing.

Low-Tech Ecash

I randomly create a very long number. I put the number and a dollar bill in an envelope and mail it to the First Bank of Cybercash. The FBC agrees – in a public statement – to do two things with money it receives in this way:

1. If anyone walks into the FBC and presents the number, he gets the dollar bill associated with that number.
2. If the FBC receives a message that includes the number associated with a dollar bill it has on deposit, instructing the FBC to change it to a new number, it will make the change and post the fact of the transaction on a publicly observable bulletin board. The dollar bill will now be associated with the new number.

Let's see how this works:

Alice has sent the FBC a dollar, accompanied by the number 59372. She now wants to buy a dollar's worth of digital images from Bill, so she emails the number to him in payment. Bill emails the FBC, sending them three numbers: 59372, 21754, and 46629.

The FBC checks to see if it has a dollar on deposit with number 59372; it does. It changes the number associated with that dollar bill to 21754, Bill's second number. Simultaneously, it posts on a publicly observable bulletin board the statement "the transaction identified by 46629 has gone through." Bill reads that message, which tells him that Alice really had a dollar bill on deposit and it is now his, so he emails her a dollar's worth of digital images.

Alice no longer has a dollar, since if she tries to spend it again the bank will report that it is not there to be spent – the FBC no longer has a dollar associated with the number she knows. Bill now has a dollar, since the dollar that Alice originally sent in is now associated with a new number and only he and the bank know what it is. He is in precisely the same situation that Alice was in before the transaction, so he can now spend the dollar to buy something from someone else. Like an ordinary paper dollar, the dollar of ecash in my system passes from hand to hand. Eventually someone who has it decides he wants a dollar of ordinary cash instead; he takes his number, the number that Alice's original dollar is now associated with, to the FBC and exchanges it for a dollar bill.

My ecash may be low-tech, but it meets all of the requirements. Payment is made by sending a message. Payer and payee need know nothing about the other's identity beyond the address to send the message to. The bank need know nothing about either party. When the dollar bill originally came in, the letter had no name on it, only an identifying number. Each time it changed hands, the bank received an email but had no information about who sent it. When the chain of transactions ends and someone comes into the bank to collect the dollar bill he need not identify himself; even if the bank can somehow identify him he has no way of tracing the dollar bill back up the chain. The virtual dollar in my system is just as anonymous as the paper dollars in my wallet.

With lots of dollar bills in the bank there is a risk that two might by chance have the same number, or that someone might make up numbers and pay with them in the hope that the numbers he invents will, by chance, match numbers associated with dollar bills in the bank. But both problems become insignificant if instead of using 5-digit numbers we use 100-digit numbers. The chance that two random 100-digit numbers will turn out to be the same is a good deal less than the chance that payer, payee, and bank will all be struck by lightning at the same time.

Robot Mechanics

It may have occurred to you that if you have to roll up a 100-digit random number every time you want to buy a dollar of ecash from the bank and two more every time you receive one from anyone else, not to mention sending off one anonymous email to the bank for every dollar you receive, ecash may be more trouble than it is worth. Don't worry – that's your computer's job, not yours. With a competently designed ecash system, the program takes care of all mathematical details; all you have to worry about is having enough money to pay your (virtual) bills. You tell your computer what to pay to whom; it tells you what other people have paid to you and how much money you have. Random numbers, checks of digital signatures, blind signing, and all the rest are done in the background. If you find that hard to believe, consider how little most of us know about how the tools we routinely use, such as cars, computers, or radios, actually work.

ECASH AND PRIVACY

When Chaum came up with the idea of ecash, email was not yet sufficiently popular to make spam an issue. What motivated him was the problem we discussed back in Chapter 4 – the loss of privacy created by the ability of modern information processing to combine publicly available information into a detailed portrait of each individual.

Consider an application of ecash that Chaum has actually worked on – automated toll collection. It would be very convenient if, instead of stopping at a toll booth when getting on or off the interstate, we could simply drive past, making the payment automatically in the form of a wireless communication between the (unmanned) tollbooth and the car. The technology to do this exists and has long been used to provide automated toll collection for busses on some roads.

One problem is privacy. If the payment is made with a credit card, or if the toll agency adds up each month's tolls and sends you a bill, someone has a complete record of every trip you have taken on the toll road, every time you have crossed a toll bridge. If we deal with auto pollution by measuring pollutants in the exhaust plumes of passing automobiles and billing their owners, someone ends up with detailed, if somewhat fragmentary, records of where you were when.

Ecash solves that problem. As you whiz past the tollbooth, your car pays it fifty cents in anonymous ecash. By the time you are thirty feet down the road, the (online) tollbooth has checked that the money is good; if it isn't an alarm goes off, a camera triggers, and if you do not stop a traffic cop eventually appears on your tail. But if your money is good you go quietly about your business – and there is no record of your passing the tollbooth. The information never came into existence, save in your head. Similarly for an automated system of pollution charges.

It works for shopping as well. Ecash – this time encoded in a smart card in your wallet, a palmtop computer in your pocket, or perhaps even a tiny chip embedded under your skin – could provide much of the convenience of a credit card with the anonymity of cash. If you want the seller to know who you are, you are free to tell him. But if you prefer to keep your transactions private, you can.

PRIVATE MONEY: A NEW OLD STORY

My examples so far assume that ecash will be produced and redeemed by private banks but denominated in government money. Both are likely, at least in the short run. Neither is necessary.

Private money denominated in dollars is already common. My money market fund is denominated in dollars, although Merrill Lynch does not actually have a stack of dollar bills in a vault somewhere that corresponds to the amount of money "in" my account. My university ID card doubles as a money card, with some number of dollars stored on its magnetic strip – a number that decreases every time I use the card to buy lunch on campus. A bank could issue ecash on the same basis. Each dollar of ecash represents a claim to be paid a dollar bill. The actual assets backing that claim consist not of a stack of dollar bills but of stocks, bonds, and the like – which have the advantage of paying the bank interest for as long as the dollar of ecash is out there circulating.

While I do not have to know anything about you in order to accept your ecash, I do have to know something about the bank that issues it – enough to be sure that the money will eventually be redeemed. That means that any ecash expected to circulate widely will be issued by organizations with reputations. In a world of almost instantaneous information transmission, those organizations will have a strong incentive to maintain their reputations, since a loss of confidence will result in money holders bringing in virtual banknotes to be redeemed, eliminating the source of income that the assets backing those banknotes provided.

Some economists, in rejecting the idea of private money, have argued that such an institution is inherently inflationary. Since issuing money costs a bank nothing and gives it the interest on the assets it buys with the money, it is always in the bank's interest to issue more. The rebuttal to this particular argument was published in 1776. When Adam Smith wrote *The Wealth of Nations*, the money of Scotland consisted largely of banknotes issued by private banks, redeemable in silver.[1] As Smith pointed out, while a bank could print as many notes as it wished, it could not persuade other people to hold an unlimited number of its notes. A customer who holds $1,000 in virtual cash – or Scottish banknotes – when he only needs $100 is giving up the interest he could have been earning if he had held the other $900 in some interest-earning asset instead. That is a good reason to limit his cash holdings to the amount he actually needs for day-to-day transactions.

What happens if a bank tries to issue more of its money than people wish to hold? The excess comes back to be redeemed. The bank is wasting its resources printing money, trying to put it into circulation, only to have each extra banknote promptly returned for cash – in Smith's case, silver. The obligation of the bank to redeem its money guarantees its value, and at that value there is a fixed amount of its money that people will choose to hold.

> Let us suppose that all the paper of a particular bank, which the circulation of the country can easily absorb and employ, amounts exactly to forty thousand pounds; and that for answering occasional demands, this bank is obliged to keep at all times in its coffers ten thousand pounds in gold and silver. Should this bank attempt to circulate forty-four thousand pounds, the four thousand pounds which are over and above what the circulation can easily absorb and employ, will return upon it almost as fast as they are issued.
>
> (*Wealth of Nations*, Bk I, chapter 2)

So far I have assumed that future ecash will be denominated in dollars. Dollars have one great advantage – they provide a common unit already in widespread use. They also have one great disadvantage – they are produced by a government, and it may not always be in the interest of that government to maintain their value in a stable, or even predictable, way. On past evidence, governments sometimes increase or decrease the value of their currency, inadvertently or for any of a variety of political purposes. In the extreme case of hyperinflation, a government tries to fund its activities with the printing press, rapidly increasing the amount of money and decreasing its value. In less extreme cases, a government might inflate in order to benefit debtors by inflating away the real value of their debts – governments themselves are often debtors, hence potential beneficiaries of such a policy – or it might inflate or deflate in the process of trying to manipulate its economy for political ends.

Dollars have a second disadvantage, although perhaps a less serious one. Because they are issued by a particular government, citizens of other governments may prefer not to use them. This has not prevented dollars from becoming a *de facto* world currency, but it is one reason why a national currency might not be the best standard to base ecash on. The simplest alternative would be a commodity standard, making the unit of ecash a gram of silver or gold or some other widely traded commodity.

Under such a commodity standard the monetary unit, while no longer under the control of a government, is subject instead to the forces that affect the value of the particular commodity it is based on. If large amounts of gold are discovered or if someone invents new and better techniques for extracting gold from low-grade ore, the value of gold, and of gold-based money, will decline.[2] If, on the other hand, important new uses for gold are found but little new gold is mined, the value of gold will rise and prices fall. Thus commodity money carries with it at least some risk of unpredictable fluctuations in its value, and hence in prices measured in it.

That problem is solved by replacing a simple commodity standard with a commodity bundle. Bring in a million Friedman dollars and I agree to give you in exchange 10 ounces of gold, 40 ounces of silver, ownership of 1,000 bushels each of grade A wheat and grade B soybeans, a ton of grade S30040 stainless steel. ... If the purchasing power of a million of my dollars is less than the value of the bundle, it is profitable for people to assemble a million Friedman dollars, exchange them for the bundle, and sell the contents of the bundle – forcing me to make good on my promise and, in the process, reducing the amount of my money in circulation. If the purchasing power of my money is more than the worth of the commodities it trades for, it is in my interest to issue more money. Since the bundle contains lots of different commodities, random changes in commodity prices can be expected to roughly average out, giving us a stable standard of value.

A commodity bundle is a good theoretical solution to the problem of monetary standards, but implementing it has a serious practical difficulty – getting all the firms issuing ecash to agree on the same bundle. If they fail to establish a common standard, we end up with a cyberspace in which different people use different currencies and the exchange rates between them vary randomly.

That is not an unworkable situation – Europeans lived with it for a very long time – but it is a nuisance. Life is easier if the money I use is the same as the money used by the people I do business with. On that fact our present world system – multiple government moneys, each with a near monopoly within the territory of the issuing government – is built. It works because most transactions are with people near you and people near you probably live in the same country you do. It works less well in Europe than in North America because the countries are smaller, which is why the European countries have largely moved from national currencies to the euro.

A system of multiple monopoly government moneys works less well in cyberspace because in cyberspace national borders are transparent. For information transactions, geography is irrelevant – I can download software or digital images from London as easily as from New York. For online purchases of physical objects geography is not entirely irrelevant, since the goods have to be delivered, but less relevant than in realspace shopping. With a system of national currencies, everyone in cyberspace has to juggle multiple currencies in the process of figuring out who has the best price and paying it. The obvious solution is to establish a single standard of value, either by adopting one national currency, probably the dollar, possibly the euro, or by establishing a private standard such as the sort of commodity bundle described earlier.

That may not be the only solution. The reason that everyone wants to use the same currency as his neighbors is that currency conversion is a nuisance. But currency conversion is arithmetic and computers do arithmetic fast and cheap. Perhaps, with some minor improvements in the interfaces on which we do online business, we could make the choice of currency irrelevant, permitting multiple standards to coexist.

I live in the United States; you live in India. You have goods to sell, displayed on a web page, with prices in rupees. I view that page through my brand new browser – Firefox v 9.0. One feature of the new browser is that it is currency transparent. You post your prices in rupees but I see them in dollars. The browser does the conversion on the fly, using exchange rates read, minute by minute, from my bank's web page. If I want to buy your goods, I pay in dollar-denominated ecash; my browser sends it to my bank, which sends rupee-denominated ecash to you. I neither know nor care what country you are in or what money you use – it's all dollars to me.

Currency transparency will be easiest online, where everything filters through browsers anyway. One can imagine, with a little more effort, realspace equivalents. An unobtrusive tag on my lapel gives my preferred currency; an automated price label on the store shelf reads my tag and displays the price accordingly. Alternatively, the price is displayed by a dumb price tag, read by a smart video camera set into the frame of my glasses, converted to my preferred currency by my pocket computer, and written in the air by the heads-up display generated by the eyeglass lenses.

As I write, the countries of Europe are in the final stages of replacing their multiple national currencies with the euro. If the picture I have just painted turns out to be correct, they may have finally achieved a common currency just as it was becoming unnecessary.

We now have three possibilities for ecash. It might be produced by multiple issuers but denominated in dollars or some other widely used national money. It might be denominated in some common nongovernmental standard of value – gold, silver, or a commodity bundle. It might be denominated in a variety of different standards, perhaps including both national monies and commodities, with conversion handled transparently, so that each individual sees a world where everyone is using his money. Any of these forms of ecash might be produced by private firms, probably banks, or by governments.[3]

WILL IT HAPPEN?

During World War II, George Orwell wrote regular articles for *Partisan Review,* an American magazine. Near the end of the war, he wrote a retrospective in which he discussed what he had gotten right and what wrong.[4] One of his conclusions was that he was generally right about the way the world was moving, wrong about how fast it would get there. He correctly saw the logical pattern but failed to allow for the enormous inertia of human society.

Similarly here. David Chaum's articles laying out the groundwork for fully anonymous electronic money were published in technical journals in the 1980s and summarized in a 1992 article in *Scientific American.* Ever since then various people, myself among them, have been predicting the rise of ecash along the lines he sketched. While pieces of his vision have become real in other contexts, there is as yet nothing close to a fully anonymous ecash available for general use. Chaum himself, working with the Mark Twain Bank of Saint Louis, attempted to get a semi-anonymous ecash into circulation – one that permitted one party to a transaction to be identified by joint action of the other party and the bank. The effort failed and was abandoned.

One reason it has not happened is that online commerce has only very recently become large enough to justify it. A second reason, I suspect but cannot prove, is that national governments are unhappy with the idea of a widely used money that they cannot control and so are reluctant to permit (heavily regulated) private banks to create such a money. A third and closely related reason is that a truly anonymous ecash would eliminate a profitable form of law enforcement. There is no practical way to enforce money-laundering laws once it is possible to move arbitrarily large amounts of money anywhere in the world, untraceably, with the click of a mouse. A final reason is that ecash is only useful to me if many other people are using it, which raises a problem in getting it started.

These factors have slowed the introduction of ecash. I do not think they will stop it. It only takes one country willing to permit it and one issuing institution in that country willing to issue it, to bring ecash into existence. Once it exists, it will be politically difficult for other countries to forbid their citizens from using it and practically difficult, if it is forbidden, to enforce the ban. There are a lot of countries in the world, even if we limit ourselves to ones with sufficiently stable institutions so that people elsewhere will trust their money. Hence my best guess is that some version of one of the moneys I have described in this chapter will come into existence sometime in the next decade or so.

SEVEN

Contracts in Cyberspace

You hire someone to fix your roof and (imprudently) pay him in advance. Two weeks later, you call to ask when he is going to get the job done. After three months of alternating promises and silence, you sue him, probably in small claims court.

Suing someone is a nuisance, which is why you waited three months. In cyberspace it will be even more of a nuisance. The law that applies to a dispute depends, in a complicated way, on where the parties live and where the events they are litigating over happened. A contract made online has no geographical location and the other party might live anywhere in the world. Suing someone in another state is bad enough; suing someone in another country is best left to professionals – who do not come cheap. If, as I suggested in an earlier chapter, the use of online encryption leads to a world of strong privacy, where many people do business without revealing their realspace identity, legal enforcement of contracts becomes not merely difficult but impossible. There is no way to sue someone if you do not know who he is.

Even in our realspace lives, however, there is another way of enforcing contracts, and one that is probably more important than litigation. The reason department stores make good on their "money back, no questions asked" promises, and the reason the people who mow my lawn keep doing it once a week even when I am out of town and so unable to pay them, is not the court system. Customers are unlikely to sue a department store, however unreasonable its grounds for refusing to take something back, and the people who mow my lawn are unlikely to sue me, even if I refuse to pay them for their last three weeks of work.

97

What enforces the contract in both cases is reputation. The department store wants to keep me as a customer and won't if I conclude that they are not to be trusted. Not only will they lose me, they may well lose some of my friends, to whom I can be expected to complain. The people who mow my lawn do a good job at a reasonable price, such people are not easy to find, and I would be foolish to offend them by refusing to pay for their work.

When we shift our transactions from the neighborhood to the Internet, legal enforcement becomes harder. Reputational enforcement, however, becomes easier. The net provides a superb set of tools for collecting and disseminating information, including information about who can or cannot be trusted.

On an informal level, this happens routinely through both Usenet and the Web. Some years back, I heard that my favorite palmtop – a full-featured computer, complete with keyboard, word processor, spreadsheet, and much else, which fitted in my pocket and ran more or less forever on its rechargeable battery – was available at an absurdly low price from a discount reseller, apparently because the attempt to sell it in the U.S. market[1] had failed and the company that made that attempt was dumping its stock of rebranded Psion Revos (aka Diamond Makos). I went on the Web, searched for the reseller, and in the process discovered that it had been repeatedly accused of failing to live up to its service guarantees and was currently in trouble with authorities in several states. The same process works in a somewhat more organized fashion through specialist web pages – MacInTouch for Macintosh users, the Digital Camera Resource Page for consumers of digital cameras, and many more.

For a different version of reputational enforcement online, consider eBay. eBay does not sell goods; it sells the service of helping other people sell goods, via an online auction system. That raises an obvious problem. Sellers may be located anywhere – quite often outside the United States. Most transactions, although not all, involve goods of modest value, so suing for failure to deliver, especially suing someone outside the United States for failure to deliver, is rarely a practical option. With millions of buyers and sellers, each individual buyer is not likely to buy many things from any particular seller, so the seller need be only mildly concerned about his reputation with that particular buyer. Why don't all sellers simply take the money and run?

One reason is that eBay provides extensive support for reputational enforcement. Anytime you win an eBay auction you have the option, after taking delivery, of reporting your evaluation of the transaction – whether the goods were as described and delivered in good condition, and anything else you care to add. Anytime you bid on an eBay auction, you have access to all past comments on the seller, both in summary form and, if you are sufficiently interested, in full. Successful eBay sellers generally have a record of many comments, very few of them negative.

There are, of course, ways that a sufficiently enterprising villain could try to game the system. One would be by setting up a series of bogus auctions, selling something under one name, buying it under another, and giving himself a good review. Eventually he builds up a string of glowing reviews and uses them to sell a dozen nonexistent goods for high prices, payable in advance.

It's possible, but it isn't cheap. eBay, after all, will be collecting its cut of each of those bogus auctions. The nominal buyers will require many different identities in order to keep the trick from being obvious, which involves additional costs. Meanwhile all the legitimate sellers have to do in order to build up their reputation is honest business as usual. And eBay itself, in order to maintain its reputation as a good place to buy and sell, attempts in various ways to prevent buyers and sellers from abusing the reputational mechanisms it has created. I am confident, on the basis of no inside information at all, that at least one villain has done it successfully – but there don't seem to be enough to seriously discourage people from using eBay.

Another way a dishonest seller could try to abuse the system is by buying goods from competitors under a false name and then posting (false) negative information about the transaction. That might be worth doing in a market with only a few sellers – and for all I know it has happened. But in the typical eBay market, with many sellers as well as many buyers, defaming one competitor merely transfers the business to another.

THE LOGIC OF REPUTATIONAL ENFORCEMENT

While reputational enforcement along the lines of what eBay currently provides is adequate for many purposes, it would be useful to have systems that are harder to cheat on. Before looking at how they might work, it is worth thinking a little more about the logic of reputational enforcement. Criminal law and tort law exist, in large part, as ways of punishing bad behavior. In the case of reputational enforcement, in contrast, punishment is only an indirect consequence of actions taken for other reasons. Consider an (imaginary) example:

The news that Charley bought an expensive suit jacket at the local department store, his wife made him take it back, and they refused to return his money, gives me no reason to want to punish the store. Ever since Charley told me what he really thought of my latest book, I have regarded his misfortunes as no more than he deserves. As the story spreads, more and more people stop shopping at that particular store. The reason is not that we wish to punish them – Charley's unfortunate habit of telling people what he really thinks has left him few friends. The reason is to protect ourselves. We too might someday buy something our wives disapproved of.

Reputational enforcement works by spreading true information about bad behavior. People who receive that information modify their actions accordingly, which imposes costs on those who have behaved badly.[2] As this example suggests, one thing determining how well reputational enforcement works is the ability of interested third parties to get information about who cheated whom.

To see this, suppose we change the story a little by making Charley not merely tactless but routinely dishonest. Now when he complains that the store refused to take the jacket back even though it was in good condition, we conclude that his idea of good condition probably included multiple ink stains and a missing sleeve, due to his wife's reaction to how he had been wasting their money – we know her too – and we continue patronizing the store.

One reason information costs are important is that if interested third parties do not know who is at fault, they do not know who to avoid future dealings with. A more subtle reason is that if third parties cannot easily find out who is at fault in a dispute, the dispute may never become public. If I accuse you of swindling me, you will of course deny it. Reasonable third parties, unable to check either side's claims, conclude that at least one of us is a crook. They have no way of finding out which, and it is therefore prudent to avoid both. Anticipating that result, I decide to swallow my losses and try to more careful next time; complaining will only make things worse.[3] So reputational enforcement requires a framework that makes it easy for interested third parties to determine who is at fault.

Such a framework exists and is used to settle intra-industry disputes in many different industries. It is called *arbitration.*

You and I make an agreement and specify the private arbitrator who will settle disagreements over its terms. A disagreement occurs; you demand arbitration. The arbitrator decides in your favor. If I refuse to obey the ruling, the arbitrator can make that fact public. An interested third party, typically another firm in the same industry, does not have to know the facts of the dispute to know who is at fault. All it has to know is that both of us agreed to the arbitrator and the arbitrator we agreed to says that I reneged on that agreement.[4]

This works well within an industry because the people involved know each other and are familiar with the industry's institutions for settling disputes. It works less well for disputes between a firm and one of its many customers. Other customers, unless they too are part of the industry, are unlikely to know enough about the institutions to be confident about who was cheating whom. What about in cyberspace?

Very Close to Zero: Third-Party Costs in Cyberspace

You and I agree to a contract online. The contract contains the name of the arbitrator who will resolve disputes and his public key – the information necessary to check his digital signature. We both digitally sign the contract and each keeps a copy.

A dispute arises; you accuse me of failing to live up to my agreement and demand arbitration. The arbitrator rules for you and instructs me to pay you $5,000 in damages. I refuse. The arbitrator writes an account of how the case came out: he awarded damages, I refused to pay them. He digitally signs it and sends you a copy.

You now have a package – the original contract and the arbitrator's verdict. My digital signature on the original contract proves that I agreed to that arbitrator; his digital signature on the verdict proves that I reneged on that agreement. That is all the information that an interested third party needs in order to conclude that I am not to be trusted.

You put the package on a web page, with my name all over it for the benefit of any search engines looking for information about me, and email the URL to anyone you think might want to do business with me in the future. Anyone who accesses the page can check the facts – more precisely, his computer can check the facts for him, by checking the digital signatures – in something under a second. Having done that, he knows that I am the one who reneged on the agreement. The most likely explanation is that I am dishonest. An alternative possibility is that I was fool enough to agree to a crooked arbitrator – but he probably doesn't want to do business with fools either. Thus the technology of digital signatures makes it possible to reduce information costs to third parties to something very close to zero, making possible effective reputational enforcement online.[5]

Private enforcement of contracts along these lines solves the problems raised by the fact that cyberspace spans many geographical jurisdictions. The relevant law is defined not by the jurisdiction but by the private arbitrator chosen by the parties. Over time, we would expect one or more body of legal rules with regard to contracts to develop, as the Law Merchant historically did develop, with many different arbitrators or arbitration firms adopting the same or similar legal rules.[6] Contracting parties could then choose arbitrators on the basis of reputation.

For small-scale transactions, you simply provide your browser with a list of acceptable arbitration firms; when you contract with another party, the software picks an arbitrator from the intersection of the two lists. If there exists no arbitrator acceptable to both parties, the software notifies both of you of the problem and you take it from there. For larger transactions, the choice of arbitrator is one of the things that the human beings negotiating the contract can bargain over.

Private enforcement also solves the problem of enforcing contracts when at least one of the parties is, and wishes to remain, anonymous. Digital signatures make it possible to combine anonymity with reputation. A computer programmer living in Russia or Iraq, where anonymity is the only way of protecting income from private or public bandits, has an online identity defined by his public key; any message signed by that public key is from him. That identity has a reputation, developed through past online transactions. The more times the programmer has demonstrated himself to be honest and competent, the more willing people will be to employ him. The reputation is valuable, so the programmer has an incentive to maintain it – by keeping his contracts.[7]

The Reputation Market

(On Earth they) even have laws for private matters such as contracts. Really. If a man's word isn't any good, who would contract with him? Doesn't he have reputation?

Manny in *The Moon is a Harsh Mistress* by Robert Heinlein

There is one way in which the online world I have been describing makes contract enforcement harder than in the real world. In the real world, my identity is tied to a physical body, identifiable by face, fingerprints, and the like. I do not have the option, after destroying my realspace reputation for honesty, of spinning off a new me, complete with new face, new fingerprints, and an unblemished reputation.

Online I do have that option. As long as other people are willing to deal with cyberspace personae not linked to realspace identities, I always have the option of rolling up a new public key/private key pair and going online with a new identity and a clean reputation.

It follows that reputational enforcement will only work for people who have reputations – sufficient reputational capital so that the cost of abandoning the current online persona and its reputation outweighs the gain from a single act of cheating. Someone who wants to deal anonymously in a trust-intensive industry may have to start small, building up his reputation to the point where its value is sufficient to make it rational to trust him with larger transactions. The same thing happens today in industries where enforcement is primarily through reputational mechanisms.[8]

The problem of spinning off new identities is not limited to cyberspace. The realspace equivalent of rolling up a new pair of keys is filing a new set of incorporation papers. Marble facing for bank buildings and expensive advertising campaigns can be seen as ways in which a new firm posts a reputational bond in order to persuade those who deal with it that they can trust it to act in a way that will preserve its reputation. Cyberspace personae do not have the option of marble, at least if they want to remain anonymous, but they do have the option of investing in a long series of transactions or in other costly activities, such as advertising or well-publicized charity, in order to establish a reputation that will bond their future performance.

What about entities – firms or individuals – that are not engaged in long-term dealings and so neither have a valuable reputation nor are willing to pay to acquire one? How are they to guarantee their contractual performance in this world?

One solution is to piggyback on the reputation of another entity engaged in such dealings. Suppose I am an anonymous online persona forming a contract that it might later be in my interest to break. How, absent a reputation, do I persuade the other party that I will keep my word? What is to keep me from making the contract, agreeing to an arbitrator, breaking the contract, ignoring the arbitrator's verdict, and walking off with my gains, unconcerned by the damage to my nonexistent reputation?

I solve the problem by offering to post a performance bond with the arbitrator – in anonymous digital currency. The arbitrator is free to allocate all or part of the bond to the other party as damages for breach. This approach – taking advantage of a third party with reputation – is not purely hypothetical. Purchasers on eBay at present can supplement direct reputational enforcement with the services of an escrow agent – a trusted third party that holds the buyer's payment until the goods have been inspected and then releases it to the seller.

This approach still depends on reputational enforcement, but this time the reputation belongs to the arbitrator. With all parties anonymous, he could simply steal bonds posted with him – but if he does, he is unlikely to stay in business very long. If I am worried about such possibilities, I can require the arbitrator to sign a contract specifying a second and independent arbitrator to deal with any conflicts between me and the first arbitrator. My signature to that agreement is worth very little, since it is backed by no reputation, but the signature of the first arbitrator to a contract binding him to accept the judgment of the second arbitrator is backed by the first arbitrator's reputation.

One problem may occur to some readers. I am identified online only by my digital signature. Someone who somehow gets a copy of my private key has a blank check against me, to the limit of the value of my reputation; he can sign contracts as me, collect payment, and then leave me to either fulfill the contracts or lose my reputation.

The obvious solution to this problem is to guard my private key. Another and partial solution is a mechanism for recalling compromised keys, perhaps a web site that exists to carry posts by people whose keys have been compromised, announcing that they will no longer be responsible for contracts signed with that key. When creating a reputation, I could explicitly state that my signature is only good for obligations up to some limit, or for some fixed length of time, with some stated mechanism for renewing it.

CONCLUSION

If the arguments I have offered are correct, we can expect the rise of online commerce to produce a substantial shift toward private law privately enforced by reputational mechanisms. While the shift should be strongest in cyberspace, it ought to be echoed in realspace as well. Digital signatures lower information costs to interested third parties whether the transactions being contracted over are occurring online or not. And the existence of a body of trusted online arbitrators will make contracting in advance for private arbitration more familiar and reliance on private arbitration easier for realspace as well as cyberspace transactions.

The use of reputational enforcement as an alternative to legal enforcement of contracts is not anything new; there are multiple historical examples.[9] In this respect as in several others discussed later, the future might resemble the past more than the present.

Relative Prices Rule the World

When I was little, one of my favorite adults was a friend of my parents named Dorothy Brady. One reason was her habit of bringing small gifts for my sister and me when she came to visit. A more important reason was that she was always doing interesting things.

One of her projects involved apple-peeling machines – the gadgets that you stick an apple on, turn a handle, and – if all goes well – end up with a peeled, cored, and sometimes even sliced apple. The conclusion of her research – done by exploring New England museums – was that over a period of about 200 years the design stayed the same but the materials changed. The earlier you went back, the more of the machine was made of wood and the less of metal.

In real life Dorothy was an economic historian. In addition to giving her an excuse to poke around museums, her research provided an example of a very common pattern in economic history. How people do things depends on the relative costs of the alternatives. When metal is expensive, wood and the labor to shape it cheap, you make things mostly out of wood, and use metal only where it is essential. As steel gets less and less expensive relative to wood and labor, people shift to using more and more of it.

This chapter is about a newer example of the same logic. The technology of the Internet reduces the cost of doing business with people far away – so we do more of it. It used to be that, as a practical matter, I only bought things from England when I was in England. Today buying a book from England is only marginally more trouble than buying it from the local Barnes & Noble. Routinely doing business with people far away raises the cost of settling disputes by use of the government court system, since the jurisdiction of courts is in large part based on geography.

Modern communications technology makes sharing information much easier than it used to be and encryption technology, in the form of digital signatures, does the same for verifying the shared information. You no longer have to check your informant's reputation and biases or look over the evidence to make sure nobody has tinkered with it. One calculation tells you a verdict came from the arbitrator it says it came from; one more tells you that that arbitrator was the one I agreed to accept. I agreed to accept his verdict, he says I reneged on that agreement, case closed.

Government courts and private reputation are alternative ways of achieving the same objective – making people keep their word. The cost of using government courts has gone up. The cost of information to interested third parties – the key ingredient in private enforcement through reputation – has gone down. The predictable result is a shift away from the one means and toward the other.

Find an apple peeler in a kitchen gadget catalog. The handle might be wood – or plastic. The rest will be steel.

EIGHT

Watermarks and Barbed Wire

Authors expect to be paid for their work. So do programmers, musicians, film directors, and lots of other people. If they cannot be paid for their work, we are likely to have fewer books, movies, songs, programs. This creates a problem if what is produced can be inexpensively reproduced. Once it is out there, anyone who has a copy can make a copy, driving the price of copies down to the cost of reproducing them. Copyright law is an attempt to solve that problem by giving the creator of a work the legal right to control the making of copies. How well it works depends on how easily that right can be enforced.

COPYRIGHT IN DIGITAL MEDIA

"The rumors of my death have been greatly exaggerated."
Mark Twain – perhaps also copyright. Or perhaps not.

To enforce his legal rights, the owner of a copyright has to be able to discover illegal copying and take legal action against those responsible. How easy that is depends in large part on the technology of copying.

Consider the old-fashioned printing press, circa 1910. It was large and expensive; printing a book required first setting hundreds of pages of type by hand. That made it much less expensive to print 10,000 copies of a book on one press than 100 copies each on a hundred different presses. Since nobody wanted 10,000 copies of a book for himself, a producer had to find customers – lots of customers. Advertising the book, or offering it for sale in bookstores, brought it to the attention of the copyright owner. If he had not authorized the copying, he could locate the pirate and sue.

Enforcement becomes much harder if copying is practical on a scale of one or a few copies – the current situation for digital works such as computer programs, digitized music, or films on DVD. Individuals making a copy for themselves or a few copies for friends are much harder to locate than mass-market copiers. Even if you can locate them, it is harder to sue 10,000 defendants than one. Hence, as a practical matter, firms mostly limit the enforcement of their copyright to legal action against large-scale infringers.

The situation is not entirely hopeless from the standpoint of the copyright holder. If the product is a piece of software widely used in business – Microsoft Word, for example – there will be organizations that use, not one copy, but thousands. If they choose to buy one and produce the rest themselves, someone may notice – and sue.

Even if copying can be done on a small scale, there remains the problem of distribution. If I get programs or songs by illegally copying them from my friends I am limited to what my friends have, which may not include what I want. I may prefer to buy from distributors providing a wide range of alternatives – and they, being potential targets for infringement suits, have an incentive to buy what they sell legally rather than produce it themselves illegally. So even in a world where many expensive works in digital form – Word, for example – can easily be copied, the producers of such works can still use copyright law to get paid for some of what they produce.

Or perhaps not. As Napster and then its peer-to-peer successors have demonstrated, distribution over the Internet makes it possible to combine individual copying with mass-market distribution, using specially designed search tools to find the individual who happens to have the particular song you want and is willing to let you copy it. A centralized distribution system is vulnerable to legal attack, as Napster discovered. But shutting down a decentralized system such as Gnutella or Freenet, which allows individuals on the net to make their music collections available for download in exchange for the ability to download songs from other people's collections, is a more difficult problem. If each user is copying one of your songs once but there are 100,000 of them, can you sue them all?

Perhaps you can – if you take proper advantage of the technology. A decentralized system must provide some way of finding someone who has the song you want and is willing to share it. Copyright owners might use the same software to locate individuals who make their works available for copying and sue all of them, perhaps in a suit that joins many defendants. Since copyright law sets a $500 statutory minimum for damages, suing 10,000 individuals, each of whom has made one copy of your copyrighted work, could in principle bring in more money than suing one individual who had made 10,000 copies.

Recent attempts along these general lines by the Recording Industry Association of America (RIAA) have gotten a good deal of publicity, at least some of it negative. They also face some practical problems. For one thing, under current law, it is not entirely clear when noncommercial file exchanges are illegal – although that situation could be changed by Congress and probably will be changed by the courts.[1] Also, it is hard to force multiple defendants into a single suit, so suing very large numbers of defendants can be expensive. On the other hand, if they expect to lose, one may not have to go very far with the suit before getting an out-of-court settlement. And one could imagine modifications in the relevant legal rules, perhaps applicable only to copyright suits, that would make the mechanics easier.

Although this approach may work for a while, its long-run problems should be clear from the earlier discussion of strong privacy. A well-designed decentralized system would locate someone willing to let you copy a song but would not let you identify the person from whom you were copying it. You do not need name, face, or social security number in order to copy the file encoding the song you want, merely some way of getting messages to and from him. This raises the possibility that the desire of people to download music without either paying for it or getting sued may be the key incentive that pushes us toward the strong privacy world of widespread encryption. As one webbed essay puts it, "to a first approximation, every PC owner under the age of 35 is now a felon." It also raises the possibility that attempts to regulate strong encryption may ultimately be fought out, not between the government and individuals with unpopular views, but between the RIAA and people downloading music.

An alternative legal approach is to sue the provider of the file-sharing software for contributory infringement, an approach that finally succeeded, after extensive litigation, in *MGM v. Grokster*. But doing that requires a provider that still exists, is under the court's jurisdiction, and has significant assets; none of those conditions can be guaranteed in future cases. A decentralized peer-to-peer system can continue to function long after the organization that created it has vanished.

There remains, for some forms of intellectual property, the possibility of collecting royalties from business customers – corporations that use Word, movie theaters performing movies. In the longer run, even that option may shrink or vanish. A world where strong privacy is sufficiently universal would permit virtual firms – groups of individuals linked via the net but geographically dispersed and mutually anonymous. Even if all of them use pirated copies of Word – or whatever the equivalent is at that point – no whistleblower can report them because nobody, inside or outside the firm, knows who they are or whether they have paid for their software.

Digital Watermarks

Consider the problem in a different context – images on the World Wide Web. Each image originated somewhere and may well belong to someone. But once webbed, anyone can copy it. Not only is it hard for the copyright owner to prevent illegal copying, but also it may be hard for even the copier to prevent illegal copying, since he may not know to whom the image belongs or whether it has been put in the public domain.

One way of dealing with these problems is *digital watermarking*. Using special software, the creator of the image imbeds in it concealed information identifying him and claiming copyright. In a well-designed system, the information has no noticeable effect on how the image looks to the human eye and is robust against transformation – meaning that it is still there after a user has converted the image from one format to another, cropped it, edited it, perhaps, if some claims are to be believed, even printed it out and scanned it back in.[2]

Digital watermarking can be used in a number of different ways. The simplest is by embedding information in an image and making the software that reads the information widely available. That lowers the cost to users of avoiding infringement, by making it easy for them to discover that an image is under copyright and who the copyright owner is. It raises the cost of committing infringement, at least on the Web, since search engines can search the Web for copyrighted images and report back to the copyright owner – who checks to see if the use was licensed and if not takes legal action. The existence of the watermark will help prove both to whom the image belongs and that the user knew or should have known and so is liable for not only infringement but deliberate infringement.

A deliberate infringer might try to remove the watermark while preserving the image. A well-designed system can make this more difficult. But as long as the watermark is observable, the infringer can try different ways of removing it until he finds one that works. And making software for reading the watermark publicly available makes it harder to keep secret the details of how it works, hence easier to design software to defeat it. So this form of watermark provides protection against inadvertent infringement, and raises the cost of deliberate infringement – the infringer must go to some trouble to remove the watermark – but cannot prevent or reliably detect deliberate infringement.

The obvious solution is an invisible watermark designed to be read only by special software not publicly available. That is of no use for preventing inadvertent infringement but substantially raises the risks of deliberate infringement, since the infringer can never be sure he has successfully removed the watermark. By imprinting an image with both a visible and an invisible watermark, the copyright holder could get the best of both worlds – provide information for those who do not want to infringe and a risk of detection for those who do.

There is another way in which watermarking could be used to enforce copyright, in a somewhat different context. Suppose we are considering, not digital images, but computer programs. Further suppose that enforcing copyright law against the sellers of pirated software is not an option – they are located outside of the jurisdiction of our court system, doing business anonymously, or both.

Even if the sellers of pirated copies of our software are anonymous, the people who originally bought the software from us are not. When we sell the program, each copy has embedded in it a unique watermark – a concealed serial number, sometimes referred to as a digital fingerprint. We keep a record of who got each copy and make it clear to our customers that permitting their copy of the program to be copied is a violation of copyright law for which we will hold them liable. If copies of our software appear on pirate archives we buy one, check the fingerprint, and sue the customer from whose copy it was made.[3]

Digital watermarking is one example of a class of technologies that can be used to get back at least some of what other technologies took away. The ease of copying digital media made enforcement of copyright harder – at first glance, impossibly hard – by enabling piracy at the individual level. But the ability of digital technologies to embed invisible, and potentially undetectable, information in digital images, combined with the ability of a search engine to check a billion web pages looking for the one that contains an unlicensed copy of a watermarked image, provide the possibility of enforcing copyright law against individual pirates. And the same technology, by embedding the purchaser's fingerprint in the purchased software, provides a potential way of enforcing copyright law even in a world of strong privacy – not against anonymous pirates or their anonymous customers but against the known purchaser from whom they got the original to copy.

While these are possible solutions, there is no guarantee that they will always work. Invisible watermarking is vulnerable to anyone sufficiently ingenious – or with sufficient inside information – to crack the code, to figure out how to read the watermark and remove it. The file representing the image or program is in the pirate's hands. He can do what he wants with it – provided he can figure out what needs to be done.

An individual who wants to pirate images or software is unlikely to have the expertise to figure out how to remove even visible watermarks, let alone invisible ones. To do so he needs the assistance of someone else who does have that expertise – most readily provided in the form of software designed to remove visible watermarks and identify and remove invisible ones. That raises the possibility of backstopping the technological solution of digital watermarks with legal prohibitions on the production and distribution of software intended to defeat it. That is the approach used by the Digital Millennium Copyright Act of 1998. It bans software whose purpose is to defeat copyright management schemes such as digital watermarking. How enforceable that ban will be, in a world of networks and widely available encryption, remains to be seen.

Each of the approaches to enforcing copyright that I have been discussing has serious limitations. The use of digital fingerprints to identify the source of pirated copies only works if the original sale is sufficiently individualized so that the seller knows the identity of the buyer – and while it would be possible to sell all software that way, it would be a nuisance. Perhaps more important, the approach works very poorly for software that is expensive and widely used. One legitimate copy of Word could be the basis for ten million illegitimate copies, giving rise to a claim for a billion dollars or so in damages – and if Microsoft limits its sales to customers both capable of satisfying such a claim and willing to put that much money at risk, it will not sell very many copies of Word. The use of digital watermarks to identify pirated copies only works if the copies are publicly displayed – for digital images on the Web but not for a pirated copy of Word on my hard drive. These limitations suggest that producers of intellectual property have good reason to look for other ways of protecting it.

One way of solving these problems would be to convert cyberspace, at least the parts of it residing on hardware under the jurisdiction of U.S. courts, into a transparent society. My computer is both a location in cyberspace and a physical object in realspace; in the latter form it can be regulated by a realspace government, however good my encryption is. One can imagine, in a world run by copyright owners, a legal regime that required all computers to be networked and all networked computers to be open to authorized search engines, designed to go through their hard drives looking for pirated software, songs, movies, or digital images.

I do not think such a legal regime will be a politically viable option in the United States anytime in the near future, although the situation might be different elsewhere. There are, however, private versions that might be more viable, technologies permitting the creator of intellectual property to make it impossible to use it save on computers that meet certain conditions – one of which could be transparency to authorized agents of the copyright holder.

For a much simpler version of the same approach, consider possible copyright enforcement strategies if each computer's central processing unit has a built-in serial number unique to that particular computer. A software company customizes each copy of its product to run on a single computer, identified by the serial number of its central processing unit (CPU). The user can freely make backups. The user can give copies to friends. But the copies will only run on the computer the original was bought for. Unless, of course, someone figures out a way to either modify the part of the program that checks the serial number or modify other software, perhaps part of the computer's operating system, to lie to the program about what its serial number is.[4]

Most readers would regard the idea of enforcing the terms of a software license by allowing a human being to randomly search their hard drive as outrageous, but might react very differently to the idea of allowing a program on their computer to check their CPU to see what its serial number is. Some may be worried about the problems that will arise if they get a new computer and want to transfer their old software to it. But nobody is likely to see such a system as an intolerable violation of privacy.

The two approaches appear very different – but consider something in between. Your hard drive must be open to searches – but the searches may be done only by computer programs. The only information the programs are capable of reporting to a human being is the fact that they found copyrighted software on your hard drive that you are not entitled to – at which point the copyright holder can go to court to ask for legal authority to look at your hard drive.

The issue raised by these examples – to what degree does being spied on by a machine violate your privacy – is one we will return to in a later chapter, where we consider the implications of using computers instead of human beings to listen to phone taps.

DIGITAL BARBED WIRE

If using technology to enforce copyright law in a world of easy copying is not always workable, perhaps we should instead use technology to replace copyright law. If using the law to keep trespassers and stray cattle off my land doesn't work, perhaps I should build a fence.

You have produced a collection of songs and wish to sell them online. To do so, you digitize the songs and insert them in a cryptographically protected container – what Intertrust, one of the pioneering firms in the industry, called a digibox. The container is a piece of software that protects the contents from unauthorized access while at the same time providing, and charging for, authorized access. Once the songs are safely inside the box you give away the package by making it available for download on your web site.

I download the package to my computer; when I run it I get a menu of choices. If I want to listen to a song once, I can do so for free. Thereafter, each play costs five cents. If I really like the song, fifty cents unlocks it forever, letting me listen to it as many times as I want. Payment is online by ecash, credit card, or an arrangement with a cooperating bank.

The digibox is a file on my hard disk, so I can copy it for a friend. That's fine with you. If he wants to listen to one of your songs more than once, he too will have to pay for it.

It may have occurred to you that there is a flaw in the business plan I have just described. The container provides one free play of each song. In order to listen for free, all the customer has to do is make lots of copies of the container and use each once. Alternatively, if I want to make copies for friends, I can pay fifty cents once to unlock the file and make copies – unlocked copies – for them. It might be prudent for the digibox to have some way of making sure that the computer it is running on is the same as the computer it was unlocked on.

Making a new copy every time you play a song is a lot of trouble to go to in order in order to save five cents. Intertrust does not have to make it impossible to defeat its protection, whether in that simple way or in more complicated ways, in order for it and the owners of the intellectual property it protects to make money. It only has to make defeating the protection more trouble than it is worth.

Between the time when I wrote the first draft of this chapter and the final revision, Intertrust went out of business, its particular approach to technological protection having failed to take off. The current incarnation of their approach is called "Digital Rights Management," usually shortened to DRM. The underlying idea is still the same. Files, typically audio or video, are distributed in a form that is only accessible with a suitable key. Information about the key is provided only to manufacturers who agree to build into their equipment – a CD player, say – restrictions on what can be done with the file. Thus, in theory, the file can only be used on equipment designed to prevent copying or in other ways restrict its use.

One problem with this approach is that files can be played not only on dedicated equipment but on computers. The firm providing DRM will, of course, refuse to tell other people how to write software that unlocks their files. But the files themselves are there to be examined, as are the devices authorized to play them, which makes it hard to prevent a sufficiently ingenious programmer from reverse engineering the protection in order to build a suitable key into software without providing the restrictions on use that the owner of the intellectual property wants.

As in the case of digital watermarking, how easy it is to defeat the protection depends very largely on who is doing it. The individual customer is unlikely to be expert in programming or encryption, and hence unlikely to be able to defeat even simple forms of technological protection. The risk comes from the person who is an expert and makes his expertise available, cheaply or for free, in the form of software designed to crack the protection.

One approach to dealing with that problem is by making it illegal to create, distribute, or possess such software – the strategy put into law by the Digital Millennium Copyright Act. That law currently faces legal challenges by plaintiffs who argue that publishing information, including information about how to defeat other people's software, is free speech, and hence protected. Even if the court declines to protect that particular sort of speech, the arguments of an earlier chapter suggest that in the online world free speech may itself be technologically protected – by the wide availability of encryption and computer networks – making the relevant parts of the act in the long run unenforceable.

If law cannot provide protection, either against piracy or against computerized safecracking tools designed to defeat technological protection, the obvious alternative is technological – safes that cannot be cracked. Is that possible?

For some forms of intellectual property – songs, for example – it is not. The problem, sometimes referred to as the "analog hole," is that, however strong the protection, at some point in the process the customer gets to play the song or watch the movie – that, after all, is what he is paying for. But if a customer is playing a song on his own computer in his own home, he can also be playing it into his own tape recorder, giving him a copy of the song outside the box. If he prefers an MP3 to a cassette he can play the song back to the computer, digitize it, and compress it. To avoid distortion due to speakers and microphone he can short-circuit the process, feeding the electrical signals that normally go to the speakers back into the computer instead to be redigitized – outside the box. A similar approach could be used to hijack a book, video, or any other work that is presented to the customer in full each time it is used. Technological protection may make the process of getting the work out of the digibox and into some usable form a considerable nuisance – but once one person has done it, in a world where copyright law is difficult or impossible to enforce, the work is available to all. Short of making everybody's hard disk searchable, the only way of protecting works of this kind is to limit their consumption to a controlled environment – showing the video in a movie theater with video cameras banned, for instance.

For other sorts of works, secure protection may be a more practical option. Consider, for example, an (imaginary) database compiled by Consumer Reports, designed to advise a user on what car to buy. A query describes price range, preferences, and a variety of other relevant information. The response is a report tailored to that particular customer. Having paid for and received the report, the customer can give a copy to a neighbor. But the neighbor is unlikely to want it, since he is unlikely to have all the same tastes, circumstances, and constraints. What the neighbor wants is his own customized report – which requires another payment.

With enough time, energy, and money, a pirate could ask a million questions and use the answers to reverse engineer the protected data – but why should he? The pirate can use the stolen information, can give it away, but has only a very limited ability to sell it. As long as the protection raises the cost of reconstructing the database high enough, it should be reasonably safe.[5] For a real-world example of almost precisely that strategy, consider LexisNexis and Westlaw, the legal databases on which lawyers and legal academics rely. There is nothing to keep me from downloading a law case from Lexis and then passing it on to a colleague who has not paid for the privilege – but the odds that my colleague is looking for the same case as I am are low.

For a different approach to the problem of protecting intellectual property, consider a program that does something very useful – high-quality speech recognition, say. I divide it into two parts. One, which contains most of the code and does most of the work, I give away to anyone who wants it. The rest, including the key elements that make my program special, resides on my server. In order for the first part to work, it must continually exchange message with the second part – access to which I charge for by the minute.

One elegant feature of this solution is that the disease is also the cure. Part of what makes copyright unenforceable is the ready availability of high-speed computer networks, enabling the easy distribution of pirated software. But high-speed computer networks are precisely what you need for the form of protection I have just described, since they allow me to make software on my server almost as accessible to you as software on your hard disk – and charge for it.

Some years after I wrote the initial draft of this section, I realized that I myself was a customer of a very successful and innovative piece of intellectual property protected in just this way. *World of Warcraft*, a massively multiplayer online role-playing game with something over ten million customers, sells the client software that goes on the customer's computer to anyone who wants to buy it. But the server software that makes it possible for thousands of individuals to coordinate their activities, to interact in a common world, is sitting on Blizzard's own servers. One can think of *World of Warcraft* and its competitors as the new technology's equivalent of the movie – one that, unlike movies, can be technologically protected. Any player who wants can record his adventures and show them to his friends. But what the friends want is to have their own adventures, and to do that they will have to pay Blizzard's monthly fee.

Another example of the same approach is provided by firms such as Pandora and Last.fm. Instead of asking for a particular song, the customer rates songs as he hears them; the service uses the ratings to decide what to play next. Think of it as your own customized DJ.

ADDING IT ALL UP

Putting together everything in this chapter, we have a picture of intellectual property protection in a near future world of widely available high-speed networks, encryption, and easy copying. Intellectual property used publicly, such as images on the Web, can be legally protected provided it is not valuable enough to make it worth going to the trouble of removing hidden watermarks and provided also that it is being used somewhere that copyright law can reach. That second proviso means that if we move all the way to a world of strong privacy such protection vanishes, since copyright law is useless if you cannot identify the infringer. But even in that world, some intellectual property can be protected by fingerprinting each original and holding the purchaser liable for any copies made from it.

Where intellectual property cannot be protected by law, it may still be possible to protect it by technology. That approach is of limited usefulness for works that must be entirely revealed every time they are accessed, such as a song. It may work better for more complicated works, such as a database or a computer program. For both sorts of works, protection will be easier if it is practical to use the law to suppress software designed to defeat it – but it probably won't be.

Does this mean that, in the near future, songs will stop being sung and novels stop being written? That is not likely. What it does mean is that those who produce that sort of intellectual property will have to find ways of getting paid that do not depend on control over copying. For songs, one obvious possibility is to give away the digitized version and charge for concerts. Filmmakers can give away the film and make money on the toys – which, being physical objects sold in realspace, are still subject to intellectual property law.[6] Another possibility is to rely on the generosity of fans – in a world where it will be easy to email a ten-cent appreciation to the creator of the song you have just enjoyed. A third is to give away the song along with a digitally signed thank you to the firm that paid you to write it and hopes to profit from your fans' goodwill, the modern equivalent of the old system of literary patronage.

Similar options are available for authors. The usual royalty payment for a book is between 5% and 10% of its face value. Many readers may be willing to voluntarily pay the author that much in a world where the physical distribution of books is essentially costless. Other books will get written in the same way that articles in academic journals are written now – to spread the author's ideas or to build up a reputation that can be used to get a job, consulting contracts, or speaking opportunities.

AND FOR OUR NEXT TRICK

Back in Chapter 4 I raised the possibility of treating transactional information as private property, with ownership allocated by agreement at the time of the transaction. Such information is a form of intellectual property and can be protected by the same technologies we have just discussed.

Suppose, for example, that you are happy to receive catalogs in the mail (or email) but do not want strangers to be able to compile enough information about you to enable identity theft, spot you as a target for extortion, or in some other way use your personal information against you. You achieve both objectives by making personal information generated by your transactions – purchases, employment, car rental, and the like – available only in a very special sort of database. The database allows users to create address lists of people who are likely customers for what they are selling but does not allow them to get individualized data about those people. It will be distributed inside a suitably designed and cryptographically protected container or on a protected server, designed to answer queries but not to reveal the underlying data. If the catalogs are going out by email, the database is combined with a forwarding service. One copy of the catalog goes to the service, along with suitable payment, and a thousand copies from there to a thousand email addresses – none of which need be revealed to the catalog company.

In the full-blown version of such a system, the company running the database doesn't know who you are either, since the information goes out by email through a chain of remailers; your email address is buried under layers of encryption, with one layer removed by each remailer. In a simpler version, or one designed to forward physical products as well as messages, you are relying on a trusted intermediary, a firm in the business of keeping its customers' secrets – a specialty that used to be associated with Swiss bankers.

The information in the database was created by your transactions. In the highest-tech version, you conduct all of them anonymously, so nobody but you has the information to start with, and you can control who gets it thereafter. In a lower-tech version, both you and the seller start with the information – what you bought and when – but the seller is contractually obliged to erase the record once the transaction is complete. In either version, you arrange for the information to be available only within the sort of protected database I have just described – and, if access to such a database is sufficiently valuable, get paid for doing so.

NINE

Reactionary Progress – Amateur Scholars and Open Source

A list of the half dozen most important figures in the early history of economics would have to include David Ricardo; it might well include Thomas Malthus and John Stuart Mill. A similar list for geology would include William Smith and James Hutton. For biology it would surely include Charles Darwin and Gregor Mendel, for physics Isaac Newton.

Who were they? Malthus and Darwin were clergymen, Mendel a monk, Smith a mining engineer, Hutton a gentleman farmer, Mill a clerk and writer, Ricardo a retired stock market prodigy. Of the names I have listed, only Newton was a university professor – and by the time he became a professor he had already come up with both calculus and the theory of gravitation.

There were important intellectual figures in the seventeenth, eighteenth, and early nineteenth centuries who were professional academics – Adam Smith, for example. But a large number, probably a majority, were amateurs. In the twentieth century, on the other hand, most of the major figures in all branches of scholarship have been professional academics. Most started their careers with a conventional course of university education, typically leading to a Ph.D. degree.

Why did things change? One possible answer is the enormous increase in knowledge. When fields were new, most scholars did not need access to vast libraries. There were not many people in the field, the rate of progress was not very rapid, so letters and occasional meetings provided adequate communication. As fields developed and specialization increased, the advantages of the professional – libraries, laboratories, colleagues down the hall – became increasingly important.

Email is as easy as walking down the hall. The Web, while not a complete substitute for a library, makes enormous amounts of information readily available to a very large number of people. In my field and many others it is becoming common for the authors of scholarly articles to make their datasets available on the Web so that other scholars can check that they really say what the articles claim they say.

An alternative explanation for the shift from amateur to professional scholarship is that it was due to the downward spread of education. In the eighteenth century, someone sufficiently well educated to invent a new science was likely to be a member of the upper class, and hence had a good chance of not needing to work for a living. In the twentieth century, the correlation between education and wealth was a good deal weaker.

We are not likely to return to the class society of eighteenth-century England. But by the standards of that society, most educated people today are rich – rich enough to make a tolerable living and still have time and effort left to devote to their hobbies. For a large and increasing fraction of the population, amateur scholarship, like amateur sports, amateur music, amateur dramatics, and much else, is a real option. These arguments suggest that, having shifted from a world of amateur scholars to a world of professionals, we may now be shifting back. That conjecture is based in large part on my own experiences. Two examples:

Robin Hanson is currently a professor of economics at George Mason University. When I first came into (virtual) contact with him, he was a NASA scientist with an odd hobby. His hobby was inventing institutions. His ideas – in particular an ingenious proposal to design markets to generate information – were sufficiently novel and well thought out to make corresponding with him more interesting than corresponding with most of my fellow economists. They were sufficiently interesting to other people to get published. Eventually he decided that his hobby was more fun than his profession and went back to school for a Ph.D. in economics.

One of my hobbies for the past thirty years has been cooking from very early cookbooks; my earliest source is a letter written in the sixth century by a Byzantine physician named Anthimus to Theoderic, king of the Franks.[1] When I started, one had to pretty much reinvent the wheel. There were no translations of early cookbooks in print and very few in libraries. Almost the only available sources in English, other than a small number of unreliable books about the history of cooking, were a few early English cookbooks – in particular a collection that had been published by the Early English Text Society in 1888. I managed to get one seventeenth-century source by finding a rare book collection that had a copy of the original and paying to have it microfilmed.

The situation has changed enormously over the past thirty years. The changes include the publication of several reliable secondary sources, additional English sources, and a few translations – all of which could have happened without the Internet. But the biggest change is that there are now at least seven English translations of early cookbooks on the Web, freely available to anyone interested, as well as several early English cookbooks. Most of the translations were done by amateurs for the fun of it. There are hundreds of worked out early recipes (the originals usually omit inessential details such as quantities, times, and temperatures) webbed. There is an email list that puts anyone interested in touch with lots of experienced enthusiasts. Some of the people on that list are professional cooks, some are professional scholars. So far as I know, none is a professional scholar of cooking history.

Similar things are happening in other areas. I am told that amateur astronomers have long played a significant role because skilled labor is an important input to star watching. There seems to be an increasing amount of interaction between historians and groups that do amateur historical recreation – sometimes prickly, when hobbyists claim expertise they don't have, sometimes cordial. The professionals, on average, know much more than the amateurs do, but there are a lot more amateurs and some of them know quite a lot. And the best of the amateurs have access not only to information but to each other, as well as to any professional more interested in the ability of the people he corresponds with than their credentials.

OPEN SOURCE SOFTWARE

Amateur scholarship is one example of the way in which rising incomes and improved communication technology make it easier to produce things for fun. Another is open source software.

The best-known example is Linux,[2] a computer operating system. The original version was created by a Finnish graduate student named Linus Torvalds. Having done a first draft himself, he invited everyone else in the world to help improve it. A lot of them accepted – with the result that Linux is now a sophisticated operating system, widely used for a variety of different tasks. Another open source project, the Apache web server, is the software on which a majority of World Wide Web pages run.

When you buy a copy of Microsoft Word you get the object code, the version of the program that the computer runs. With an open source program, you get the source code, the human-readable version that the original programmer wrote and that other programmers need if they want to modify the program. You can compile it into object code to run it, but you can also modify it and then compile and run your new version of the program.

The mechanics of open source are simple. Someone comes up with a first version of the software. He publishes the source code. Other people interested in the program modify it – which they are able to do because they have the source code – and send their modifications to him. Modifications that he accepts go into the code base, the current standard version that other programmers will work from. At the peak of Linux development, Torvalds was updating the code base daily.

There are lots of programmers, each working on the parts of the code that interest him, so when someone reports a problem there is likely to be someone else to whom its source and solution are obvious. "With enough eyeballs, all bugs are shallow."[3] And with the source code open, bugs can be found and improvements suggested by anyone interested.

Eric Raymond, a prominent spokesman for the movement and the author of a book about it,[4] has pointed out that open source has its own set of norms and property rights. There is nobody who can forbid you from copying or modifying an open source program. But there is ownership in two other and important senses.

Linus Torvalds owns Linux. Eric Raymond owns Fetchmail. A committee owns Apache. Under an open source license anyone is free to modify the code any way he likes, provided that he makes the source code to his modified version public, thus keeping it open source. But programmers want to all work on the same code base so that each can take advantage of improvements made by the others. If Torvalds rejects your improvements to Linux, you are still free to use them – but don't expect any help. Everyone else will be working on his version. Thus ownership of a project – the ability to decide what goes into the code base – is a property right enforced entirely by private action.

As Eric Raymond has pointed out, such ownership is controlled by rules similar to the common law rules for owning land. Ownership of a project goes to the person who creates it, homesteads that particular programming opportunity by creating the first rough draft of the program. If he loses interest he can transfer ownership to someone else. If he abandons the program, someone else can claim it – publicly check to be sure nobody else is currently in charge of it and then publicly take charge of it himself. The equivalent in property law is adverse possession, the legal rule under which, if you openly treat property as yours for long enough and nobody objects, it is yours.

There is a second form of ownership in open source – credit for your work. Each project is accompanied by a file identifying the authors. Meddle with that file – substitute in your name, thus claiming to be the author of code someone else wrote – and your name in the open source community is Mud. The same is true in the scholarly community. From the standpoint of a professional scholar, copyright violation is a peccadillo, theft someone else's problem, plagiarism the ultimate sin.

As this example suggests, the open source movement is simply a new variation on the system under which most of modern science was created. Programmers create software; scholars create ideas. Ideas, like open source programs, can be used by anyone. The source code, the evidence and arguments on which the ideas are based, is public information. An article that starts out "The following theory is true, but I won't tell you why" is unlikely to persuade many readers.

Scientific theories do not have owners in quite the sense that open source projects do, but at any given time in most fields there is considerable agreement as to what the orthodox body of theory is. Scholars can choose to ignore that consensus, but if they do, their work is unlikely to be taken seriously. Apache's owner is a committee. Arguably neoclassical economics belongs to a somewhat larger committee. A scholar can defy the orthodoxy to strike out on his own; some do. Similarly, if you don't like Linux, you are free to start your own open source operating system project based on your variant of it. Heretical ideas sometimes succeed and open source projects are sometime successfully forked but, in both cases, the odds are against it.

JIMMY WALES'S IMPOSSIBLE SUCCESS

Few projects seem less suited to the open source approach than writing an encyclopedia. For it to be a success readers must rely on it, so a mistake in one article casts doubt on others. The structure is interdependent; an article on one subject may frequently need to refer to articles on related subjects. Clearly the only way to do it is with a central editorial board coordinating the whole thing and hiring experts in various fields to write the articles. Indeed, I have seen it argued that the reason for the decline of the *Encyclopedia Britannica* from its high point early in the twentieth century – the eleventh edition is widely regarded as a classic – was the shift away from paying substantial sums for articles, on the theory that the prestige of being published in the *Britannica* was itself sufficient reward. That meant that they were offering the smallest reward to the most qualified writers, the experts whose prestige was unlikely to be raised by one more encyclopedia article. If a little bit of reliance on volunteers, status, nonpecuniary payments could weaken the market leader, surely a complete reliance on such would be fatal to a new startup.

It did not turn out that way. In 2001, Jimmy Wales created Wikipedia as an open-source, online encyclopedia. Not only was everyone in the world invited to contribute, everyone in the world got the last word – until someone else showed up. When Linus Torvalds invited the world to write Linux he retained control over the code base; changes he did not approve of did not get included. Nobody has a corresponding power over Wikipedia. With rare exceptions, any article can be edited anytime by anyone.

Amazingly enough, it works. Once in a while there is a minor flap when a group of true believers tries to edit an article to make it support their view of the world – only to discover that every time they make a change, some wicked outsider undoes it. More often than one might expect, the article evolves to a consensus, a statement of differing views that both sides can agree on. However it works – I have not entirely rejected the possibility of magic – the result six years later is a massive reference work that, if not perfect, is arguably as reliable as the encyclopedias produced by more conventional models, free for everyone to use and very widely used – almost certainly more widely, online, than any competitor.

MARKET AND HIERARCHY

One of the odd features of a capitalist system is how socialist it is. Firms interact with customers and other firms through the decentralized machinery of trade. But firms themselves are miniature socialist states, hierarchical organizations controlled, at least in theory, by orders from above.

There is one crucial difference between Microsoft and Stalin's Russia. Microsoft's interactions with the rest of us are voluntary. It can get people to work for it or buy its products only by offering them a deal they prefer to all alternatives. I do not have to use the Windows operating system unless I want to, and in fact I don't and don't. Stalin did not face that constraint.

One implication is that, however bad the public image of large corporations may be, they exist because they serve human purposes. Employees work for them because they find doing so a better life than working for themselves; customers buy from them because they prefer doing so to making things for themselves or buying from someone else. The disadvantages associated with taking orders, working on other people's projects, depending for your reward on someone else's evaluation of your work, are balanced by advantages sufficient, for many people, to outweigh them.[5]

The balance between the advantages and disadvantages of large hierarchical organizations depends in part on technologies associated with exchanging information, arranging transactions, enforcing agreements, and the like. As those technologies change, so does that balance. The easier it is for a dispersed group of individuals to coordinate their activities, the larger we would expect the role of decentralized coordination, market rather than hierarchy, in the overall mix. This has implications for how goods are likely to be produced in the future – open source is a striking example. It also has implications for political systems, social networks, and a wide range of other human activities.

One example occurred some years ago in connection with one of my hobbies, one at least nominally run by a nonprofit corporation controlled by a self-perpetuating board of directors. The board responded to problems of growth by hiring a professional executive director. Acting apparently on his advice, they announced, with no prior discussion, that they had decided to double dues and to implement a controversial proposal that had been previously dropped in response to an overwhelmingly negative response by the membership.

If it had happened ten years earlier there would have been grumbling but nothing more. The corporation, after all, controlled all of the official channels of communication. When its publication, included in the price of membership, commented on the changes, the comments were distinctly one-sided. Individual members, told by those in charge that the changes were necessary to the health of the hobby, would for the most part have put up with them.

That is not what happened. The hobby in question had long had an active Usenet newsgroup associated with it. Members included individuals with professional qualifications, in a wide range of relevant areas, arguably superior to those of the board members, the executive director, or the corporation's officers. Every time an argument was raised in defense of the corporation's policies, it was answered – and at least some of the answers were persuasive. Only a minority of those involved in the hobby read the newsgroup, but it was a large enough minority to get the relevant arguments widely dispersed. And email provided an easy way for dispersed members unhappy with the changes to communicate, coordinate, act. The corporation's board of directors was self-perpetuating – membership in the organization did not include a vote – but it was made up of volunteers, people active in the hobby who were doing what they thought was right. They discovered that quite a lot of others, including those they respected, disagreed and were prepared to support their disagreement with facts and arguments. By the time the dust cleared, every member of the board of directors that made the decision, save those whose terms had ended during the controversy, had resigned; their replacements reversed the most unpopular of the decisions. It struck me as an interesting example of the way in which the existence of the Internet had shifted the balance between center and periphery.

For a more commercial example, consider the announcement some years ago that Eli Lilly had decided to subcontract part of its chemical research to the world at large. Lilly created a subsidiary, InnoCentive LLC, to maintain a web page listing chemistry problems that Lilly wanted solved and the prices, up to $100,000, that they were offering for the solutions. InnoCentive has invited other companies to use their services to get their problems solved too. By late 2001, according to a story in the *Wall Street Journal*, they had gotten "about 1,000 scientists from India, China, and elsewhere in the world" to work on their problems.[6] A number of other projects along similarly decentralized lines, volunteer or commercial, either are in practice or have been proposed – including one for open source development of drugs to deal with third-world diseases.[7]

One problem InnoCentive raises is that the people who are solving Lilly's problems may be doing so on someone else's payroll. Consider a chemist hired to work in an area related to one of the problems on the list. He has an obvious temptation to slant the work in the direction of the $100,000 prize, even if the result is to slow the achievement of his employer's objectives. A chemist paid by firm A while working for firm B is likely to be caught – and fired – if he does it in realspace. But if he combines a realspace job with cyberspace moonlighting – still more if parts of the realspace job are done by telecommuting from his home – the risks may be substantially less. So one possibility if InnoCentive's approach catches on is a shift from paying for time to paying for results, at least for some categories of skilled labor. In the limiting case, employment vanishes and everyone becomes a subcontractor, selling output rather than time.

INFORMATION WARFARE

So far we have been considering ways in which the Internet supports decentralized forms of cooperation. It supports decentralized forms of conflict as well. A communication system can be used as a weapon, a way of misleading other people, creating forged evidence, accomplishing your objectives at the expense of your opponents. Consider two academic examples.

Case 1: The Tale of the Four Little Pigs

The year is 1995, the place Cornell University. Four freshmen have compiled a collection of misogynist jokes entitled "75 Reasons Why Women
(Bitches) Should Not Have Freedom of Speech" and sent copies to their
friends. The collection reaches someone who finds it offensive and pro-
ceeds to distribute it to many other people who share that view, producing
a firestorm of controversy inside and outside the university. The central
question is whether creating such a list and using email to transmit it
is an offense that ought to be punished or a protected exercise of free
speech.

Eventually, Cornell announces its decision. The students have violated
no university rules and so will be subject to no penalties. They have,
however, recognized the error of their ways:

... in addition to the public letter of apology they wrote that was printed by
the *Cornell Daily Sun* on November 3, 1995, the students have offered to do the
following:

Each of them will attend the "Sex at 7:00" program sponsored by Cornell Advo-
cates for Rape Education (CARE) and the Health Education Office at Gannett
Health Center. This program deals with issues related to date and acquaintance
rape, as well as more general issues such as gender roles, relationships, and
communication.

Each of them has committed to perform 50 hours of community service. If
possible, they will do the work at a nonprofit agency whose primary focus relates
to sexual assault, rape crisis, or similar issues. Recognizing that such agencies may
be reluctant to have these students work with them, the students will perform
the community service elsewhere if the first option is not available.

The students will meet with a group of senior Cornell administrators to apologize
in person and to express regret for their actions and for the embarrassment and
disruption caused to the University.

Public statement by Barbara L. Krause, Judicial Administrator

There are at least two ways to interpret that outcome. One is that Ms.
Krause is telling the truth, the whole truth, and nothing but the truth –
Cornell imposed no penalty on the students, they imposed an entirely
voluntary penalty on themselves. It seems a bit strange – but then, Cornell
is a rather unusual university.

The alternative interpretation starts with the observation that university administrators have a lot of ways of making life difficult for students.

By publicly announcing that the students had broken no rules and were subject to no penalty, while privately making it clear to the students that if they planned to remain at Cornell they would be well advised to "voluntarily" penalize themselves, Cornell engaged in a successful act of hypocrisy. They publicly maintained their commitment to free speech while covertly punishing students for what they said.

Someone who preferred the second interpretation thought up a novel way of supporting it. An email went out during Thanksgiving break to thousands of Cornell students, staff, and faculty – 21,132 of them according to its authors.

CONFIDENTIAL

I would like to extend my heartfelt thanks to the many faculty members who advised me regarding the unfortunate matter of the "75 Reasons" letter that was circulated via electronic mail. Your recommendations for dealing with the foul-mouthed "four little pigs" (as I think of them) who circulated this filth was both apposite and prudent.

Now that we have had time to evaluate the media response, I think we can congratulate ourselves on a strategy that was not only successful in defusing the scandal, but has actually enhanced the reputation of the university as a sanctuary for those who believe that "free speech" is a relative term that must be understood to imply acceptable limits of decency and restraint — with quick and severe punishment for those who go beyond those limits and disseminate socially unacceptable sexist slurs.

I am especially pleased to report that the perpetrators of this disgusting screed have been suitably humiliated and silenced, without any outward indication that they were in fact disciplined by us. Clearly, it is to our

```
advantage to place malefactors in a position
where they must CENSOR THEMSELVES, rather than
allow the impression that we are censoring
them.

...
Yours sincerely
Barbara L. Krause Judicial Administrator
```

The letter was not, of course, actually written by Barbara Krause — as anyone attentive enough to check the email address could have figured out. It was written, and sent, by an anonymous group calling themselves OFFAL – Online Freedom Fighters Anarchist Liberation. The letter was a satire, and an effective one, giving a believable and unattractive picture of what its authors suspected Ms. Krause's real views were. It was also a fraud — some readers would never realize that she was not the real author. In both forms it provided propaganda for its authors' view of what had really happened.

But it did more than that. Email is not only easily distributed, it is easily answered. Some recipients not only believed the letter, they agreed with it and said so. Since OFFAL had used, not Ms. Krause's email address, but an email address that they controlled, those answers went back to them. OFFAL produced a second email, containing the original forgery, an explanation of what they were doing, and a selection of responses.

```
I happen to support your actions and the res-
olution of this incident, but put into the
wrong hands, this memo could perhaps be used
against you.
— — —

Thank god you sent this memo — something with
a little anger and fire — something that speaks
to the emotion and not just the legalities. I
hope you are right in stating that what went
on behind the scenes was truly humiliating for
"them."
— — —
```

I agree with what your memo states about the
"four little pigs" (students who embarrassed
the entire Cornell community), but I don't
think I was one of the people really intended
for your confidential memo. ...Great Job in the
handling of a most sensitive issue.

— — —

The authors of the list have received
richly — deserved humiliation

Their summary:

We believe that ridicule is a more powerful weapon than bombs or death threats. And we
believe that the Internet is the most powerful system ever invented for channeling grass-
roots protests and public opinion in the face
of petty tyrants who seek to impose their con-
stipated values on everyday citizens who merely
want to enjoy their constitutionally protected
liberties.

It is hard not to have some sympathy for the perpetrators. They were
making a defensible argument, although I am not certain it was a correct one, and making it in an ingenious and effective way. But at the
same time they, like the purveyors of other sorts of propaganda, were
combining a legitimate argument with a dishonest one, and it was the
latter that depended on their ingenious use of modern communications
technology.

The correct point was that Cornell's actions could plausibly be inter-
preted as hypocritical – attacking free speech while pretending to support
it. The dishonest argument was the implication that the responses they
received provided support for that interpretation. The eight replies that
OFFAL selected consisted of six supporting the original email, one criti-
cizing it, one doing neither. If that were a random selection of responses,
it would be impressive evidence for their view of what had happened –
but we have no reason to think the selection was random. All it showed

was that about half a dozen people out of more than 20,000 supported the idea of covert punishment, which tells us very little about whether that was what was really happening.

What I find interesting about the incident is that it demonstrates a form of information warfare made practical by the nature of the net – very low transaction costs, anonymity, no face-to-face contact. Considered as parody, it could have been done with old technology. As fraud, a way of tricking people into revealing their true beliefs by pretending that they were revealing them to someone who shared them, it could have been done with old technology, although not as easily. But as mass production fraud, a way of fooling thousands of people in order to get a few of them to reveal their true beliefs, it depended on the existence of email.

Some years ago on a Usenet group, I read the following message:

> I believe that it is okay to have sex before marriage unlike some people. This way you can expirence different types of sex and find the right man or woman who satifies you in bed. If you wait until marriage then what if your mate can not satisfy you, then you are stuck with him. Please write me and give me your thoughts on this. You can also tell me about some of your ways to excite a woman because I have not yet found the right man to satisfy me.

It occurred to me that what I was observing might be a commercial variant of the OFFAL tactic. The message is read by thousands, perhaps tens of thousands, of men. A hundred or so take up the implied offer and email responses. They get suitably enticing emails in response – the same emails for all of them, with only the names changed. They continue the correspondence. Eventually they receive a request for fifty dollars – and a threat to pass on the correspondence to the man's wife if the money is not paid. The ones who are not married ignore it; some of the married ones pay. The responsible party has obtained $1,000 or so at a cost very close to zero. Mass production blackmail.[8]

One of my students suggested a simpler explanation. The name and email address attached to the message belonged not to the sender but to someone the sender disliked. Whether or not he was correct, that form of information warfare has been used frequently enough online to have acquired its own nickname: "Joe job." It is not a new technique – the classical version is a phone number on the wall of a men's room. But the net greatly expands the audience.

A Sad Story

The following story is true; names and details have been changed to protect the innocent.

SiliconTech is an institution of higher education where the students regard Cornell, OFFAL and all, as barely one step above the Stone Age. If they ever have a course in advanced computer intrusion – for all I know they do – there will be no problem finding qualified students.

Alpha, Beta, and Gamma were graduate students at ST. All three came from a third-world country that, in the spirit of this exercise, I will call Sparta. Alpha and Beta were a couple for most of a year, at one point planning to get married. That ended when Beta told Alpha that she no longer wanted to be his girlfriend. Over the following months Alpha attempted, unsuccessfully, to get her back.

Eventually the two met at a social event held by the Spartan Student Association; in the course of the event, Alpha learned that Beta was now living with Gamma. This resulted in a heated discussion among the three of them; there were no outside witnesses and the participants later disagreed about what was said. Alpha's version is that he threatened to tell other members of the Spartan community at ST things that would damage the reputation of Beta and her family. Sparta was a sexually conservative and politically oppressive society, so it is at least possible that spreading such information would have had serious consequences. Beta and Gamma's version is that Alpha threatened to buy a gun and have a duel with Gamma.

Later that evening, someone used Alpha's account on the computer he did his research on to log onto another university machine and from that machine forge an obscene email to Beta that purported to come from Gamma. During the process the same person made use of Alpha's account on a university supercomputer. A day or so later, Beta and Gamma complained about the forged email to the ST computer organization, which traced it to Alpha's machine, disabled his account on their machine, and left him a message. Alpha, believing (by his account) that Beta and Gamma had done something to get him in trouble with the university, sent an email to Gamma telling him that he would have to help Beta with her research, since Alpha would no longer be responsible for doing so.

The next day, a threatening email was sent from Alpha's account on his research computer to Gamma. Beta and Gamma took the matter to the ST authorities. According to their account, Alpha had

1. Harassed Beta since they broke up, making her life miserable and keeping her from doing her research.
2. Showed her a gun permit he had and told her he was buying a gun.
3. Threatened to kill her.
4. Threatened to have a duel with Gamma.

They presented the authorities with copies of four emails – the three described so far, plus an earlier one sent at the time of the original breakup. According to Alpha, two of them were altered versions of emails that he had sent, two he had never seen before.

Two days later, Beta and Gamma went to the local police with the same account plus an accusation that, back when Alpha and Beta were still a couple, he had attempted to rape her. Alpha was arrested on charges of felony harassment and terrorism, with bail set at more than $100,000. He spent the next five and half months in jail under quite unpleasant circumstances. The trial took two weeks; the jury then took three hours to find Alpha innocent of all charges. He was released. ST proceeded to have its own trial of Alpha on charges of sexual harassment. They found him guilty and expelled him.

When I first became interested in the case – because it involved issues of identity and email evidence in a population technologically a decade or two ahead of the rest of the world – I got in touch with the ST attorney involved. According to her account, the situation was clear. Computer evidence proved that the obscene and threatening emails had ultimately originated on Alpha's account, to which only he had the password, having changed it after his breakup with Beta. While the jury may have acquitted him on the grounds that he did not actually have a gun, Alpha was clearly guilty of offenses against (at least) ST rules.

I then succeeded in reaching both Alpha's attorney and a faculty member sympathetic to Alpha who had been involved in the controversy. From them I learned a few facts that the ST attorney had omitted.

1. All of Alpha's accounts used the same password. Prior to the breakup with Beta, the password had been "Beta." Afterwards, it was Alpha's mother's maiden name.

2. According to the other graduate students who worked with Alpha, and contrary to Beta's sworn testimony, the two had remained friends after the breakup and Alpha had continued to help Beta do her research on his computer account. Hence it is almost certain that Beta knew the new password. Hence she, or Gamma, or Gamma's older brother, a professional systems manager who happened to be in town when the incidents occurred, could have accessed the accounts and done all of the things that Alpha was accused of doing.

3. The "attempted rape" was supposed to have happened early in their relationship. According to Beta's own testimony at trial, she subsequently took a trip alone with him during which they shared a bed. According to other witnesses, they routinely spent weekends together for some months after the purported attempt.

4. In the course of the trial there was evidence that many of the statements made by Beta and Gamma were false. In particular, Beta claimed never to have been in Alpha's office during the two months after the breakup (relevant because of the password issue); other occupants of the office testified that she had been there repeatedly. Beta claimed to have been shown Alpha's gun permit; the police testified that he did not have one.

5. One of the emails supposedly forged by Alpha had been created at a time when he not only had an alibi – he was in a meeting with two faculty members – but had an alibi he could not have anticipated having, hence could not have prepared for by somehow programming the computer to do things when he was not present.

6. The ST hearing was conducted by a faculty member who had told various other people that Alpha was guilty and ST should get rid of him before he did something that they might be liable for. Under existing school policy, the defendant was entitled to veto suggested members of the committee. Alpha attempted to veto the chairman and was ignored. According to my informant, the hearing was heavily biased, with restrictions by the committee on the introduction of evidence and arguments favorable to Alpha.

7. During the time Alpha was in jail awaiting trial, his friends tried to get bail lowered. Beta and Gamma energetically and successfully opposed the attempt, tried to pressure other members of the Spartan community at ST not to testify in Alpha's favor, and even put

together a booklet containing not only material about Alpha but stories from online sources about Spartan students killing lovers or professors.

Two different accounts of what actually happened are consistent with the evidence. One, the account pushed by Beta and Gamma and accepted by ST, makes Alpha the guilty party and explains the evidence that Beta and Gamma were lying about some of the details as a combination of exaggeration, innocent error, and perjury by witnesses friendly to Alpha. The other, the account accepted by at least some of Alpha's supporters, makes Beta and Gamma the guilty parties and ST at the least culpably negligent. On that version, Beta and Gamma conspired to frame Alpha for offenses he had not committed, presumably as a preemptive strike against his threat to release true but damaging information about Beta – once he was in jail, who would believe him? They succeeded to the extent of getting him locked up for five and a half months, beaten in jail by fellow prisoners, costing him and his friends some $20,000 in legal expenses, and ultimately getting him expelled.

I favor the second account, in part because I think it is clear that the ST attorney I originally spoke with was deliberately trying to mislead me by concealing facts that not only were relevant but directly contradicted the arguments she was making. I am suspicious of people who lie to me. On the other hand, attorneys, even attorneys for academic institutions, are hired to serve the interest of their clients, not to reveal truth to curious academics, so even if she believed Alpha was guilty she might have preferred to conceal the evidence that he was not. For my present purposes what is interesting is not which side was guilty but the fact that either side could have been, and the problems that fact raises for the world that they were, and we will be, living in.

Lessons

Women have simple tastes. They can take pleasure in the conversation of babes in arms and men in love.

H.L. Mencken, *In Defense of Women*

Online communication, in this case email, normally carries identification that, unlike one's face, can readily be forged. The Cornell case demonstrated one way in which that fact could be used: to extract unguarded statements from somebody by masquerading as someone he has reason to trust. This case, on one interpretation, demonstrates another: to injure someone by persuading third parties that he said things he in fact did not say.

The obvious solution is some way of knowing who sent what message. The headers of an email are supposed to provide that information. As these cases both demonstrate, they do not do it very well. On the simplest interpretation of the events at ST, Alpha used a procedure known to practically everyone in that precocious community to send a message to Beta that purported to come from Gamma. On the alternative interpretation, Beta or Gamma masqueraded as Alpha (accessing his account with his password) in order to send a message to Beta that purported to come from Gamma – and thus get Alpha blamed for doing so.

ST provided a second level of protection – passwords. The passwords were chosen by the user, hence in many cases easy to guess; users tend to select passwords that they can remember. And even if they had been hard to guess, one user can always tell another his password. However elaborate the security protecting Alpha's control over his own identification, up to and including the use of digital signatures, it could not protect him against betrayal by himself. Alpha was in love with Beta, and men in love are notoriously imprudent.

Or perhaps it could. One possible solution is the use of *biometrics*, identification linked to physical characteristics such as fingerprints or retinal patterns. If ST had been twenty years ahead of the rest of us instead of only ten, they might have equipped their computers with scanners that checked the users' fingerprints and retinas before letting them sign on. Even a man in love is unlikely to give away his retinas. With that system, we would know which party was guilty. Provided, of course, that none of the students at SiliconTech, the cream of the world's technologically precocious young minds, figured out how to trick the biometric scanners or hack the software controlling them.

Even if the system works, it has some obvious disadvantages. In order to prevent someone from editing a real email he has received and then presenting the edited version as the original – what Alpha claims that Beta and Gamma did – the system must keep records of all email that passes through it. Many users may find that objectionable on the grounds of privacy – although there are possible technological ways around that problem.[9] And the requirement of biometric identification eliminates not only forged identity but anonymity as well – which arguably could have a chilling effect on free speech.

So far I have implicitly assumed a single computer network with a single owner, like the one at Silicon Tech. With a decentralized network such as the Internet, creating a system of unforgeable identity becomes an even harder challenge. It can be done via digital signatures, but only if the potential victims are willing to take the necessary precautions to keep other people from getting access to their private keys. Biometric identification, even if it becomes entirely reliable, is still vulnerable to the user who inserts additional hardware or software between the scanner and the computer of his own system and uses it to lie to the computer about what the scanner saw.

OPEN SOURCE CRIME CONTROL

A few years ago, a college student named Jason Eric Smith sold a Mac laptop and some accessories on eBay and sent it COD to the buyer. The buyer paid with a $2,900 cashier's check that turned out to be forged. Jason, understandably upset, "posted my tale of woe and call for assistance on every Mac bulletin board I could think of" and received more than 100 responses offering help and/or oral support, one of which provided a pointer to an online private investigator who, from the buyer's cell phone number, was able to get his real name and landline phone number. Attempts to interest the Chicago police department, the FBI, and the Secret Service were unsuccessful – "will call you back later" from the first, "not large enough to interest us" from the others.

Eventually Jason got an email response from another seller who had been the victim of the same buyer and knew of the existence of others. Unable to get law enforcement interested, he decided on a little private entrapment, set up an auction on eBay of the same computer under his girlfriend's name, and within three hours received an offer – from the same buyer. Fellow Mac users in Chicago provided additional information about the neighborhood, which turned out to be not in the city at all but in the suburb of Markham. He called the Markham police and this time found an officer enthusiastically interested in catching crooks. The police officer, dressed in a FedEx uniform, made the delivery and arrested the criminal with more than $10,000 in bogus checks in his possession.[10]

The story got a good deal of news coverage at the time, but I missed it. The reason I know about it is that, when looking for material for this part of the chapter, I put a post on my blog asking for examples of open source crime control. The next day I had responses with links to several stories, including Jason's. I found his story the same way he found his criminal.

The same pattern can be seen in a number of more recent cases. One[11] involved stamp collectors swindled by someone who bought low-quality stamps, "improved them," and then resold the altered versions for higher prices. The victims succeeded in persuading eBay to join with them and shut down those of the swindler's accounts that could be identified. Total losses were apparently more than $1,000,000. One of the private investigators was a retired FBI agent and they succeeded in identifying the man responsible, but as of the most recent story I have seen on the case they have not yet succeeded in getting law enforcement to act; unfortunately, this swindler doesn't live in Markham.

The existence of the Internet facilitates open source law enforcement by victims in two ways. It makes it easier for a crime victim to get information just as it makes it easier for an amateur economist or historian to get information. And it makes it much easier for victims to find each other, pool their information, and work together to find the criminal. Only the final stage of the process requires the intervention of professionals paid to catch criminals.

Or perhaps not even the final stage. One recent news story described tactics organized online for harassing email scammers, using tactics rather like their own. And a decentralized approach can also be applied to the problem of identifying and filtering out spam, a form of enforcement entirely legal and entirely outside the legal system.

All of which raises the interesting question of whether there are opportunities for open source crime as well as open source crime control. If any occur to me I will keep them to myself.

TEN

Intermission

What's a Meta Phor?

I am typing these words into a metaphorical document in a metaphorical window on a metaphorical desktop; the document is contained in a metaphorical file folder represented by a miniature picture of a real file folder. I know the desktop is metaphorical because it is vertical; if it were a real desktop, everything would slide to the bottom.

All this is familiar to anyone whose computer employs a graphical user interface (GUI). We use that collection of layered metaphors for the same reason we call unauthorized access to a computer a break-in and a machine language program burned into a computer chip, unreadable by the human eye, a writing. The metaphor lets us transport a bundle of concepts from one thing, about which that bundle first collected, to something else to which we think most of the bundle is appropriate. Metaphors reduce the difficulty of learning to think about new things. Well-chosen metaphors do it at a minimal cost in wrong conclusions.

Consider the metaphor that underlies modern biology: evolution as intent. Evolution is not a person and does not have a purpose. Your genes are not people either and also do not have purposes. Yet the logic of Darwinian evolution implies that each organism tends to have those characteristics that it would have if it had been designed for reproductive success. Evolution produces the result we would get if each gene had a purpose – increasing its frequency in future generations – and acted to achieve that purpose by controlling the characteristics of the bodies it built.

Everything stated about evolution in the language of purpose can be restated in terms of variation and selection, Darwin's original argument. But since we have dealt with purposive beings for much longer than we have dealt with the logic of Darwinian evolution, the restated version is further from our intuitions; putting the analysis that way makes it harder to understand, clumsier. That is why biologists routinely speak in the language of purpose, as when Dawkins titled his brilliant exposition of evolutionary biology "The Selfish Gene."

For a final example, consider computer programming. When you write your first program, the approach seems obvious: Give the computer a complete set of instructions telling it what to do. By the time you have gotten much beyond telling the computer to type "Hello World," you begin to realize that a complete set of instructions for a complicated set of alternatives is a bigger and more intricate web than you can hold in your mind at one time.

People who design computer languages deal with that problem through metaphors. Currently the most popular are the metaphors of object-oriented languages such as Java and C++. A programmer builds classes of objects. None of these objects are physical things in the real world; each exists only as a metaphorical description of a chunk of code. Yet the metaphor – independent objects, each owning control over its own internal information, interacting by sending and receiving messages – turns out to be an extraordinarily powerful tool for writing and maintaining programs, programs more complicated than even a very talented programmer could keep track of if he tried to conceptualize each as a single interacting set of commands.

METAPHORICAL CRIMES

From time to time I read a news story about an intruder breaking into a computer, searching through the contents, and leaving with some of them – but I don't believe it. Looking at the computer sitting on my desk, it is obvious that intrusion is impractical for anything much bigger than a small cat. There isn't room. And if one of my cats wants to get into my computer, it doesn't have to break anything – just hook its claws into the plastic loop on the side (current Macs are designed to be easily upgradeable) and pull.

"Computer break-in" is a metaphor. So are the fingerprints and watermarks of Chapter 8. Computer programmers have fingers and occasionally leave fingerprints on the floppy disks or CDs that contain their work, but copying the program does not copy the prints.

New technologies make it possible to do things that were not possible, sometimes not imagined, fifty years ago. Metaphors are a way of fitting those things into our existing pattern of ideas, instantiated in laws, norms, language. We already know how to think about people breaking into other people's houses and what to do about it. By analogizing unauthorized access to a computer to breaking into a house we fit it into our existing system of laws and norms.

The choice of metaphor matters. What actually happens when someone "breaks into" a computer over the Internet is that he sends the computer messages, the computer responds to those messages, and something happens that the owner of the computer does not want to happen. Perhaps the computer sends out what was supposed to be confidential information. Perhaps it erases its hard disk. Perhaps it becomes one out of thousands of unwitting accessories to a distributed denial of service attack, sending thousands of requests to read someone else's web page – with the result that the overloaded server cannot deal with them all and the page temporarily vanishes from the Web. Perhaps it spews out spam at the command of its new master.

The computer is doing what the cracker[1] wants instead of what its owner wants. One can imagine the cracker as an intruder, a virtual person traveling through the net, making his way to the inside of the computer, reading information, deleting information, giving commands. That is how we are thinking of it when we call the event a break-in.

To see how arbitrary the choice of metaphor is, consider a lower tech equivalent. I want to serve legal papers on you. In order to do so, my process servers have to find you. I call your home number. If you do not answer, I tell the servers to look somewhere else. If you do answer, I hang up and send them in.

Nobody is likely to call what I have just described a break-in. Yet it fits almost precisely the earlier description. Your telephone is a machine that you have bought and connected to the phone network for a purpose. I am using your machine without your permission for a different purpose, one you disapprove of – finding out whether you are home, something you do not want me to know. With only a little effort, you can imagine a virtual me running down the phone line, breaking into your phone, peeking out to see if you are in, and reporting back. An early definition of cyberspace was "where a telephone conversation happens."

We now have two metaphors for unauthorized access to a computer – housebreaking and an unwanted phone call. They have very different legal and moral implications.

Consider a third – what crackers refer to as "human engineering," tricking people into giving them the secret information needed to access a computer. It might take the form of a phone call to a secretary from a company executive outside the office who needs immediate access to the company's computer. The secretary, whose job includes helping company executives with their problems, responds with the required passwords. The name of the executive may not be immediately familiar, but would you, if you were the secretary, want to expose your ignorance of the names of the top people in the firm you work for?

Human engineering is both a means and a metaphor for unauthorized access. What the cracker is going to do to the computer is what he has just done to the secretary – call it up, pretend to be someone authorized to get the information it holds, and trick it into giving that information. If we analogize a computer not to a house or a phone but to a person, unauthorized access is not housebreaking but fraud – against the computer.

We now have three quite different ways of fitting the same act into our laws, language, and moral intuitions – as housebreaking, fraud, or an unwanted phone call. The first is criminal, the second often tortious, the third legally innocuous.

In the early computer crime cases, courts were uncertain what the appropriate metaphor was. Much the same problem arose in the early computer copyright cases. Courts were uncertain whether a machine language program burned into the ROMs of a computer was properly analogized to a writing (protectable), a fancy cam (unprotectable, at least by copyright), or (the closest equivalent for which they had a ruling by a previous court) the paper tape controlling a player piano.[2]

In both cases, the legal uncertainty was ended by legislatures – Congress when it revised the copyright act to explicitly include computer programs, state legislatures when they passed computer crime laws that made unauthorized intrusion a felony. The copyright decision was correct, at least as applied to literal copying, for reasons I have discussed at some length elsewhere.[3] The verdict on the intrusion case is less clear.

Choosing a Metaphor

We have three different metaphors for fitting unauthorized use of a computer into our legal system. One suggests that it should be a felony, one a tort, one a legal if annoying act. To choose among them, we consider how the law will treat the acts in each case and why one treatment or the other might be preferable.

The first step is to briefly sketch the difference between a crime and a tort. A *crime* is a wrong treated by the legal system as an offense against the state. A criminal case has the form *"The State of California v. D. Friedman."* So far as the law is concerned, the state of California is the victim – the person whose computer was broken into is merely a witness. Whether to prosecute, how to prosecute, whether and on what terms to settle (an out of court settlement in a criminal case is called a plea bargain) are decided by employees of the state of California. The cost of prosecution is paid by the state and the fine, if any, paid to the state. The punishment has no necessary connection to the damage done by the wrong, since the offense is not "causing a certain amount of damage" but "breaking the law."

A *tort* is a wrong treated by the legal system as an offense against the victim; a civil case has the form *"A. Smith v. D. Friedman."* The victim decides whether to sue, hires and pays for the attorney, controls the decision of whether to settle out of court, and collects the damages awarded by the court. In most cases, the damage payment awarded is supposed to equal the damage done to the victim by the wrong – enough to "make whole" the victim.

An extensive discussion of why and whether it makes sense to have both kinds of law and why it makes sense to treat some kinds of offenses as torts and some as crimes is matter for another book; interested readers can find it in Chapter 18 of my book *Law's Order*. For our purposes it will be sufficient to note some of the legal rules associated with the two systems, some of their advantages and disadvantages, and how they might apply to a computer intrusion.

One difference we may start with is that, as a general rule, criminal conviction does, and tort does not, require intent – although the definition of intent is occasionally stretched pretty far. On the face of it, unauthorized access clearly meets that requirement. Or perhaps not. Consider three stories – two of them true.

The Boundaries of Intent

The year is 1975. The computer is an expensive multi-user machine located in a dedicated facility. An employee asks it for a list of everyone currently using it. One of the sets of initials he gets belongs to his supervisor – who is standing next to him, obviously not using the computer.[4]

The computer was privately owned but used by the Federal Energy Administration, so they called in the FBI. The FBI succeeded in tracing the access to Bertram Seidlitz, who had left six months earlier after helping to set up the computer's security system. When they searched his office, they found forty rolls of computer printout paper containing source code for WYLBUR, a text-editing program.

The case raised a number of questions about how existing law fit the new technology. Did secretly recording the "conversation" between Seidlitz and the computer violate the law requiring that recordings of phone conversations be made only with the consent of one of the parties (or a court order, which they did not have)? Was the other party the computer; if so could it consent? Did using someone else's code to access a computer count as obtaining property by means of false or fraudulent pretenses, representations, or promises – the language of the statute? Could you commit fraud against a machine? Was downloading trade secret information, which WYLBUR was, a taking of property? The court found that it could, you could, and it was; Seidlitz was convicted.

One further question remains: Was he guilty? Clearly he used someone else's access codes to download and print out the source code to a computer program. The question is why.

Seidlitz's answer was quite simple. He believed the security system for the computer was seriously inadequate. He was demonstrating that fact by accessing the computer without authorization, downloading stuff from inside the computer, and printing it out. When he was finished, he planned to send all forty rolls of source code to the people now in charge of the computer as a demonstration of how weak their defenses were. One may suspect – although he did not say – that he also planned to send them a proposal to redo the security system for them. If he was telling the truth, his access, although unauthorized, was not in violation of the law he was convicted under – or any then existing law that I can think of.

The strongest evidence in favor of his story was forty rolls of printer output. In order to make use of source code, you have to compile it – which means that you first have to get it into a form readable by a computer. In 1975, optical character recognition, the technology by which a computer turns a picture of a printed page back into machine-readable text, did not yet exist; even today it is not entirely reliable. If Seidlitz was planning to sell the source code to someone who would actually use it, he was also planning at some point to have someone type all forty rolls back into a computer – making no mistakes, since a mistake might introduce a bug into the program. It would have been far easier, instead of printing the source code, to download it to a tape cassette or floppy disk. Floppy disks capable of being written to had come out in 1973, with a capacity of about 250K; a single 8" floppy could store about 100 pages worth of text. Forty rolls of printout would be harder to produce and a lot less useful than a few floppy disks. On the other hand, the printout would provide a more striking demonstration of the weakness of the computer's security, especially for executives who did not know very much about computers.

One problem with using law to deal with problems raised by a new technology is that the legal system may not be up to the job. It is likely enough that the judge in *U.S. v. Seidlitz* (1978) had never actually touched a computer and more likely still that he had little idea what source code was or how it was used.

Seidlitz had clearly done something wrong. But deciding whether it was a prank or a felony required some understanding of both the technology and the surrounding culture and customs – which a random judge was unlikely to have. In another unauthorized access case,[5] decided a year earlier, the state of Virginia had charged a graduate student at Virginia Polytechnic Institute with fraudulently stealing more than $5,000. His crime was accessing a computer that he was supposed to access in order to do the work he was there to do – using other students' passwords and keys to access it, because nobody had gotten around to allocating computer time to him and he was embarrassed to ask for it. He was convicted and sentenced to two years in the State penitentiary. The sentence was suspended, he appealed, and on appeal was acquitted – on the grounds that what he had stolen was services, not property. Only property counted for purposes of the Virginia statute, and the scrap value of the computer cards and printouts was less than the $100 that the statute required. While charges of grand larceny were still pending against him VPI gave him his degree, demonstrating what they thought of the seriousness of his offense.

When I tell my students the sad case of Bertram Seidlitz, I like to illustrate the point with another story, involving more familiar access technologies. This time I am the hero, or perhaps villain.

The scene is the front door of the University of Chicago Law School. I am standing there because, during a visit to Chicago, it occurred to me that I needed to check something in an article in the *Journal of Legal Studies* before emailing off the final draft of an article. The University of Chicago Law School not only carries the *JLS*, it produces the *JLS*; the library is sure to have the relevant volume. While checking the article, perhaps I can drop in on some of my ex-colleagues and see how they are doing.

Unfortunately, it is a Sunday during Christmas break; nobody is in sight inside and the door is locked. The solution is in my pocket. When I left the Law School last year to take up my present position in California I forgot to give back my keys. I take out my key ring, find the relevant key, and open the front door of the law school.

In the library another problem arises. The volume I want is missing from the shelf, presumably because someone else is using it. It occurs to me that one of the friends I was hoping to see is both a leading scholar in the field and the editor of the *JLS*. He will almost certainly have his own set in his office – as I have in my office in California.

I knock on his door; no answer. The door is locked. But at the University of Chicago Law School – a very friendly place – the same key opens all faculty offices. Mine is in my pocket. I open his door, go in, and there is the *Journal of Legal Studies* on his office shelf. I take it down, check the article, and go.

The next day, on the plane home, I open my backpack and discover that, as usual, I was running on autopilot; instead of putting the volume back on the shelf I took it with me. When I get home, I mail the volume back to my friend with an apologetic note of explanation.

Let us now translate this story into a more objective account and see where I stand, legally speaking.

Using keys I had no legal right to possess I entered a locked building I had no legal right to enter, went into a locked room I had no legal right to enter and left with an item of someone else's property that I had no authorization to take. Luckily for me, the value of one volume of the *Journal of Legal Studies* is considerably less than $5,000 so although I may possibly be guilty of burglary under Illinois law, I am not covered by the federal law against interstate transportation of stolen property. Aside from the fact that the Federal government has no special interest in the University of Chicago Law School, the facts of my crime were nearly identical to the facts of Seidlitz's. Mine was just the low-tech version.

As it happens, this story is almost entirely fiction – inspired by the fact that I really did forget to give back my keys until a year or so after I left Chicago, so could have gotten into both the building and a faculty office if I had wanted to. But even if it were true, I would have been at no serious risk of anything worse than embarrassment. Everyone involved in my putative prosecution would have understood the relevant facts – that not giving keys back is the sort of thing absent-minded academics do, that using those keys in the same way you have been using them for most of the past eight years, even if technically illegal, is perfectly normal and requires no criminal intent, that looking at a colleague's copy of a journal without his permission when he isn't there to give it is also perfectly normal, and that absent-minded people sometimes walk off with things instead of putting them back where they belong. Seidlitz – assuming he really was innocent – was not so lucky.

My third story, like my first, is true.[6] The scene this time is a building in Oregon belonging to Intel. The year is 1993. The speaker is an Intel employee named Mark Morrissey.

On Thursday, October 28, at 12:30 in the afternoon, I noticed an unusual process running on a Sun computer which I administer. Further checking convinced me that this was a program designed to break, or crack, passwords. I was able to determine that the user "merlyn" was running the program. The username "merlyn" is assigned to Randal Schwartz, an independent contractor. The password-cracking program had been running since October 21st. I investigated the directory from which the program was running and found the program to be Crack 4.1, a powerful password cracking program. There were many files located there, including passwd.ssd and passwd.ora. Based on my knowledge of the user, I guessed that these were password files for the Intel SSD organization and also an external company called O'Reilly and Associates. I then contacted Rich Cower in Intel security.

Intel security called in the local police. Randy Schwartz was interrogated at length; the police had a tape recorder but did not use it. Their later account of what he said was surprisingly detailed, given that it dealt with subjects the interrogating officers knew little about, and strikingly different from his account of what he said. The main facts, however, are reasonably clear.

Randy Schwartz was a well-known computer professional, the author of two books on PERL, a language used in building things on the Web. He had a reputation as the sort of person who would rather apologize afterwards than ask permission in advance. One reason Morrissey was checking the computer Thursday afternoon was to make sure Schwartz wasn't running any jobs on it that might interfere with its intended function. As he put it in his statement, "Randal has a habit of using as much CPU power as he can find."

Schwartz worked for Intel as an independent contractor running parts of their computer system. He accessed the system from his home using a gateway through the Intel firewall that he had created on instructions from Intel for the use of a group working offsite but retained for his own use. In response to orders from Intel he had first tightened its security and later shut it down completely – then quietly recreated it on a different machine and continued to use it.

How to Break Into Computers[7]

The computer system at Intel, like many others, used passwords to control access. This raises an obvious design problem. In order for the computer to know if you typed in the right password, it needs a list of passwords to check yours against. But if there is a list of passwords somewhere in the computer's memory, anyone who can get access to that memory may be able to find the list.

You can solve this problem by creating a public key/private key pair and throwing away the private key – more generally, by creating some procedure that encrypts but does not decrypt.[8] Every time a new password is created, encrypt it and add it to the computer's list of encrypted passwords. When a user types in a password, encrypt that and see if what you get matches one of the encrypted passwords on the list. Someone with access to the computer's memory can copy the list of encrypted passwords, can copy the procedure for encrypting them, but cannot copy a procedure for decrypting them because it is not there. So he has no way of getting from the encrypted version of the password in the computer's memory to the original password that he has to type to get the desired level of access to (and control over) the computer.

A program such as Crack solves that problem by guessing passwords, encrypting the guesses, and comparing the result to the list of encrypted passwords. If it had to guess at random, the process would take a very long time. But despite the instructions of the people running the system, people who create passwords frequently insist on using their wife's name, or their date of birth, or something else easier to remember than V7g9H47ax. It does not take all that long for a computer program to run through a dictionary of first names and every date in the past seventy years, encrypt each, and check it against the list. One of the passwords Randy Schwartz cracked belonged to an Intel vice president. It was the word PRE$IDENT.

Randy Schwartz's defense was the same as Bertram Seidlitz's. He was responsible for parts of Intel's computer system. He suspected that its security was inadequate. The obvious way to test that suspicion was to see whether he could break into it. Breaking down doors is not the usual way of testing locks, but breaking into a computer does not, by itself, do any damage.

By correctly guessing one password, using that to get at a file of encrypted passwords, and using Crack to guess a considerable number of them, Randy Schwartz demonstrated the vulnerability of Intel's system. I suspect, knowing computer people although not that particular computer person, that he was also entertaining himself by solving the puzzle of how to get through Intel's barriers while proving how much cleverer he was than the people who set up the system he was cracking – including one particularly careless Intel vice president. He was simultaneously (but less successfully) running Crack against a password file from a computer belonging to O'Reilly and Associates, the company that publishes his books.

Since Intel's computer system contains a lot of valuable intellectual property protected (or not) by passwords, demonstrating its vulnerability might be considered a valuable service. Intel did not see it that way. They actively aided the state of Oregon in prosecuting Randy Schwartz for violating Oregon's computer crime law. He ended up convicted of two felonies and a misdemeanor – unauthorized access to, alteration of, and copying information from a computer system.

Two facts lead me to suspect that Randy Schwartz may have been the victim, not the criminal. The first is that Intel produced no evidence that he had stolen any information from them other than the passwords themselves. The other is that, when Crack was detected running, it was being run by "merlyn" – Randy Schwartz's username at Intel. The Crack program was in a directory named "merlyn." So were the files for the gate through which the program was being run. I find it hard to believe that a highly skilled computer network professional attempting to steal valuable intellectual property from one of the world's richest and most sophisticated high-tech firms would do it under his own name. If I correctly interpret the evidence, what actually happened was that Intel used Oregon's computer crime law to enforce its internal regulations against a subcontractor in the habit of breaking them. Terminating the offender's contract is a more conventional, and more reasonable, response.

In fairness to Intel, I should add that almost all my information about the case comes from an extensive web site set up by supporters of Randy Schwartz – extensive enough to include the full transcript of the trial.[9] Neither Intel nor its supporters has been willing to web a reply. I have, however, corresponded with an acquaintance who is in a position to know something about the case. My friend believed that Schwartz was guilty but was unwilling to offer any evidence.

Perhaps he was guilty; Intel might have reasons for keeping quiet other than a bad conscience. Perhaps Seidlitz was guilty. It is hard, looking back at a case with very imperfect information, to be sure my verdict on its verdict is correct. But I think both cases, along with my own fictitious burglary, show problems in applying criminal law to something as ambiguously criminal as unauthorized access to a computer, hence provide at least a limited argument for rejecting the break-in metaphor in favor of one of the alternatives.

Is Copying Stealing? The Bell South Case

One problem with trying to squeeze unauthorized access into existing criminal law is that intent may be ambiguous. Another is that it does not fit very well. The problem is illustrated by *U.S. v. Neidorf*, entertainingly chronicled in *The Hacker Crackdown*, Bruce Sterling's account of an early and badly bungled campaign against computer crime.

The story starts in 1988 when Robert Riggs, a college student, succeeded in accessing a computer belonging to Bell South and downloading a document about the 911 emergency system. He had no use for the information in the document, which dealt with bureaucratic organization – who was responsible for what to whom – not technology. But written at the top was "WARNING: NOT FOR USE OR DISCLOSURE OUTSIDE BELLSOUTH OR ANY OF ITS SUBSIDIARIES EXCEPT UNDER WRITTEN AGREEMENT," which made getting it an accomplishment and the document a trophy. He accordingly sent a copy to Craig Neidorf, who edited a virtual magazine – distributed from one computer to another – called Phrack. Neidorf cut out about half of the document and included what was left in Phrack.

Eventually someone at Bell South discovered that their secret document was circulating in the computer underground – and ignored it. Somewhat later, federal law enforcement agents involved in a large-scale crackdown on computer crime descended on Riggs. He and Neidorf were charged with interstate transportation of stolen property valued at more than $5,000 – a Federal offense. Riggs agreed to a guilty plea; Neidorf refused and went to trial.

Bell South asserted that the twelve-page document had cost $79,449 to produce – well over the $5,000 required for the offense. It eventually turned out that they had calculated that number by adding to the actual production costs – mostly the wages of the employees who created the document – the full value of the computer it was written on, the printer it was printed on, and the computer's software. The figure was accepted by the federal prosecutors without question. Under defense questioning, it was scaled back to a mere $24,639.05. The case collapsed when the defense established two facts: that the warning on the 911 document was on every document that Bell South produced for internal use, however important or unimportant, and that the information it contained was routinely provided to anyone who asked for it. One document, containing a more extensive version of the information published in Phrack, information Bell South had claimed to value at just under $80,000, was sold by Bell South for $13.

In the ancient days of single-sex college dormitories there was a social institution called a panty raid. A group of male students would access, without authorization, a dormitory of female students and exit with intimate articles of apparel. The objective was not acquiring underwear but defying the authority of the college administration. Robert Riggs engaged in a virtual panty raid – and ended up pleading guilty to a felony. Craig Neidorf received the booty from a virtual panty raid and displayed it in his virtual window. For that act, the federal government attempted to convict him of offenses that could have led to a prison term of over sixty years.

Part of the problem, again, was that the technology was new, hence unfamiliar to many of the people – cops, lawyers, judges – involved in the case. Dealing with a world they did not understand, they were unable to distinguish between a panty raid and a bank robbery.

Another part of the problem was that the law the case was prosecuted under was designed to deal with the theft and transportation of physical objects. It was natural to ask the questions appropriate to that law – including how much the stolen object cost to produce. But what was labeled theft was in fact copying; after Neidorf copied the document, Bell

South still had it. The real measure of the damage was not what it cost to produce the document but the cost to Bell South of other people having the information. Bell South demonstrated, by its willingness to sell the same information at a low price, that it regarded that cost as negligible. Robert Riggs was prosecuted under a metaphor. On the evidence of that case, it was the wrong metaphor.

Crime or Tort?

Bell South's original figure for the cost of creating the 911 document was one that no honest person could have produced. If you disagree, ask yourself how Bell South would have responded to an employee who, sending in his travel expenses for a 100-mile trip, included the full purchase price of his car – the precise equivalent of what Bell South did in calculating the cost of the document. Bell's testimony about the importance and secrecy of the information contained in the document was also false, but not necessarily dishonest; the Bell South employee who gave it may not have known that the firm provided the same information to anyone who asked for it. Those two false statements played a major role in a criminal prosecution that could have put Craig Neidorf in prison and did cost him, his family, and his supporters hundreds of thousands of dollars in legal expenses.

Knowingly making false statements that cost other people money is usually actionable. But the testimony of a witness in a trial is privileged – even if deliberately false, the witness is not liable for the damage done. He can be prosecuted for perjury – but that decision is made not by the injured party but by the state.

Suppose the same case had occurred under tort law. Bell South sues Riggs for $79,449. In the course of the trial it is established that the figure was wildly inflated by the plaintiff, that in any case the plaintiff still has the property, so has a claim only for damage done by the information getting out, and that that damage is zero since the information was already publicly available from the plaintiff. Not only does Bell South lose its case, it is at risk of being sued for malicious prosecution, which is not privileged. In addition, of course, Bell South, rather than the federal government, would have been paying the costs of prosecution. Putting such cases under tort law would have given Bell South an incentive to check its facts and figure out whether it had really been injured before, not after, it initiated the case – saving everyone concerned a good deal of time, money, and unpleasantness.

One advantage of tort law is that the plaintiff might have been liable for the damage it did by claims that it knew were false. Another is that it would have focused attention on the relevant issue – not the cost of producing the document but the injury to the plaintiff from having it copied. That is a familiar issue in the context of trade secret law, which comes considerably closer than criminal law to fitting the actual facts of the case.

A further problem with criminalizing such acts is illustrated by the fate of Robert Riggs. Unlike Craig Neidorf, he accepted a plea bargain and could have spent a substantial amount of time in prison – although in fact his sentence was cancelled after the trial made it clear that he had done nothing seriously wrong. One reason for agreeing to a guilty plea, presumably, was the threat of a much longer jail term if the case went to trial and he lost. Criminal law, by providing the prosecution with the threat of very severe punishments, poses the risk that innocent defendants may agree to plead guilty to a lesser offense. If the case had been a tort prosecution by the victim, the effective upper bound on damages would have been everything that Riggs owned.

There is, however, another side to that argument. Under tort law, the plaintiff pays for the prosecution. If winning the case is likely to be expensive and the defendant does not have the money to pay large damages, it may not be worth suing in the first place – in which case there is no punishment and no incentive not to commit the tort. That problem – providing an adequate incentive to prosecute when prosecution is private – is one we already touched on in Chapter 5 and will return to in Chapter 12.

PART FOUR

CRIME AND CONTROL

ELEVEN

The Future of Computer Crime

The previous chapter discussed computer crime but its subject was metaphor. This time it is crime.

THE PAST AS PROLOGUE

In the early years, computers were large stand-alone machines; most belonged to governments, large firms, or universities. Frequently they were used by those organizations to control important real-world actions – writing checks, keeping track of orders, delivering goods. The obvious tactic for computer criminals was to get access to those machines and change the information they contained – creating fictitious orders and using them to have real goods delivered, arranging to have checks written in payment for nonexistent services, or, if the computer was used by a bank, transferring money from other people's accounts to their own.

As time passed, it became increasingly common for large machines to be accessible from offsite over telephone lines. That was an improvement from the standpoint of the criminal. Instead of having to gain admission to a computer facility – with the risk of being caught – he could access the machine from a distance, evading computer defenses rather than locked doors.

While accessing computers to steal money or stuff was the most obvious form of computer crime, there were other possibilities. One was vandalism. A discontented employee or ex-employee could crash the firm's computer or erase its data. But this was a less serious problem with computers than with other sorts of machines. If a vandal smashes your truck, you have to buy another truck. If he crashes your computer, all you have to do is reboot. Even if he wipes your hard drive you can still restore from your most recent backup, losing only the most recent data.

A more interesting possibility was extortion. In one British case, a supervisor of computer operations for a large multinational firm decided that it was time to retire. He took the reels of tape that were the mass storage for the firm's computer, the backup tapes, and the extra set of backups that were stored offsite, erased the information actually in the computer, and departed. He then offered to sell the tapes – containing information that the firm needed for its ordinary functioning – back to the firm for a mere £275,000 (about $700,000).[1]

In a world with anonymous ecash, the payoff could have been made and the information delivered over the net via a remailer. In a world of strong privacy, he could have located a criminal firm in the business of collecting payoffs and subcontracted the collection end of his project. Unfortunately for the executive, he committed his crime too early. He tried to collect the payoff himself – on a motorcycle – and was caught doing it.

WONDERS OF A NETWORKED WORLD

Large computers controlling lots of valuable stuff still exist, but nowadays they are usually connected to networks. So are hundreds of millions of small computers. This opens up some interesting possibilities.

A few years back, the Chaos Computer Club of Hamburg, Germany, demonstrated one of them on German television. What they had written was an ActiveX control, a chunk of code downloaded from a web site onto the user's computer. It was designed to work with Quicken, a widely used accounting package. One of the things Quicken can do is pay bills online. The control they demonstrated modified Quicken's files to add one additional payee. Trick a million people into downloading it, have each of them pay you ten marks a month – a small enough sum so that it might take a long time to be noticed – and retire.

One of the classic computer crime stories – possibly apocryphal – concerns a programmer who computerized a bank's accounting system.

After a few months, bank officials noticed that something seemed to be wrong – a slow leakage of money. But when they checked the individual accounts, everything balanced. Eventually someone figured out the trick. The programmer had designed the system so that all rounding errors went to him. If you were supposed to receive $13.436 in interest, you got $13.43, his account got .6 cents. It was a modest fraud – six-tenths of a cent is not much money, and nobody normally worries about rounding errors anyway. But if the bank has a million accounts and calculates interest daily, the total comes to about $5,000 a day.

That sort of fraud is called a "salami scheme" – nobody notices one more thin slice missing from a salami.[2] The Chaos Computer Club had invented a mass production version. Hardly anyone notices a leakage of a few dollars a month from his account but, with millions of accounts, it adds up fast. It is the old computer crime of tricking a computer into transferring money to you modernized for a world with lots of networked computers that each control only small amounts. So far as I know, nobody has yet put this particular form of computer crime into practice, despite the public demonstration that it could be done. But someone will.

A modern criminal who preferred extortion to theft could hold the contents of computers for ransom using either a downloaded ActiveX control or a computer virus – and take advantage of the power of public key encryption. Once the software gets onto the victim's computer it creates a large random number and uses it as the key to encrypt the contents of the hard drive, erasing the unencrypted version as it does so. The final step is to encrypt the key using the criminal's public key and erase the original.

The next time the computer is turned on, its screen shows a message offering to unencrypt the contents of the hard drive for twenty dollars in anonymous ecash, sent to the criminal through a suitable remailer. The money must be accompanied by the encrypted key, which the message includes. The extortionist will send back the decrypted key and the software to decrypt the hard drive.

From the standpoint of the criminal, the scheme has two attractive features. The first is that since each victim's hard drive is encrypted with a different key, there is no way one victim can share the information about how to decrypt it with another – each must pay separately. The second is that, with lots of victims, the criminal can establish a reputation for honest dealing; after the first few cases, everyone will know that if you pay you really do get your hard drive back. So far as I know, nobody has done it yet, although there was an old case involving a less sophisticated version of the scheme, using floppy disks instead of downloads.

What else can be done in a world of lots of small networked computers? One answer is vandalism, familiar in the form of computer viruses. A more productive possibility is to imitate some of the earliest computer criminals and steal, not money, but computing power. At any instant, millions of desktop computers are twiddling their thumbs while their owners are eating lunch or thinking about what to type next. When you operate at millions of instructions a second, there's a lot of time between keystrokes.

The best-known attempt to harness that wasted power is SETI – the Search for Extra-Terrestrial Intelligence. It is a volunteer effort by which large numbers of individuals permit their computers, whenever they happen to be idle, to work on a small part of the immense project of searching the haystack of interstellar radio noise for the needle of information that might tell us that, somewhere in the galaxy, someone else is home. Similar efforts on a smaller scale have been used in experiments to test how hard it is to break various forms of encryption, another project that requires very large-scale number crunching.

One could imagine an enterprising thief stealing a chunk of that processing power – perhaps justifying the crime on the grounds that nobody was using it anyway. The approach would be along SETI's lines, but without SETI's public presence. Download a suitable bit of software to each of several million unknowing helpers, then use the Internet to share the burden of very large computing projects among them. Charge customers for access to the worlds' biggest computer while keeping its exact nature a trade secret. Think of Randy Schwartz – who, whether or not he stole trade secrets, had the reputation of grabbing all the CPU power he could get his hands on. Nobody has done it. My guess is that nobody will, since the continuing access is too easy to detect. But two more destructive versions have been implemented repeatedly.

One is called a Distributed Denial of Service attack – DDOS, for short. To do it, you temporarily take over a large number of networked computers and instruct each to spend all of its time trying to access a web page belonging to some person or organization you disapprove of. A web server can send out copies of its web page to a lot of browsers at once, but not an unlimited number. With enough requests coming fast enough, the server is unable to handle them all and the page vanishes from the Web.

A second reason to temporarily take over lots of computers that don't belong to you is to solve the spam problem – not the problem that you and I face in dealing with in-boxes clogged by hundreds of offers to expand various parts of our anatomy but the problem faced by the people sending spam. If you send it from your own computer, you might get into trouble – if not with the recipients, then with your own ISP. One solution is to use a computer virus to modify lots of other people's computers in a way that gives you temporary access to them and then use them as your unwitting accessories.

Spam itself provides multiple examples of computer crimes made possible by the existence of enormous numbers of networked computers. Nobody with any sense would believe an email from a stranger in Nigeria offering to give him millions of dollars – after he first provides some small financial evidence of his reliability. But if you send out such an offer to a billion email addresses, ten million of which turn out to be actual people, you will reach the small minority of those ten million who are sufficiently credulous, or sufficiently greedy, to fall for the scam. A small minority of ten million people can still be a large number.

Distributed Computing: The Solution
the Problem Comes From

Most of the problems we have been discussing involve software downloaded from a web page to a user's computer. Such software originated as a solution to one of the problems of networked computing: server overload.

You have a web page that does something for the people who access it – draws a map showing them how to get to a particular address, say. Drawing that picture – getting from information on a database to a map a human being can read – takes computing power. Even if it does not take very much power, when 1,000 people each want a different map drawn at the same time it adds up and your system slows down.

Each of those people is accessing your page from his own computer. Reading a web page does not take much in the way of computing resources, so most of those computers are twiddling their thumbs – operating at far below capacity. Why not put them to work drawing maps?

The web page copies to each of the computers a little map-drawing program – an ActiveX control or Java applet. That only has to be done once. Thereafter, when the computer reads the web page, the page sends it the necessary information and it draws the map itself. Instead of putting the whole job on one busy computer, it is divided up among 1,000 idle computers. The same approach – distributed computing – works for multiplayer webbed games and many other applications. It is a solution – but a solution that, as we have just seen, raises a new problem. Once that little program gets on your computer, who knows what it might do there?

Microsoft deals with that problem by using digital signatures authenticated by Microsoft to identify where each ActiveX control comes from. Microsoft's response to the Chaos Computer Club's demonstration of a new use for an ActiveX control was that there was really no problem. All a user had to do to protect himself was to tell his browser, by an appropriate setting of the security level on Explorer, not to take controls from strangers.

This assumes that nobody can fool Microsoft into signing bogus code. I can think of at least two ways of doing it. One is to get a job with a respectable software company and insert extra code into one of their ActiveX controls, which Microsoft would then sign. The other is to start your own software company, produce useful software that makes use of an ActiveX control, add an additional unmarked feature inspired by the Chaos Computer Club, get it signed by Microsoft, put it up on the Web, then close up shop and decamp for Brazil.

Sun Computer has a different solution to the same problem. Java applets, their version of software for distributed computing, are only allowed to play in the sandbox, designed to have a very limited ability to affect other things in the computer, including files stored on the hard drive. One problem with that solution is that it limits the useful things an applet can do. Another is that even Sun sometimes makes mistakes. The fence around the sandbox may not be entirely applet-proof.

The odds are that both ActiveX and applets will soon be history. Whatever form of distributed computing succeeds them will face the same problem and the same set of possible solutions. In order to be useful, it has to be able to do things on the client computer. The more it can do, the greater the danger of its doing things that the owner of that computer would disapprove of. That can be controlled either by controlling what gets downloaded and holding the firm that certified it responsible for the software's behavior or by strictly limiting what any such software is allowed to do – Microsoft's and Sun's approaches, respectively.

Growing Pains

Readers with high-speed Internet connections may at this point be wondering if they ought to pull the plug. I don't think so – and I haven't.

There are two important things to remember about the sort of problem we have been discussing. The first is that it is your computer, sitting on your desktop. A bad guy may be able to get control of it by some clever trick, by getting you to download bogus software or a virus. But you start with control – and whatever the bad guy does, you can always turn the machine off, boot from a CD, wipe the hard drive, restore from your backup, and start over. The logic of the situation favors you. It is only bad software design and careless use that makes it possible for other people to take over your machine.

The second thing to remember is that this is a new world and we have just arrived. Most desktop computers are running under software originally designed for stand-alone machines. It is not surprising that such software frequently proves vulnerable to threats that did not exist in the environment it was designed for. As software evolves in a networked world, a lot of the current problems will gradually vanish. Until the next innovation.

The Worm Turns: Clients Fooling Servers

We have been discussing crimes committed by a server against clients – downloading chunks of code to them that do things their owners would

not approve of. I once got into an interesting conversation with someone who had precisely the opposite problem. He was in the computer
gaming business – online role-playing games in which large numbers of
characters, each controlled by a different player, interact in a common
universe, allying, fighting each other, gaining experience, becoming more
powerful, acquiring enchanted swords, books of spells, and the like.

People running online games want lots of players. As more and more
players join, the burden on the server supporting the game increases, since
it has to keep track of the characteristics and activities of an increasing
number of characters. Ideally, a single computer should keep track of
everything in order to maintain a consistent universe, but there is a limit
to what one computer can do.

One solution is distributed computing. Offload most of the work to
the player's computer. Let it draw the pretty pictures on the screen, maps
of a dungeon or a fighter's eye view of the monster he is fighting. Let it
keep track of how much gold the character has, how much experience he
has accumulated, what magic devices are in his pouch, what armor on
his back. The server still needs to keep track of the shared fundamentals –
who is where – but not the details. Now the game scales; when you double
the number of players you almost double the computing power available,
since the new players' computers are now sharing the load.

Like many solutions, this one comes with a problem. If my computer
is keeping track of how strong my character is and what goodies he
has, that information is stored in files on my hard drive. My hard drive
is under my control. With a little specialized knowledge about how the
information is stored – provided, perhaps, by a fellow enthusiast online –
I can modify those files. Why spend hundreds of hours fighting monsters
in order to become a hero with muscles of steel, lightning reactions, and
a magic sword, when I can get the same result by suitably editing the
file describing my character? In the online gaming world, where many
players are technically sophisticated, competitive, and unscrupulous –
or, if you prefer, where many players regard competitive cheating as
merely another dimension of the game – it is apparently a real problem.
I offered him a solution; I do not know if he, or anyone else, has tried
implementing it.

The server cannot be bothered to keep track of all the details of all
the characters, but it can probably manage 1 in 100. Pick a character

at random and, while his computer is calculating what is happening to him, run a parallel calculation on the server. Follow him for a few days, checking to make sure that his characteristics remain what they should be. If they do, switch to someone else.

What if the character has mysteriously jumped twenty levels since the last time he logged off? Criminal law solves the problem of deterring offenses that are hard to detect – littering, for example – by scaling up the punishment to balance the low probability of imposing it. It should work here too.

I log into the game where my character, thanks to hundreds of hours of playing assisted by some careful hacking of the files that describe him, is now a level 83 mage with a spectacular collection of wands and magic rings. There is a surprise waiting:

```
"You wake up in the desert, wearing only a
   loin cloth. Clutched in your hand is a
   crumpled parchment."
"Look at the Parchment."
"It looks like your handwriting, but unsteady
   and trailing off into gibberish at the end."
"Read the Parchment."
The parchment reads:
"I shouldn't have done it. Dabbling in
   forbidden arts. The Demons are coming. I can
   feel myself pouring away. No, No, No...."
"Show my statistics."
Level: 1.
Possessions: 1 loincloth.
```

Crime doesn't pay.

HIGH-TECH TERRORISM: NIGHTMARE OR EMPLOYMENT PROJECT?

A few years ago, I participated in a conference called to advise a presidential panel investigating the threat of high-tech terrorism. So far as I could tell, the panel originated with an exercise by the National Security Agency in which they demonstrated that, had they been bad guys, they could have done a great deal of damage by breaking into computers controlling banks, hospitals, and much else.

I left the conference uncertain whether what I had just seen was a real threat or an NSA employment project, designed to make sure that the end of the Cold War did not result in serious budget cuts. Undoubtedly a group of highly sophisticated terrorists could do a lot of damage by breaking into computers. But then, a group of sophisticated terrorists could do a lot of damage in low-tech ways too. I had seen no evidence that the same team could not have done as much damage – or more – without ever touching a computer. A few years after that conference, a group of not very sophisticated terrorists demonstrated just how much damage they could do by flying airplanes into buildings. No computers required.

I did, however, come up with one positive contribution to the conference. If you really believe that foreign terrorists breaking into computers in order to commit massive sabotage is a problem, the solution is to give the people who own computers adequate incentives to protect them, to set up their software in ways that make it hard to break in. One way of doing so would be to decriminalize ordinary intrusions. If the owner of a computer cannot call the cops when he finds that some talented teenager has been rifling through his files, he has an incentive to make it harder to do so in order to protect himself. Once the computers of America are safe against Kevin Mitnick,[3] Osama bin Laden won't have a chance.

TWELVE

Law Enforcement × 2

The previous chapter dealt with the use of new technologies by criminals; this chapter deals with the other side of the picture. I begin by looking at ways in which new technologies can be used to enforce the law and some associated risks. I then go on – via a brief detour to the eighteenth century – to consider how technologies discussed in earlier chapters may affect not only how law is enforced but by whom.

HIGH-TECH CRIME CONTROL

Criminals are not the only ones who can use new technologies; cops can too. Insofar as enforcing law is a good thing, new technologies that make it easier are a good thing. But the ability to enforce the law is not an unmixed blessing – the easier it is to enforce laws, the easier it is to enforce bad laws.

There are two different ways in which our institutions can prevent governments from doing bad things. One is by making particular bad acts illegal. The other is by making them impossible. That distinction appeared back in Chapter 3, when I argued that unregulated encryption could serve as the twenty-first-century version of the Second Amendment – a way of limiting the ability of governments to control their citizens.

For a less exotic example, consider the Fourth Amendment's restrictions on searches – the requirement of a warrant issued upon showing of reasonable cause. At least some searches under current law – wiretaps, for instance – can be done without the victim even knowing about it. What's the harm? If you have nothing to hide, why should you object?

One answer is that the ability to search anyone at anytime, to tap any phone, puts too much power in the hands of law enforcement agents. Among other things, it lets them collect information irrelevant to crimes but useful for blackmailing people into doing what they are told. For similar reasons, the United States, practically alone among developed nations, has never set up a national system of required ID cards – although that may have changed by the time this book is published. Such a system would make law enforcement a little easier. It would also make abuses by law enforcement easier.

The underlying theory, which I think everyone understands although few put it into words, is that a government with only a little power can only do things that most of the population approves of. With a lot of power, it can do things that most people disapprove of – including, in the long run, converting a nominal democracy into a *de facto* dictatorship. Hence the delicate balance intended to provide government with enough power to prevent most murder and robbery but not much more. How might new technologies available for law enforcement affect that balance?

KNOWING TOO MUCH

A police officer stops me and demands to search my car. I ask him why. He replies that my description fits closely the description of a man wanted for murder. Thirty years ago, that would have been a convincing argument. It is less convincing today. The reason is not that police officers know less but that they know more.

In the average year, there are about 20,000 murders in the United States. With 20,000 murders and (I am guessing) several thousand wanted suspects, practically everyone fits the description of at least one of them. Thirty years ago, police officers would have had information only on those in their immediate area. Today they can access a databank listing all of them.

Consider the same problem as it might show up in a courtroom. A rape/murder is committed in a big city. The jury is told that the defendant's DNA matches that of the perpetrator – well enough so that there is only a one in a million probability that the match would happen by chance. Obviously he is guilty – those odds easily satisfy the requirements of "beyond a reasonable doubt."

There are two problems with that conclusion. The first is that the one-in-a-million statement is false. The reason it is false has to do not with DNA but with people. The figure was calculated on the assumption that all tests were done correctly. But we have plenty of evidence from past cases that the odds that someone in the process, whether the police officer who sent in the evidence or the lab technician who tested it, was either incompetent or dishonest are a great deal higher than one in a million.[1]

The second problem is not yet relevant but soon may be. To see it, imagine that we have done DNA tests on everyone in the country in order to set up a national database of DNA information, perhaps as part of a new nationwide system of ID cards. Under defense questioning, more information comes out. The way the police located the suspect was by going through the DNA database. His DNA matched the evidence, he had no alibi, so they arrested him.

Now the odds that he is guilty shift down dramatically. The chance that the DNA of someone chosen at random would match the sample as closely as his did is only one in a million. But the database contains information on seventy million men in the relevant age group. By pure chance, about seventy of them will match. All we know about the defendant is that he is one of those seventy, does not have an alibi, and lives close enough to where the crime happened so that he could conceivably have committed it. There might easily be three or four people who meet all of those conditions, so the fact that the defendant is one of them is very weak evidence that he is guilty.

Consider the same problem in a very different context, one that has existed for the past twenty years or so. An economist interested in crime has a theory that the death penalty increases the risk to police of being killed, since cornered murder suspects have nothing to lose. To test that theory, he runs a regression, a statistical procedure designed to see how different factors affect the number of police killed in the line of duty. The death penalty is not the only factor, so he includes additional terms for variables such as the fraction of the population in high-crime age groups, racial mix, poverty level, and the like. When he publishes his results, he reports that the regression fits the theory's prediction at the .05 level: there is only one chance in twenty that the result would fit as well as it did by pure chance.

What the economist does not mention in the article is that the reported regression was one of sixty that he ran – varying which other factors were included, how they were measured, how they were assumed to interact. With sixty regressions, the fact that at least one came out as predicted does not tell us very much – by pure chance, about three of them should.

Fifty years ago, running a regression was a lot of work – done by hand or, if you were lucky, on an electric calculating machine that did addition, multiplication, and not much else. Doing sixty of them was not a practical option, so the fact that someone's regression fit his theory at the .05 level was evidence that the theory was right. Today, any academic – practically any schoolchild – has access to a computer that can do sixty regressions in a few minutes. That makes it easy to do a specification search, to try lots of different regressions, each specifying the relationship a little differently, until you find one that works. You can even find statistical packages that do it for you.

So the fact that your article reports a successful regression no longer provides much support for your theory. At the very least, you have to report the different specifications you tried, give a verbal summary of how they came out, and detailed results for a few of them. If you really want to persuade people you have to make your dataset freely available, ideally over the Internet, and let other people run as many regressions on it in as many different ways as they want until they convince themselves that the relationship you found is really there, not an illusion created by carefully selecting which results you reported.

All of these examples – the police stop on suspicion, the DNA evidence, the specification search – involve the same issue. By increasing access to information you make it easier to find evidence for the right answer. But you also make it easier to find evidence for the wrong answer.

If you are the one looking for evidence, the additional information is an asset. The researcher can report the specification search and use its results to improve the theory. The traffic cop can check the database of wanted suspects, see that the person whose description I fit was last reported on the other side of the country, and decide not to bother stopping me. The police, having located several suspects who fit the DNA evidence, can engage in a serious attempt to see if one of them is guilty and only make an arrest if there is enough additional evidence to convict. Develop the technology a little further and the police, unable to find a match for the suspect's DNA in their database, can instead search it for his relatives – and, having found plausible candidates, continue their investigation from there.

But in each case, the additional information also makes it easier to generate bogus evidence. The traffic cop who actually wants to stop me because of the color of my skin or my out-of-state plates, or in the hope of finding something illegal and being offered a bribe not to report it, can honestly claim that I met the description of a wanted man. The district attorney who wants a good conviction rate before his next campaign for high office can report the DNA fit and omit any explanation of how it was obtained and what it really means. And the academic researcher, desperate for publications to bolster his petition for tenure, can selectively remember only those regressions that came out right. If we want to prevent such behavior we must alter our rules and customs accordingly, raising the standard for how much evidence it takes in order to reflect how much easier it has become to produce evidence – even for things that are not true.

EVERY PHONE

The hero of *The President's Analyst* (James Coburn), having spent much of the film evading various bad guys who want to kidnap him and use him to influence his star patient, has temporarily escaped his pursuers and made it to a phone booth. He calls up a friendly CIA agent (Godfrey Cambridge) to come rescue him. When he tries to leave the booth, the door won't open. Down the road comes a phone company truck loaded with booths. The truck's crane picks up the one containing the analyst, deposits it in the back, replaces it with an empty booth, and drives off. A minute later a helicopter descends containing the CIA agent and a KGB agent who is his temporary ally. They look in astonishment at the empty phone booth. The American speaks first:

"It can't be. Every phone in America tapped?"
The response (you will have to imagine the accent)
"Vhere do you think you are – Russia?"

A great scene in a very funny movie. But it may not be a joke much longer.

Fast forward to the debate over the digital wiretap bill, legislation pushed by the FBI to require phone companies to provide law enforcement agents facilities to tap digital phone lines. One point made by critics of the legislation was that the FBI appeared to be demanding the ability to simultaneously tap about 1 phone out of 100. While that figure was probably an exaggeration – there was disagreement as to the exact meaning of the capacity the FBI was asking for – it was not much of an exaggeration.

As the FBI pointed out, that did not mean they would be using all of that capacity. To be able to tap 1% of the phones in any particular place – say a place with lots of drug dealers – they needed the ability to tap 1% of the phones in every place. And the 1% figure would only apply in parts of the country where the FBI thought it might need such a capacity and included not only wiretaps but also less intrusive forms of surveillance, such as keeping track of who called whom but not of what they said.

At the time they made the request, wiretaps were running at a rate of under 1,000 a year – not all at the same time. Even after giving the FBI the benefit of all possible doubt, the capacity they asked for was only needed if they were contemplating an enormous increase in telephone surveillance.

The FBI defended the legislation as necessary to maintain the status quo, to keep developments in communications technology from reducing the ability of law enforcement to engage in court-ordered interceptions. Critics argued that there was no evidence such a problem existed. My own suspicion is that the proposal was indeed motivated by technology – but not that technology.

The first step is to ask why, if phone taps are as useful as law enforcement spokesmen claim, there are so few of them and they produce so few convictions. The figure for 1995 was a total of 1,058 authorized interceptions at all levels, federal, state, and local. They were responsible for a total of 494 convictions, mostly for drug offenses. Total drug convictions for that year, at the federal level alone, were over 16,000.

The answer is not the reluctance of courts to authorize wiretaps. The National Security Agency, after all, gets its wiretaps authorized by a special court, widely reported to have never turned down a request. The answer is that wiretaps are very expensive. Some rough calculations by Robin Hanson[2] suggest that on average, in 1993, they cost more than $50,000 each. Most of that was the cost of labor, police officers' time listening to 1.7 million conversations at a cost of about $32 per conversation.

That problem has been solved. Software to convert speech into text is now widely available on the market. Using such software, you can have a computer listen, convert the speech to text, search the text for keywords and phrases, and notify a human being if it gets a hit. Current commercial software is not very reliable unless it has first been trained to the user's voice. But an error level that would be intolerable for using a computer to take dictation is more than adequate to pick up keywords in a conversation. And the software is getting better.

Computers work cheap. If we assume that the average American spends half an hour a day on the phone – a number created out of thin air by averaging in two hours for teenagers and ten minutes for everyone else – that gives, on average, about six million phone conversations at any one time. Taking advantage of the wonders of mass production, it should be possible to produce enough dedicated computers to handle all of that for less than a billion dollars. And it's getting cheaper every year.

Every phone in America.

A Legal Digression: My Brief for the Bad Guys

Law enforcement agencies still have to get court orders for all of those wiretaps; however friendly the courts may be, persuading judges that every phone in the country needs to be tapped, including theirs, might be a problem.

Or perhaps not. A computer wiretap is not really an invasion of privacy – nobody is listening. Why should it require a search warrant? If I

were an attorney for the FBI facing a friendly judge, I would argue that
a computerized tap is at most equivalent to a pen register, which keeps
track of who calls whom and does not currently require a warrant. The
tap only rises to the level of a search when a human being listens to the
recorded conversation. Before doing so, the human being will, of course,
go to a judge, offer the judge the computer's report on keywords and
phrases detected, and use that evidence to obtain a warrant. Thus law
enforcement will be free to tap all our phones without requiring permission from the court system – until, of course, it finds evidence that
we are doing something wrong. If we are doing nothing wrong, only a
computer will hear our words, so why worry? What do we have to hide?

LIVING ID CARDS

In the wake of the attack on the World Trade Center there has been
political pressure to establish a national system of ID cards; currently
(defined by when I write, not when you read) it is unclear whether it
will succeed. In the long run, it may not matter very much. Each of us
already has a variety of built-in identification cards – face, fingerprints,
retinal patterns, DNA. Given adequate technologies for reading that
information, a paper card is superfluous.

In low-density populations, face alone is enough. Nobody needs to ask
a neighbor for identification because everybody already knows everybody
else.

That system breaks down in the big city because we are not equipped
to store and search a million faces. But we could be. Facial recognition
software exists and is getting better. There is no technical reason that,
sometime fairly soon, someone, most probably law enforcement, could
not compile a database containing every face in the country. Point the
camera at someone and read off name, age, citizenship, criminal history,
and whatever else is in the database.

Faces are an imperfect form of identification, since there are ways
to change your appearance. Fingerprints are better. There already exist
commercial devices to recognize fingerprints, used to control access to
laptop computers. I do not know how close we are to an inexpensive

fingerprint reader matched with a filing system, but it does not seem like an inherently difficult problem. Nor does the equivalent using a scan of retinal patterns. Cheap DNA recognition is a little further off, but there, too, technology has been progressing rapidly.

We could make laws forbidding law enforcement bodies from compiling and using such databases, but it does not seem likely that we will, given the obvious usefulness of the technology for the job we want them to do. Even if we did forbid it, enforcing the ban against both law enforcement and everyone else would be difficult. When the Social Security system was set up, the legislation explicitly forbade the use of the Social Security number as a national identifier. Nonetheless, the federal government – and a lot of other people – routinely ask you for it. Even if there is no official national database of faces, each police department will have its own collection of faces that interest it. If expanding that collection is cheap – and it will be – "interest" will become a weaker and weaker requirement. And there is nothing to stop different police departments from talking to each other.

THE OBSOLESCENCE OF CRIMINAL LAW

A few chapters back, I raised the question of whether unauthorized access to a computer ought to be treated as a tort or a crime. It is now time to return to that issue in a broader context.

Most of us think of law enforcement as almost entirely the province of government. In fact it is not and, so far as I know, never has been.[3] In the United States, total employment in private crime prevention – security guards, burglar alarm installers, and the like – has long been greater than that in public law enforcement. Catching and prosecuting criminals is mostly done by agents of government, but that is only because crime is defined as the particular sort of offense that is prosecuted by the government. The same action – killing your wife, for example – can be prosecuted either by the state as a crime or by private parties as a tort, as O. J. Simpson discovered.

That fact suggests that we might not need criminal law. Perhaps we could manage, even manage better, with a system in which all wrongs were privately prosecuted by the victim or the victim's agents. Such systems have existed in the past. They may again.

A Brief Temporal Digression

Consider, for one of my favorite examples, criminal prosecution in eighteenth-century England. On paper, their legal system made the same distinction between crimes and torts that ours does. A crime was an offense against the Crown – the case was *Rex v. Friedman*.[4]

The Crown owned the case but it did not prosecute it. England in the eighteenth century had no police as we understand the word – no professionals employed by government to catch and convict criminals. There were constables, sometimes unpaid, with powers of arrest, but figuring out whom to arrest was not part of their job description. It was not until the 1830s that the situation changed, when Robert Peel created the first English police force.

Not only were there no police, there were no public prosecutors, either; the equivalent of the district attorney in the modern American system did not exist in England until the 1870s, although for some decades prior to that police officers functioned as *de facto* prosecutors. With neither police nor public prosecutors, criminal prosecution was necessarily private. The legal rule was that any Englishman could prosecute any crime. In practice, prosecution was usually by the victim or his agent.

That raises an obvious puzzle. When I sue someone under tort law, I have the hope of winning and being paid damages, with luck more than enough to cover my legal bills. A private prosecutor under criminal law had no such incentive. If he got a conviction the criminal would be hanged, transported, permitted to enlist in the armed services, or pardoned, none of which put any money in the prosecutor's pocket. So why did anyone bother to prosecute?

One answer is that the victim prosecuted in order to deter – not crimes in general but crimes against himself. That makes sense if he is a repeat player, such as the owner of a store or factory at continual risk from thieves. Hang one and the others will get the message. That is why, even today in a system where prosecution is nominally entirely public, department stores have signs announcing that they prosecute shoplifters. Arguably it is why Intel prosecuted Randy Schwartz.

Most potential victims were not repeat players. For them, the eighteenth-century English came up with an ingenious solution: societies for the prosecution of felons. There were thousands of them. The members of each contributed a small sum to a pooled fund, available to pay the cost of prosecuting a felony committed against any member of the society. The names of the members were published in the newspaper for the felons to read. Potential victims thus precommitted themselves to prosecute. They had made deterrence into a private good.

That set of institutions was eventually abandoned. One possible explanation is that, in order for it to work, criminals had to know their victims, at least well enough to know whether the victim either had a reputation for prosecuting or was a member of a prosecution association. As England became increasingly urbanized, crime became increasingly anonymous. It did no good to join a prosecution association and publish your membership in the local paper if the burglar didn't know your name. Another possible explanation, argued by some scholars, is that the police were introduced as a solution to other problems – perhaps reforming the poor, perhaps providing government with the ability to make sure that the French Revolution, or something similar, did not happen in England.[5]

Forward into the Past

One consequence of modern information-processing technology is the end of anonymity, at least in realspace. Public information about you is now truly public; not only is it out there, anyone who wants it can find it. In an earlier chapter, I discussed that in the context of privacy. Privacy through obscurity is no longer an option. We can now see a different consequence. In the nineteenth century, big cities made victims anonymous. With nobody anonymous any more, we are back in the eighteenth century.

Consider our earlier discussion of how to handle unauthorized access to computers. One problem with using tort law is inadequate incentive to prosecute, since the random cracker may not be able to pay a large enough sum in damages to cover the cost of finding and suing him. That problem was solved 250 years ago. Under criminal law there were no damages to collect, so eighteenth-century Englishmen found a different incentive – private deterrence.

Imagine the online version of a society for the prosecution of felons. Subscribers pay an annual fee, in exchange for which they are guaranteed prosecutorial services if someone accesses their computer in ways that impose costs on them. The names of subscribers and their IP addresses are posted on a web page, for prudent crackers to read and avoid. If the benefit of deterrence is worth the cost, there should be lots of customers. If it is not, why provide deterrence at the taxpayers' expense?

There remains one problem. Under ordinary tort law, the penalty is either the damage done or the largest amount the offender can pay, whichever is less. If computer intruders are hard to catch, that penalty might not be adequate to deter them. One time out of ten, the intruder must pay for the damage if he can. The other nine times he goes free.

Criminal law solves that problem by permitting penalties larger, sometimes much larger, than the damage done, thus making up for the fact that only some fraction of offenders are caught, convicted, and punished. Punitive damages in tort law achieve the same effect. But punitive damages are limited by the assets of the offender, and criminal punishment is not – the criminal law can impose nonmonetary punishments such as imprisonment.

So we have two possibilities for private enforcement of legal rules against unauthorized access. One is to use ordinary tort law, with private deterrence as the incentive to prosecute. That works so long as the assets of offenders are large enough so that taking them via a tort suit is an adequate punishment to deter most offenses. The other is to go all the way back to the eighteenth century – private prosecution with criminal penalties.

I have discussed the problems with private prosecution – what are the advantages? The main one is the advantage that private enterprise usually has over state enterprise. The proprietors of an online prosecution firm are selling a service to their customers on a competitive market. The better they do their job, the more likely they are to make money. If costs are high and quality low, they will not have the option of getting bailed out by the taxpayers.

The argument applies to more than the defense of computers against unwanted intruders. Information-processing technology eliminates the anonymity that urbanization created; in that respect, at least, it puts us back in villages. Doing so eliminates what was arguably the chief reason for the shift from private to public prosecution. Of all crime.

Private Enforcement Online

My interest in the future of private enforcement online was in part inspired by history and economic theory, in part by news stories about criminals who were caught by their victims, using the Internet to coordinate their efforts – open source crime control, as discussed in an earlier chapter.

Such stories suggest another way in which modern technology may make private law enforcement more practical than it has been in the recent past. Many crimes involve a single criminal but multiple victims. Each victim has reasons, practical and moral, to want the criminal caught, but no one victim can do the job on his or her own. The Internet, by drastically reducing the cost of finding fellow victims and coordinating with them, helps solve that problem.

PART FIVE

BIOTECHNOLOGIES

THIRTEEN

Human Reproduction

Through most of the past century, improved reproductive technology has consisted in large part of better ways of not reproducing. Better contraception has been accompanied by striking changes in human mating patterns: a steep decline in traditional marriage, a corresponding increase in nonmarital sex, and, perhaps surprisingly, extraordinarily high rates of childbirth outside of marriage. While the long-term consequences of reliable contraception will continue to play out over the next few decades, they will not be discussed here. This chapter deals with more recent developments in the technology of human reproduction.

BUILDING BETTER BABIES

Eugenics, the idea of improving the human species by selective breeding, was supported by quite a lot of people in the late nineteenth and early twentieth centuries.[1] Currently it ranks, in the rhetoric of controversy, only a little above Nazism. Almost any reproductive technology capable of benefiting future generations is at risk of being attacked as "eugenics" by its opponents.

That argument confuses, sometimes deliberately, two quite different ways of achieving similar objectives. One is to treat human beings like show dogs or racehorses – have someone, presumably the state, decide which ones get to reproduce in order to improve the breed. Such a policy involves forcing people who want to have children not to do so and perhaps forcing people who do not want to have children to do so. In addition, it imposes the eugenic planner's desires on everyone; there is

189

no reason to assume that the result would be an improvement from the point of view of the rest of us. A prudent state might decide that submissiveness, obedience to authority, and similar characteristics were what it wanted to breed for.

Libertarian Eugenics

The alternative is what I think of as libertarian eugenics. The earliest description I know of is in a science fiction novel, *Beyond This Horizon*, by Robert Heinlein, arguably one of the ablest and most innovative science fiction writers of the twentieth century.

In Heinlein's story, genetic technology is used by couples to control which of the children they could produce they do produce. With the assistance of expert advice, they select among the eggs produced by the wife and the sperm produced by the husband the particular combination of egg and sperm that will produce the child they most want to have, the one that does not carry the husband's gene for a bad heart or the wife's for poor circulation, but does carry the husband's good coordination and the wife's musical ability. Each couple gets its own child, yet characteristics that parents do not want their children to have are gradually eliminated from the gene pool. Since the decision is made by each set of parents for their own children, not by someone for everyone, it should maintain a high degree of genetic diversity; different parents will want different things. And since parents, unlike state planners, can usually be trusted to care a great deal about the welfare of their children, the technology should mostly be used to benefit the next generation, not to exploit it.

Heinlein's technology does not exist but its result, in a crude form, does. The current, more primitive, method is for a woman to conceive, obtain fetal cells by extracting amniotic fluid ("amniocentesis"), have the cells checked to see if they carry any serious genetic defect – in particular, the extra copy of chromosome 21 that produces Down syndrome – and abort the fetus if they do.[2]

A version that eliminates the emotional (some would say moral) costs of abortion is now coming into use. Obtain eggs from the intended mother, sperm from the intended father. Fertilize in vitro – outside the mother's body. Let the fertilized eggs grow to the eight-cell level. Extract one cell – which at that point can be done without damage to the rest. Analyze its genes. Select from the fertilized eggs one that does not carry whatever serious genetic defect they are trying to avoid. Implant that egg back in the mother.

At present there are two major limitations to this process. The first is that in vitro fertilization (IVF) is still a difficult and expensive process. The second is that genetic testing is a new technology, so only a small number of genetic characteristics can actually be identified in the cell. Some genetic diseases, yes; musical ability or intelligence, no. The use of IVF is, however, increasing; for the cohort of Danish women born in 1978, 6% of their babies were produced with the help of artificial reproductive technologies such as IVF. Given current rates of progress, the second limitation is likely to be rapidly reduced over the next decade or two. We will then be in a world where at least some people are able to deliberately produce "the best and the brightest" of the children those people could have had. That ability will be greatly increased when and if we get the ability to determine the genetic structure of egg and sperm before they are combined, greatly increasing the number of alternatives that parent can choose among.[3]

So far I have been considering a reproductive technology that already exists, although at a fairly primitive level: selecting among the fertilized eggs produced by a single couple. We come next to some newer technologies. The one that has gotten most of the attention is *cloning*, producing an individual who is genetically identical to another.[4] One form of cloning is natural and fairly common; identical twins are genetically identical to each other. The same effect has been produced artificially in animal breeding: get a single fertilized egg, from it produce multiple fertilized eggs, and implant them to produce multiple genetically identical offspring. In agriculture, cloning to reproduce particularly desirable varieties of grapevines or apple trees – grafting – is a technology that has been practiced for more than 2,000 years.

The form of cloning that has recently become controversial starts instead with a cell from an adult animal and uses it to produce a baby that is the identical twin of that adult. Much of the initial hostility to the technology seemed to be rooted in the bizarre belief that cloning replicates an adult – that, after I am cloned, one of me can finish writing this chapter while the other puts my children to bed. That is not how cloning works – although we will discuss something very similar in a later chapter, where the copying will be into silicon instead of carbon.

Another technology, a little further into the future, is genetic engineering. If we knew enough about how genes work and how to manipulate them, it might be possible to take genetic material from sperms, eggs, or adult cells contributed by two or more individuals and combine it, producing a single individual with a tailor-made selection of genes.

Sexual reproduction already combines genes from our parents in us. Genetic engineering would let us choose which genes came from which, instead of accepting a random selection. It would also let us combine genes from more than two individuals without taking multiple generations to do it, as well as splicing in useful genes from other species. Primitive versions of the technology have already been used successfully to insert genes from one species of plant or animal into another.

Another possibility is to create artificial genes, perhaps an entire additional chromosome.[5] Such genes would be designed to do things within our cells that we wanted done – prevent aging, say, or fight AIDS – but that no existing gene did. Constructing them would be a project at the intersection of biotechnology and nanotechnology.

Current and near-future technologies to control what sort of children we have depend on IVF, a technology originally developed to make it possible for otherwise infertile women to have children. It also makes possible artificial cloning of eggs, by letting the fertilized egg divide and then separating it into two. It makes possible cloning of adult cells, by replacing the nucleus of a fertilized egg with a nucleus from an adult cell. And it may yet make possible genetic engineering and artificial genes. It has also already made it possible for surrogate mothers to bear children produced from other women's fertilized eggs.

Other new technologies may make possible reproduction by a different sort of infertile parents: same-sex couples. At present a pair of women who wish to rear a child can, in at least some states, adopt one. Alternatively, one of the women can bear a child using donated sperm. But they cannot do what most other couples desiring children do: produce a child who is the genetic offspring of both of them. The closest that can be managed with traditional technology is to use sperm donated by a father or brother of one to inseminate the other, producing a child who is, genetically speaking, half one of them and a quarter the other.

That situation is changing. Techniques have been developed for producing artificial sperm containing genetic material from an adult cell. They may make it possible in the fairly near future for two women to produce a child who is, in the full sense, theirs. At some point an analogous technology might make possible artificial eggs, permitting two men, with the assistance of a borrowed womb, to produce a child who is, in the same sense, theirs.[6]

HOW TO RETROFIT A CHROMOSOME

If your goal is to genetically manipulate a human being, you need to insert a gene into every relevant cell, or start with a single-celled embryo.

Matt Ridley, *Genome*, p. 247

The genetic engineering we have been discussing is applied to a single cell, a fertilized ovum. Doing that is an elegantly simple way of changing things, since the altered characteristics of a single cell will be passed on to every cell of the body built from that cell and to any new bodies descended from that one. For the same reason some find the application of such technologies to humans frightening, a way of permanently changing at least part of the human race.

The technical term for this is *germ-line genetic engineering*. Surprisingly enough, it is not the only way of altering living things by changing their genes. The alternative is to alter genes in the cells of an already existing organism. This raises an obvious problem. Altering the genes in a single cell is a difficult and chancy procedure. A single human body contains about 100 trillion cells.[7] How can one possibly alter enough of them to make a difference?

This problem was solved a very long time ago, and not by humans. Viruses reproduce by hijacking the mechanism of a cell, modifying it, and using it to produce more viruses. Since viruses hijack us, it seems only fair for us to hijack them.

A retrovirus contains a message written in RNA which reads, in essence: 'Make a copy of me and stitch it into your chromosome.' All a gene therapist need do is take a retrovirus, cut out a few of its genes . . . , put in a human gene, and infect the patient with it. The virus goes to work inserting the gene into the cells of the body and, lo, you have a genetically modified person.

Ridley, *Genome*, p. 247

This form of genetic engineering has already been used to combat severe combined immune deficiency – SCID – the genetic disease that makes children's bodies unable to defend themselves against infection.[8] It used to be that such children could be kept alive only in a sterile environment and died young. Later a method was discovered of treating the disease by monthly injections of the protein that the defective genes were failing to make. Currently, that approach is combined with genetic therapy that repairs some of the defective genes and so reduces the victim's dependency on the injected protein. Similar cures are being developed for a variety of other diseases.

SCID is a rare disease. Cancer, on the other hand, is one of the chief causes of death in modern societies, second only to heart disease and soon expected to overtake it. And cancer is a genetic disease.

My development from a fertilized ovum to an adult was made possible by cell division, starting with a single cell. So is the process of healing wounds by building new tissue to replace the old. Once I reach my full size, most of those cells must stop dividing, since otherwise I will keep growing. Cells are provided with mechanisms to make them divide – oncogenes – which get turned off when division is no longer necessary. They are provided with additional mechanisms to stop them dividing, in case the oncogene gets somehow stuck on "divide." And, just to play safe, they have a third mechanism to make the cell self-destruct if the first two fail.

Mutation changes genes. If enough changes happen in the same cell to make all three mechanisms fail, you get cancer; that, at least, is the current theory. For three different things to break in the same cell is, of course, very unlikely. But with 100 trillion cells, even very unlikely things can happen. Which suggests a possible tactic for curing cancer. Genetically modify the cancer cells in a way that fixes at least one of the three things that is wrong with them. If you fix one of the first two, the cancer cells stop dividing. If you fix the third, they die.

The possibility of retrofitting cells with new genes also suggests a tempting, and disturbing, possibility for high-tech law enforcement. Suppose we conclude that some of the causes of criminal behavior are genetic; perhaps that there is a gene, more likely a group of genes, for psychopathy. Instead of sentencing a criminal to be imprisoned we sentence him to have his genes revised – a brand-new, high-tech version of the old dream of reforming criminals instead of deterring them.

When we are finished altering some of the genes in every cell in his body – I am assuming a more advanced version of the technology than we have at present – is he still the same person? Have we reformed or replaced him?

Maybe Huxley Got It Right

So far I have been discussing ways of changing what people are like by changing their genes. Another possibility is by changing their environment – their very early environment. There is now good evidence that subtle features of the prenatal environment, the mother's womb, have significant and interesting effects on how the occupant turns out.

Look at one of your hands and compare the length of the first and third ("ring") fingers. On average, the greater the relative length of the third finger, the higher the level of testosterone (and the lower the level of estrogen) in the womb you occupied. Finger length does not matter very much, but finger length is not all that is affected; the relative length of those two fingers also correlates with children's relative scores on numeracy and literacy tests.[9] It has long been observed that, on average, males seem to do relatively better at mathematical learning, females on verbal. Apparently the difference is at least in part due to their different uterine environments. Not only does a womb with a male fetus have, on average, a higher level of testosterone than a womb with a female fetus, but among males or among females the level of testosterone correlates with relative mathematical and verbal abilities.

In *Brave New World*, Aldous Huxley described a future dystopia in which the state produced different sorts of people for different purposes, each designed to be good at and contented with a particular role in life. They did it by controlling not genes but uterine chemistry, using artificial wombs for the purpose. He may have been on to something.

WHY BOTHER?

New technologies make it possible to do new things; there remains the question of whether they are worth doing. In the case of reproductive technology, the initial driving force, still important, was the desire of people to have their own children. From that we get IVF and the use of surrogate mothers to permit a mother unable to bring her fetus to term to get someone else to do it for her. The desire to have your own children also provides a possible incentive for cloning – to permit a couple unable to produce a child of both (because one is infertile) to produce instead a child who is an identical twin of one – and for technologies to allow same-sex couples to reproduce.

A second and increasingly important motive is the desire to have better children. In the early stages of the technology this means avoiding the catastrophe of serious genetic defects. As the technology gets better, it opens the possibility of eliminating less serious defects – the risk of a bad heart, say, which seems to be in part genetic, or alcoholism, which may well be – and selecting in favor of desirable characteristics. Parents want their children to be happy, healthy, smart, strong, beautiful. These technologies provide ways of improving the odds.

One can imagine the technologies used for other purposes. A dictatorial government might try to engineer the entire population, to breed some inconvenient characteristic, say aggressiveness or resistance to authority, out of it.[10] A less ambitious government might use cloning to produce multiple copies of the perfect soldier, or secret policeman, or scientific researcher, or dictator – although multiple identical dictators might be asking for trouble.

Such scenarios are more plausible as movie plots than as policies. It takes about twenty years to produce an adult human; few real-world governments can afford to plan that far ahead. And while a clone will be genetically identical to the donor, its environment will not be identical, so while cloning produces a more predictable result than sexual reproduction, it is far from perfectly predictable.[11] Getting your soldiers, secret police, scientists, or dictators the old-fashioned way has the advantage of letting you select them from a large population of people already adult and observable.

One further argument against the idea is that if it is an attractive strategy for a dictatorial state, it ought already to have happened. Selective breeding of animals is a very old technology. Yet I know of no past society that made any serious large-scale attempt at selective breeding of humans in order to produce in the ruled traits desired by the rulers.[12] Insofar as we have observed selective breeding of humans it has been at the individual or family level, people choosing mates for themselves or their children in part on the basis of what sort of children they think those mates will help produce.

A more serious danger is the exploitation of cloned children on a smaller scale. In a version sometimes offered as an argument against cloning humans, an adult produces a clone of himself in order to disassemble it for body parts to be used for future transplants. One obvious problem with that scenario is that even if the cloning were legal, the disassembly would not be – in the United States at present or in any reasonably similar society. But one can imagine a future society in which it was. On the other hand, the process again involves a substantial time lag, and becomes increasingly less useful as improved medical technology reduces the problems of transplant rejection.

There has been at least one real-world case distantly analogous to this, however. Looking at it suggests that producing a human being at least partly to provide tissue for transplant may not be such an ugly idea after all. In 1988, Anissa Ayala, then a high school sophomore, was diagnosed with a slow progressing but ultimately fatal form of leukemia. Her only hope was a treatment that would kill off all her existing blood stem cells and replace them by a transplant from a compatible donor. The odds that a random donor would be compatible were about 1 in 20,000.

Her parents spent two years in an unsuccessful search for a compatible donor, then decided to try to produce one. The odds were not good. A second child would have only a 25% chance of compatibility. Even with a compatible donor the procedure had a survival probability of only 70%. The mother was already forty-two, the father had been vasectomized. The alternative was worse; Anissa's parents took the gamble. The vasectomy was successfully reversed. Their second daughter Marissa was born – and compatible. Fourteen months later she donated the bone marrow that – as she put it five years later in a television interview – saved her sister's life.

Marissa was produced by conventional methods; the controversial element, loudly condemned by a variety of bioethicists, was producing a child in the hope that she could donate the bone marrow required to save another. But cloning, had it been practical, would have raised the odds of a match from 25% to 100%.

For another potentially controversial use of cloning, consider parents whose small child has just been killed in an auto accident. Parents have a very large emotional investment in their children, not children in the abstract but this particular small person whom they love. Cloning could let them, in a real although incomplete sense, get her back – in the form of a second child very nearly identical to the first.[13]

Reasons Not To Do It

I disagree with your principles, and will require you to die for mine.

Voltaire's view, bioethically revised

Reproductive technologies – most recently cloning, earlier contraception, IVF, and artificial insemination – have aroused widespread opposition. One reason, the idea that such a technology might be particularly useful to a dictatorial state, I have already dismissed as implausible. There are at least three others.

The first is the "yecch" factor. New technologies involving things as intimate as reproduction feel weird, unnatural, and for many people, frightening and ugly. That was true for contraception, it was true for IVF and artificial insemination, it is strikingly true for cloning, and it will no doubt be true for genetic engineering when and if we can do it. That reaction may slow the introduction of new reproductive technologies but is unlikely to prevent it, so long as those technologies make it possible for people to do things they very much want to do.

A second reason is that new technologies usually do not work very well at first. Judging by experience so far with cloning large mammals, if someone tries tomorrow to clone a human it will take many unsuccessful tries to produce one live infant and that infant may suffer from a variety of problems. That is a strong argument against cloning a human being today. But it is an argument that will get weaker and weaker as further experiments in cloning other large mammals produce more and more information about how to do it right.

The final reason is the most interesting of all. It is the possibility that individual reproductive decisions might have unintended consequences – perhaps seriously negative ones.

Where Have All the Women Gone?

Consider a simple example: gender selection. Parents often have a preference as to whether they want a boy or a girl. The simplest technology to give them what they want – selective infanticide – has been in use for thousands of years. A less costly alternative – selective abortion – is already being used extensively in some parts of the world.[14] And we now have ways to substantially alter the odds of producing male or female offspring by less drastic methods.[15] As such techniques become more reliable and more widely available, we will move toward a world where parents have almost complete control over the gender of the offspring they produce. What will be the consequences?

For the most extreme answer, consider the situation under China's one-child policy, imposed on a society where families strongly desire at least one son. The result is that a substantial majority of the children born are male; some estimates suggest about 120 boys for 100 girls. A similar but weaker effect has occurred in India even without a restriction on number of children; recent figures suggest about 107 boys for 100 girls. With better technologies for gender selection the ratios would be higher. The consequence is likely to be societies where many men have difficulty finding a wife.

The problem may be self-correcting – with a time lag. In a society with a high male-to-female ratio women are in a strong bargaining position, able to take their pick of mates and demand favorable terms in marriage.[16] As that becomes clear, it will increase the payoff to producing daughters. There is not a lot of point to preserving the family name by having a son if he cannot find a woman willing to produce grandchildren for you. A high ratio of men to women might also result in a shift in mating patterns in the direction of polyandry: two or more husbands sharing the same wife. Even without changes in marriage laws there is still the possibility of serial polyandry. A woman marries one man, produces a child for him, divorces him, and marries a second husband.[17]

Class Genes

What about technologies allowing parents to choose among the children they might have, or even to add useful genes, perhaps artificial, that neither parent carries? Lee Silver, a mouse geneticist and the author of a fascinating book on reproductive technology,[18] worries that the long-term result might be a society divided into two classes: generich, the genetically superior descendants of people who could afford to use new technologies to produce superior offspring, and genepoor.

There are two reasons this is not likely to happen. The first is that human generations are long and technological change is fast. We might have a decade or two in which higher-income people have substantially better opportunities to select their children. After that the new technology, like many old technologies, will probably become inexpensive enough to be available to almost anyone who really wants it. It was not that long ago, after all, that television was a new technology restricted to well-off people. Currently, about 97% of American families below the poverty line own at least one color television.

The second reason is that human mating is not strictly intraclass. Rich men sometimes marry poor women and vice versa. Even without marriage, if rich men are believed to carry superior genes – as, after a generation or two of Lee Silver's hypothetical future, they would be – that is one more reason for less rich women to conceive by them, a pattern that, however offensive to egalitarian sensibilities, is historically common. Put in economic terms, sperm is a free good, hence provides a low-cost way of obtaining high-quality genes for one's offspring. I doubt we will get that far, but if we do we can rely on the traditional human mating pattern – monogamy tempered by adultery – to blur any sharp genetic lines between social or economic classes.

SLOWING THE BIOLOGICAL CLOCK

Everything not forbidden is compulsory.
        Sign over the entrance to the ant colony in *The Once and Future King*

In our society people are not supposed to become sexually active until they become adults. In practice, it doesn't work that way, leading to problems with which anyone who reads newspapers, watches television, or worries about his or her own children is familiar. The essential problem is that we are physically ready to reproduce before we are emotionally or economically ready. That has become increasingly true as the age of physical maturity has fallen – by about two years over the past century, probably as a result of improved nutrition. With the continuing progress of medical science, we may soon be able to reverse that change.

Suppose a drug company announces a new medication – one that will safely delay puberty for a year, or two years, or three years. I predict that there will be a considerable demand for the product. Are parents who artificially delay the physical development of their daughters guilty of child abuse? May schools pressure parents to give the medication to boys about to reach puberty, as many now do for other forms of medication designed to make children behave more as schoolteachers wish them to? If schools do require it, are parents who refuse to artificially delay the development of their sons guilty of child abuse – or at least subject to the same pressures as parents who today refuse to put their sons on Ritalin?

While we are at it, what about the application of a similar technology to other species? Cats are lovely creatures, but kittens are much more fun. If only they stayed kittens a little longer. . . .

FOURTEEN

The More You Know...

The previous chapter discussed changes in what we can do to ourselves and our descendants, and possible consequences. This chapter discusses changes in what we know – and possible consequences. More knowledge is, on the whole, a good thing – but there may be exceptions.

WISE FATHERS

Human mating patterns have varied a good deal across time and space, but long-term monogamy is far and away the most common. This pattern – male and female forming a mated pair and remaining together for an extended period of time – is uncommon in other mammalian species. It is, oddly enough, very common among birds, possibly because their offspring, like ours, require extended parental care.[1] Swans and geese, for example, have long been known to mate for life.

Modern research has shown that the behavior of most varieties of mated birds is even closer to that of humans than we once supposed. As with humans, the norm is monogamy tempered by adultery. While a mated pair will raise successive families of chicks together, a significant fraction of those chicks – genetic testing suggests figures from 10 to 40% – are not the offspring of the male member of the pair. Similar experiments are harder to arrange with humans, but such work as has been done suggests that some significant percentage – estimates range from about 1 in 100 to 1 in 3 – of the children of married women cohabiting with their husbands are fathered by someone else.[2]

From an evolutionary standpoint, the logic of the situation is clear. Males play two different roles in human (and avian) reproduction. They contribute genes to help produce children and resources to help rear them. The latter contribution is costly; the former is not. A male who can successfully impregnate another male's mate gets reproductive success – more copies of his genes in the next generation – at negligible cost. So it is not surprising that males, whether men or ganders, invest substantial effort both in attempting to impregnate females they are not mated to and in attempting to keep the females they are mated to from being impregnated by other males.

A faithful female gets both genes and support from her mate, trading her contribution to producing offspring for his. But an unfaithful female can do even better. She pairs up with the best provider who will have her and then, given the opportunity, becomes pregnant by the highest quality male available, where "quality" is defined by whatever observable characteristics signal heritable characteristics that can be expected to result in reproductive success for her offspring – tail length in swallows, income and status in humans. As Henry Kissinger is supposed to have said, "Power is the ultimate aphrodisiac."[3]

This strategy works, for geese and women, because of a curious feature of our biology: the inability of males to reliably identify their offspring. If that were not the case, if males were equipped with some built-in system of biometric identification based on scent, appearance, or the like, they could and would refuse to provide support for the offspring of other males.[4]

Technological Wisdom

This feature of human biology has just vanished. Paternity testing now does what evolution failed to do; it provides men a reliable way of determining which children are theirs. What are the likely consequences? I started thinking about this question in response to a hypothetical by a colleague: Suppose it became customary to check the paternity of every child at birth. What would happen?

The obvious consequence is that some men would discover that their wives had been unfaithful and some marriages would break up as a result.

The slightly less obvious consequence is that married women conducting affairs would take more care with contraception. The still less obvious consequence – except to economists and evolutionary biologists – is that men would take better care of their children.

From the economist's standpoint, the reason is that people value the welfare of their own offspring above the welfare of other people's off-spring. From the biologist's standpoint, the reason is that human beings, like other living creatures, have been designed by evolution to act in ways that maximize their reproductive success, and one way of doing so is to concentrate your limited resources on your own children. Either way, the conclusion is the same. Routine paternity testing would mean that men knew that their children were really theirs and so would be willing to invest more resources in them. They would invest less in children that turned out not to be theirs, but there would be fewer of those than before, due to the desire of wives to have children that their husbands will help support. And those children that did have a father who was not their mother's husband could prove it, and so have at least a hope of support from him.

Readers who question the assumption that parents are biased in favor of their own children might want to look at the literary evidence. Across a very wide variety of cultures, it is taken for granted that stepparents cannot be trusted to care for their stepchildren.[5] Across a variety of cultures there is evidence from statistics on child abuse and child murder that the literature is right – judging by one study, stepparents are about forty times as likely to kill children as real parents.[6] And, going beyond our species, there is evidence that male birds adjust the amount of parental care they give chicks to take account of the probability that the chicks are not theirs.[7]

So far I have been considering a straightforward consequence of the combination of a new technology and a new social practice. The technology has already happened; the practice, so far, has not changed in response.

The law, however, has. Under Lord Mansfield's rule, a common-law doctrine going back to the eighteenth century, a married man cohabiting with his spouse was legally forbidden from challenging the legitimacy of her offspring. This appears in modern statutes as the rule that the mother of a child is the woman from whose body the child is born and, if that woman was married and cohabiting with her husband when the child was conceived, he is conclusively presumed to be the father.

That was a reasonable legal rule as long as there was no practical way of demonstrating paternity. Most of the time it gave the right answers. When it did not, there was usually no good way of doing better and no point in using up time, effort, and marital goodwill trying.

It is no longer a reasonable legal rule and, increasingly, it is no longer the rule embodied in modern statutes. In California, for example, a state whose family law we shall be returning to at the end of this chapter, the current statute provides that the presumption may be rebutted by scientific evidence that the husband is not the father.

If All Fathers Are Wise...

So much for the present and the immediate future. A more interesting question is the long-term effect of the technology. One function of the marriage institutions of most human societies we know of, past and present, is to give males a reasonable confidence of paternity by providing that under most circumstances no more than one male has sexual access to each female. With modern paternity testing, that is no longer necessary.

This raises some interesting possibilities. We could, at one extreme, have a society of casual promiscuity – Samoa, at least as imagined by Margaret Mead. When a child was born, the biological father, as demonstrated by paternity testing, would have the relevant parental rights and responsibilities. There are problems with that system. It is easier for two parents to raise a child jointly if they are living together, and the fact that two people enjoy sex together is very weak evidence that they will enjoy living together. An alternative that is both more attractive and more interesting is some form of group marriage – three or more people living together and rearing children together. Such arrangements have been attempted in the past and no doubt some currently exist. The only form that has ever been common – polygyny, one husband with several wives – is the one that does not require paternity testing to determine paternity. The question is whether other forms will now become more common.

That in turn comes down to a simple question to which I do not know the answer: Is male sexual jealousy hardwired?[8] Do men object to other men sleeping with their mates because evolution has built into them a strong desire for sexual exclusivity or because they have chosen, or been taught, that strategy as a way of achieving the (evolutionarily determined) objective of not spending their resources rearing another man's children? Weak evidence for the latter explanation is provided by an anthropologist's observation that men spent less time monitoring their wives when the wives were pregnant, and hence could not conceive.[9]

One person I have discussed the question with reported that he and people he knew did not experience sexual jealousy; readers interested in joining that discussion should be able to find him and some of his friends on the Usenet newsgroup alt.polyamory, which means what it sounds like. But what he was observing may have been only the tail of the distribution – the small fraction of men who, because they have abnormally low levels of sexual jealousy, are willing to experiment with unconventional mating patterns.

Suppose that male sexual jealousy is hardwired. There still remains an interesting possibility: the professional mother. Consider a woman who likes children, is good at bearing and rearing them, and herself has characteristics that men would like in the mother of their child – healthy, intelligent, good looking. Match her up with men who would like to have children but have not been successful in finding a willing mate with whom they would like to have them. The man fathers the child, whether by artificial insemination or more traditional means. The woman bears and rears the child. The man provides financial support and perhaps a paternal role.

One problem with this is that the ideal mother for your children is beautiful, brilliant, and healthy – and a woman like that may be able to find a more attractive career than being a surrogate mother. Modern reproductive technology has a solution. There is already a thriving market in human eggs, with the price dependent on the characteristics of the woman who donated them; good genes are for sale. The professional mother could be only a host mother, bearing the better baby constructed by combining your sperm with the best egg money can buy.

What if we reverse the roles? Suppose it is the mother who wishes to build her own baby, combining her egg with the best genes she can find? Being provided with her own womb, she doesn't have to rent one from someone else, assuming she is willing to accept the costs of bearing the child herself. She has a second advantage as well. Eggs are relatively scarce, since harvesting them from a woman's ovary is an unpleasant and uncomfortable process. Sperm is, for most practical purposes, a free good. Given a well-developed market for sperm, properly labeled with the characteristics of the donor or perhaps his gene map, the intentional single mother should have a wider range of choice, at a lower cost, than the intentional single father.

There are two trends in modern society that might make such a pattern of increasing importance. One is rising real incomes; it is easier for a single parent to raise a child the richer he or she is. The other is the improvement in our knowledge of genetics. Eventually it should be possible for a couple to build better babies mostly from their own genes, as described later in this chapter. But it requires much less progress – genetic knowledge, not genetic engineering – to do it using someone else's.

Will it happen? We will have to wait and see.[10]

THE PARENT PROBLEM

Whether or not new reproductive technologies are going to generate new problems for people in the future, they are already producing problems for the legal system and the social institutions in which it is embedded.

The first, and currently the biggest, is the paternity problem. State welfare agencies and unmarried or no-longer-married mothers would like to find a man who can be made responsible for supporting the mothers' children. If their genetic father can be identified, he is the obvious candidate. But what if he cannot?

The view of some states is that the man who was the mother's mate ought to be responsible whether or not he is the actual father – a reversion to Lord Mansfield's rule, extended to cover unmarried couples. It was workable before modern paternity testing because the state could argue that the man she had been living with, perhaps married to, was likely to be the genetic father of her children even if he denied it. That argument no longer works now that he can prove he isn't.

The obvious argument on the other side is that a man who has been cuckolded by his wife is already a victim of her betrayal; to make him responsible for supporting someone else's child only adds injury to insult. The counterargument is that even if the mother is at fault her child is not – and requires support from someone. That argument becomes more convincing if the man has functioned as father to the child for long enough to establish an emotional bond between the two.

One possibility a little farther down the road is a genetic database that could be used to identify the genetic father and make him liable, bringing us back to the idea of paternity testing at birth. A less ambitious alternative is to require the mother to identify the father or possible fathers and have the state compel him to permit testing. But if the mother is unwilling or unable to identify the father, we are back with the problem of who, other than the state, can be made responsible.

Paternity testing could also create problems for men who, under current law, are not responsible for supporting children who, genetically speaking, really are theirs. In many states, if a woman conceives by artificial insemination using sperm from a sperm bank, she has no claims for support from the donor. Prior to paternity testing, that legal rule could be enforced by simply not keeping the relevant records. Today the records establishing paternity are stamped into every cell of father and child. If law and custom change, as they have changed in the past in the direction of making it easier for adopted children to locate birth parents, including ones who do not want to be located, some men may be in for a surprise.

Two, Four, Many

Paternity testing can establish the fact of paternity. But it does not tell us what paternity, or maternity, or parenthood, means. We can do a better job than in the past of determining who has what relation to a child. But we can also produce a more complicated set of relations, making it harder to fit the new reality into the old law.

With current technology and practice, the term "mother" has at least three different meanings. One is intentional mother: the woman who intended to play the social role of mother when the arrangements for producing the child were made. One is womb mother: the mother in whose womb the fetus grew. A third is egg mother: the mother who provided the egg. Once we start cloning humans a fourth category will be mitochondrial mother: the woman who provides the egg whose nucleus is replaced by the nucleus of a cell from the clone donor, retaining the woman's extranuclear DNA.

Fathers still come in only two varieties. The intentional father is the man who intended to play the social role of father; the biological father is the man who provided the sperm. The one change associated with the newer technology is that it is more common than it used to be for the intentional father to know he is not the biological father.[11] With three or four varieties of mother and two of father, the definition of "parents" becomes seriously ambiguous.

That problem was mentioned back in Chapter 2, where I described the (real, California) case of the child with five parents. All five were different people – and the intentional parents, John and Luanne, separated a month before the baby was born. The court decided that the intentional parents were the ones that counted. Although neither had any biological connection to the child, Luanne ended up with the baby, John liable for supporting it.

The same legal approach could be used to resolve the issues of parenthood raised by cloning. The human clone gets all of his or her nuclear DNA from one donor. Genetically speaking, one might describe that donor as both parents. If we actually did the usual genetic tests, they would show the clone as a child of the donor's parents. Further complications arise from extranuclear DNA, which comes from the woman who donated the egg used in the procedure and might or might not be the donor of the nuclear DNA. And, since cells can be obtained from a donor without his consent, we have the possibility that a woman could bear the clone of a rich and prominent man and then sue him for child support on a scale appropriate to his income. The nearest real-world case I know of under current technology is one in which a woman apparently impregnated herself with sperm fraudulently obtained and succeeded in establishing a claim for child support against the father.[12]

The definition established by the California court – parenthood determined by intention – provides a single rule to cover nearly all circumstances, whatever the reproductive technology; in order for the child to come into existence, at least one person had to intend it, or at least choose to take actions that could lead to it, and that person counts as a parent. It still leaves some problems.

Conventional reproduction involves one male and one female. Once the biology can be subcontracted, intentional reproduction could involve one male and one female, two males, two females, a partnership of four of each, or a corporation – say Microsoft, looking to breed a successor for Bill Gates. Only the conventional pattern fits legal rules designed for that pattern. Once we accept intentional parenthood, the law must either restrict who can be an intentional parent – require, for example, that before any form of assisted reproduction can legally take place, one man and one woman (in the most conservative version) must identify themselves as intentional parents – or specify parental rights and obligations broadly enough so that any of the permitted arrangements can fit them.

A similar problem has existed, and been dealt with by the law, for a long time: the firm. For many purposes, we treat firms as if they were persons; we make contracts with them, sell them things, buy things from them, sue them for damages. To do so, we have had to map the rights and responsibilities of a single individual onto organizations of a wide variety of sorts. We have to decide what it means for a firm to agree to something, to be responsible for doing something, to be liable for something, what actual acts by living and breathing human beings count as acts by the fictional person in whose name they are acting. Defining parenthood, in the world being created by modern reproductive technology, presents a closely analogous problem.

PEOPLE CONSIDERED AS INTELLECTUAL PROPERTY

When Monsanto, the leading agricultural biotech company, creates a transgenic soybean, it gets to patent it; if other people make copies without permission by using this year's crop for next year's seed without paying Monsanto for the right to do so, they are infringing Monsanto's patent. Some of the problems raised by that situation will be discussed in the next chapter.

What if Monsanto applies its new technologies not to soybeans but to people, producing an improved version with some novel genes, transplanted from another species or created in the lab? On the face of it, the same law would appear to apply. You now have human beings who partly belong to someone else; one or more of the genes in every cell are Monsanto's intellectual property.

Living creatures, including humans, are continually creating new cells to replace old ones, so it looks as though the patented baby infringes the patent with every breath he draws. The obvious solution is for the contract by which the baby is produced to include a lifetime license to use the patent within that child's body, just as the contract by which a farmer buys genetically engineered soybeans includes the right to have the resulting plants reproduce their patented genes in the process of growing.

What about making copies that end up outside the child's body? If I am the child, do I require Monsanto's permission to reproduce? To engage in any activity that might lead to reproduction? Perhaps the original license ought to include some additional terms, with prices set in advance.

Considering the attitude our legal system takes to private ownership of human beings by anyone other than themselves, I doubt that Monsanto could get very far enforcing its intellectual property rights in this novel context, but one never knows. The issue is unlikely to come up. Human beings mature slowly. By the time I become seriously interested in infringing the patent on me it will probably have expired.

Soybeans, on the other hand, do not have individual rights to self-ownership and their generations are only a year long. For soybeans, the issue of intellectual property rights in things that live and reproduce is a real one, currently faced by courts in a variety of countries.

IS IGNORANCE BLISS?

... and *the* thousand natural *shocks*/That flesh is heir to ...

Hamlet

Of the ills that human flesh is heir to, some are entirely due to having the wrong genes – sickle cell anemia, for example. Many others, such as heart disease and Alzheimer's,[13] appear to have a substantial genetic component.[14] As knowledge and technology improve, we will increasingly be able to identify individuals who do or do not have the genes that make them more likely to die young of a heart attack, become alcoholics, or suffer other undesirable consequences. It is already possible to do a complete gene map of an individual for less than $1,000,000 and the cost is predicted to get below $1,000 in the not very distant future. Combine that with adequate knowledge linking genes to outcomes and it becomes possible to know a great deal about your future prospects.

Someone who knows he is genetically predisposed to heart disease has good reasons to take greater precautions against it – exercise, diet, testing, and the like. That my grandfather died of a heart attack and my father has twice had bypass surgery are good reasons for me to take cholesterol-lowering medication and try to maintain regular exercise. But I would have better grounds for such decisions if I knew whether or not I carried the genes that caused those problems for my father and grandfather; while we do not yet have a complete account of the genetics of heart disease, we do know that carrying certain variants of certain genes substantially increases your chances of dying of a heart attack. And someone who knew he was, for genetic reasons, particularly vulnerable to alcoholism might choose to avoid the problem by never taking the first drink.

What if I have a genetic problem for which there is no solution, such as a gene that results in abnormally rapid aging? Knowing I have it at least lets me do a better job of planning my life – have children early or not at all, for example. But knowledge is not inevitably desirable. If I carry a death sentence in my genes, I might prefer not to know about it. Sometimes ignorance is bliss, at least for a while.

So far I have been considering the effect of my knowledge of my genes. Rather different problems might arise from what other people know about them. Consider an insurance company offering insurance against a disease that is entirely genetic in a future where reliable genetic testing is readily available. Once testing is available, the risk of the disease becomes uninsurable. Only people who know they have the relevant genes will buy the insurance, and the sellers, knowing that, will price it accordingly.

What about the more realistic situation where a problem is in part genetic? The expected cost of insuring me against that problem then depends on what genes I have. If insurance companies are permitted to insist on testing clients before selling them insurance, both those with and without bad genes will be able to buy insurance but at different prices. The part of the risk due to having bad genes becomes uninsurable, leaving insurance only for the residual risk, the uncertainty of the disease for someone with a known genetic propensity. In the more realistic case where what you are insuring against is not a particular risk but the combined effect of lots of risks – the case of life or health insurance – the result is the same. Your life expectancy depends in part on your genetic makeup and in part on other things. Uncertainty due to the former becomes uninsurable; uncertainty due to the latter does not.

The solution some have recommended is to make it illegal for insurance companies to require testing. Individuals still can and will get themselves tested. If I discover that I am, genetically speaking, extraordinarily lucky, I also know that both life insurance and health insurance, priced on the assumption that I am average, are bad gambles. If, on the other hand, I know that I am likely to drop dead at age forty, then lots of life insurance – provided I expect to have survivors I care about – is obviously a good deal.

This effect is known in the insurance literature as *adverse selection*; it occurs when one party to a transaction has information about the quality of what is being sold that the other party does not have and cannot get. A standard example is the used car market. The ignorant buyers pay the same price for good cars (cream puffs) and bad cars (lemons), making the sale of your car a good deal if you have a lemon and a poor deal if you have a cream puff. Lemons sell and cream puffs, for the most part, do not. Buyers, anticipating that, make their offer on the assumption that if the offer is accepted the car is probably a lemon – and at lemon prices, few cream puffs are offered for sale.

The logic is the same here. Imagine that insurance companies start out by charging a rate that just covers their costs for an average customer. Insurance is a much better deal for customers with genes that make them likely to collect than for customers with genes that make them unlikely to collect, so the purchasers of insurance include a more than average number of bad risks. Insurance companies discover that and raise their rates, driving out still more of the good risks. In the limiting case, where all good risks are driven out, the result is even worse than it would be with testing by the insurance companies. Nobody can insure against genetic risk, because the decision to buy insurance tells the seller that the buyer knows he has bad genes. Those who have bad genes can still insure against risk from other causes; those who have good genes cannot.

One solution would be to somehow make it possible to prove that you have never been tested. Now people can get insured first, and then arrange to be tested and modify their life plans accordingly. Unfortunately, such a system provides a large incentive to cheat, to get tested on the black market or in a foreign country so as not to leave any record and then decide what insurance to buy after seeing the results.

An alternative solution would be for parents to buy insurance for their children before the children are conceived. The price might still depend on the parents' genes, but it cannot depend on the children's, since that is information that nobody has. Not, at least, until we have worked our way through the developments described in the previous chapter, at which point there should no longer be any bad genes left to worry about.

Insurance companies are not, of course, the only people who might be interested in your genes. There is now some evidence that a tendency toward sexual fidelity – or infidelity – is in part genetic. Requesting genetic testing of your intended just before the marriage seems a bit crass but perhaps, in a future where the relevant technologies are well developed and fully exploited, the questions will be asked – of the online matchmaker – prior to the first date.

AMBIGUOUS GENDER

We are used to taking it for granted that each of us is either male or female. For a long time that was quite a good approximation.[15] But not for much longer. One reason is the knowledge provided by modern biology. Almost all men have an X and a Y chromosome and a male body; almost all women have two X chromosomes and a female body. But there are exceptions. Some humans are XY but have female bodies: genetically male but morphologically female. Some are the reverse – XX with male bodies. And some humans are genetically XYY, with male bodies and a mild tendency toward aggressive personalities, or XXY, or. . . .

So far we are dealing with genetics and morphology, both fairly unambiguous even if the combinations are wilder than we thought. The situation gets more confused if you add in psychology. Some people who are genetically and morphologically male claim to be psychologically female, to think of themselves as women. Others have the reverse pattern. There is some evidence that this is more than a delusion – that in a way not yet clearly understood, such people have brains designed for the wrong gender. Modern surgical techniques make it possible to at least partly correct the error – for someone who self-identifies as a woman in a man's body to have the body altered to at least a reasonable facsimile of a woman's body, although an infertile one. Similarly the other way around.

All of this raises interesting problems for both individuals and the law. Am I to think of Deirdre, a professional colleague who used to be Donald, as a woman, a man surgically altered to look like a woman, or something neither man nor woman? If I had discussed these issues with Donald back when he/she/it possessed, in his/her/its view, the body of a man but the mind of a woman – as it happens I didn't – how should I have thought of the person I was discussing them with? If Deirdre marries a wealthy man and he later dies intestate, can his heirs successfully challenge her claim to part of his estate on the grounds that she was a he, hence could not contract a legal marriage with a man? That particular case – with a different transsexual – was recently litigated in Kansas. The wife lost.

It's going to be an interesting century.

FIFTEEN

As Gods in the Garden

In the day ye eat thereof, then your eyes shall be opened, and ye shall be as gods...

Genesis 3:5

The previous chapter dealt with a narrow slice of biotechnology – its application to humans. This chapter deals with applications of the same technology to other living things.

DESIGNER CROPS

Agricultural biotechnology is one of the oldest forms of high tech, going back at least 8,000 years. That, by current estimates, is when the breeding program began that eventually produced maize – the cereal Americans call "corn" – possibly from teosinte, a plant most of us would describe as a weed. Similar programs of selective breeding are responsible for creating all of our major food plants.

Not only is the creation of genetically superior strains by random mutation and selective breeding an ancient technology, so is cloning. It has been known for a very long time that fruit trees do not breed true to seed. To prove it for yourself, remove the seeds from a golden delicious apple, plant them, wait ten or twenty years, and see what you get. The odds are overwhelmingly high that it will not be a golden delicious and moderately good that it will not be anything you would want to eat.

The solution is grafting. Once your little apple tree has its roots well grown, replace the top section of trunk with a piece of a branch cut from a golden delicious tree. If you do it right, the new wood grows onto the old;

everything above the graft will be golden delicious, genetically speaking, including the apples. You have just produced a clone, an organism (at least most of an organism) that is genetically identical to another. Like Dolly, the cloned sheep, your cloned tree was created using cells from a mature organism.

To be even fancier, let your tree grow until it has a few little branches and then replace the end of one branch with a piece of wood from a golden delicious, a second with a piece from a Swaar (ugly but delicious), and a third with a bit from a lady apple (tiny, pretty, tasty). You now have that staple of plant catalogs, a three-in-one apple. You have also just employed, in your own backyard, a form of biotechnology that has been known at least since Roman times and is in large part responsible for the quality of fruit, grapes, and wine over the last few thousand years.

New under the Sun

Modern agricultural biotech adds at least two new elements to the ancient technologies of selective breeding and grafting. One gives us the ability to do what we have been doing better. The other gives us the ability to do something almost entirely new.

The traditional way of breeding a better apple is to create a very large number of seeds, plant them all, let them all grow up, and see how they come out. If, by great good luck, one turns out to be a superior variety, it can be propagated thereafter by grafting. With enough expert knowledge the plant breeder can improve the odds a little by picking the right parents, choosing a pair of trees that there is some reason to hope might produce superior progeny, pollinating one with pollen from the other and using the resulting seeds. But it is still very much a gamble.

As our knowledge of genetics and our ability to manipulate genes improve, we may be able to do better than that. If we discover that particular sequences of genes are related to particular desirable traits, we can mix and match to produce trees – or grapevines, or tomato plants – with the traits we want. We will be doing the same thing we could have done with the old technologies, but in a lot fewer than 8,000 years.

An odder and more interesting possibility is to add to one species genes from another, producing transgenic plants. A famous – and commercially important – example uses *Bacillus thuringiensis*, or Bt, a bacterium that produces proteins poisonous to some insects but not to humans or other animals. Varieties of plants have been produced by adding to them the genes from the Bt bacterium responsible for manufacturing those proteins. Such plants produce, in effect, their own insecticide. Other transgenic plants are designed to be resistant to widely used herbicides, permitting a farmer to kill weeds without harming the crop.

The same technology can also be used to alter the final crop, producing peanuts or tomatoes with longer shelf life or sunflower oil that combines long shelf life with low levels of saturated fats and trans fats. It is also possible to insert genes into a plant (or animal) that result in its producing something unrelated to its normal crop. Examples include bacteria modified to produce insulin, a cow whose milk contains human milk proteins, and a sheep whose milk contains a clotting factor missing from the blood of hemophiliacs.

Insect-resistant plants permit us to grow crops at lower cost and with much less use of insecticides. Other applications of the technology increase crop yields, reduce costs, improve quality, and provide low cost ways of producing valuable pharmaceuticals, including some that cannot, at least so far, be produced in any other way. Yet the technology has been fiercely attacked; in some parts of the world, most notably Europe, agricultural applications are severely restricted. Why?

A Nest of Serpents?

Abu Hurairah (may Allah be pleased with him) reported that the Prophet (peace and blessings of Allah be upon him) said: "Allah, may He be exalted, says: 'Who does more wrong than the one who tries to create something like My creation? Let him create a grain of wheat or a kernel of corn.'"

Reported by al-Bukhari, *Fath al-Baari, 10/385*

One reason is obvious – hostility to anything new, combined with a romanticized view of nature. Lots of people like the idea of "natural foods," although practically nothing we eat is natural in the sense of not having been substantially altered by human activity. And we have the term "chemical" used pejoratively, despite the fact that everything we eat and everything we are made out of is a combination of chemicals. The same attitude shows up in the description of the products of agricultural biotech as "Frankenfoods." The Muslim tradition quoted above reflects a religious version of this view: Creating living things is God's business, not ours.[1]

This attitude is of considerable importance today; over the next decade or two, it may result in European consumers getting lower quality food at higher prices than they otherwise would. One reason that may happen is that European farmers are subsidized by their governments and protected from foreign competition by trade barriers. The more European consumers can be persuaded that foreign foods are evil and dangerous, the easier it is for European farmers to sell what they grow.

While irrational hostility may be important in the short run, it is likely to be less so in the long. There are large parts of the world where increasing agricultural output means fewer people going hungry, making symbolic issues of natural or unnatural unimportant by comparison. And over time, new things become old things. Contraception was widely viewed as unnatural, wicked, dirty, and sinful 100 years ago. In vitro fertilization met at first with considerable suspicion. Both are now widely accepted. From a point of view that goes beyond the next decade, the interesting question is whether there are any real problems associated with this sort of technology. The answer is almost certainly yes. These are powerful technologies, and powerful things can do damage as well as good. Consider a simple example.

Our common food plants were bred from preexisting wild plants. Many of the latter are still around and to some degree cross-fertile with their domesticated descendants. That means that genetic traits introduced into crop plants may find their way, as pollen blown in the wind, to related wild plants. Herbicide resistance is a useful feature in a crop plant. It is a considerable nuisance in a weed. How serious this sort of problem is depends on whether transgenically improved crop plants are grown near wild relatives, whether the modification is of benefit to weeds, and whether the modification makes the weed more of a problem for humans.

Consider a transgenic tomato designed for better flavor or longer shelf life. Even if there are related wild plants, those characteristics are of no particular use to them, so wild plants with those characteristics would have no advantage over wild plants without them and be no more of a problem for farmers.

The same does not hold for resistance to herbicides. Suppose that weed beets grow near the fields containing sugar beets transgenically modified to make them resistant to herbicides. Weed beets that have had the good luck to acquire the genes for resistance will be more successful in that location than ones that have not – and more of a nuisance.

Can We Compete with Mother Nature?

Stepping back a moment, it is worth looking at the general argument for why such problems cannot exist and seeing why it is sometimes wrong. That argument starts with the observation that existing plants, including weeds, have been "designed" by Darwinian evolution for their own reproductive success. Our current biotechnology is a much more primitive design system than evolution; that is why we produce new crops not by designing the whole plant from scratch but by adding minor modifications to plants provided by nature. One might therefore expect that if a genetic characteristic that we could give a weed were useful, the weed would already have it.

There are two things wrong with that argument. The first is that evolution is slow. Weeds are adapted to their environment, but that environment has only recently included farmers spraying herbicides on them. So they are not adapted, or at least not yet very well adapted, to resist those herbicides. If we deliberately create crop plants resistant to specific herbicides and the resistance spreads to related weeds we provide an evolutionary shortcut, a way of generating resistant weeds substantially faster than nature would.

The second error in the argument is more complicated. Evolution works not by designing new organisms from scratch but by a series of small changes. The more simultaneous changes are required to make a feature work, the less likely it is to appear. Complicated structures – the standard example is the eye – are produced by a long series of changes, each of which provides the organism at least a small gain in reproductive success. Features that cannot be produced in that way are unlikely to be produced at all.

Genetic engineering also works by small changes – introducing one gene from a bacterium into a variety of corn, for instance. But the available range of small changes is different. There may be some changes in an organism that result in greater reproductive success, and hence would have been selected for by evolution, that can be produced by genetic engineering but are unlikely to come about naturally. The introduction of genes that code for a particular protein lethal to particular insect pests, genes borrowed from an entirely unrelated living creature, is an example. This is a subject we will return to in a later chapter, when we consider nanotechnology's still more ambitious attempts to compete with natural design.[2]

The possibility that engineered genes will spread into wild populations and so produce improved weeds is one example of a class of issues raised by genetic technology. Others include the possibility of indirect ecological effects – improved weeds, or crop plants gone wild, that compete with other plants and so alter the whole interrelated system. They also include such unanticipated effects as crop plants designed to be lethal to insect pests turning out to also be lethal to harmless, perhaps beneficial, species of insects. I started with the case of transgenic weeds because I think that is the clearest case of a problem that is likely to happen, although not one likely to have catastrophic consequences. If, after all, weed beets become resistant to the farmers' favorite herbicide, they can always switch to their second favorite, putting them back where they started, with an herbicide to which neither weeds nor crop is especially resistant.

I am more skeptical about the other examples, mostly because I am skeptical about the idea that nature is in a delicate balance likely to produce catastrophe if disturbed. The extinction of old species and the evolution of new is a process that has been going on for a very long time. But while I am skeptical about particular examples, I believe that they illustrate a real potential problem arising from technological change – probably the most serious problem.

The problem arises when actions taken by one person have substantial dispersed effects on many others. The reason it is a problem is that we have no adequate set of institutions to deal with such affects. Markets, property rights, and trade provide a very powerful set of tools for coordinating the activities of a multitude of individual actors. But their functioning requires some way of defining property rights so that most of the effect of my actions is born by me, my property, and some reasonably small and identifiable set of other people.

If there is no way of defining property rights that meets that requirement, we have a problem. The alternative institutions – courts, tort law, government regulation, intergovernmental negotiations, and the like – that we use to deal with that problem work very poorly. The more dispersed the effects, the worse they work. If technological changes result in making actions with such dispersed effects play a much larger role in our lives, if, for example, genetic engineering means that my engineered genes eventually show up in the weeds in your garden 1,000 miles away, we have a problem for which no known institutions provide a reasonably good solution. This is an issue I will return to in later chapters.

Technological Protection for Biotechnology

Back in Chapter 8, we considered the problem of protecting intellectual property in digital form in a world where reproducing it is cheap and easy. The same problem arises with agricultural biotechnology, where the product comes complete with its own copier. One possible solution is to use intellectual property law to prevent farmers from buying the genetically engineered crop once and producing their own seeds thereafter. That should work better for crops than for computer programs since infringement, if it occurs, happens on a large scale in large open spaces.

A different solution is technological protection, some way of selling the object that contains the intellectual property while preventing the purchaser from copying what it contains. In an older version of agricultural biotech, hybrid seed varieties, it happened automatically. A farmer bought hybrid seeds, planted them, harvested the crop. If he then replanted from what he had harvested, the result, thanks to the magic of sexual reproduction, would be a crop with varying characteristics, reflecting the random process determining which genes from each parent ended up in each seed. Such a crop was harder to deal with than the uniform crop from purchased hybrid seeds, so the seed company could sell him more seeds each year.

That does not work with those transgenic species that do not depend on controlled hybridization, species that grow sufficiently true to seed for the farmers' purposes. To deal with that problem, researchers developed and patented a way of accomplishing the same objective artificially.

The obvious approach is to engineer a plant whose seeds will be sterile. There is, however, a small practical problem. In the case of hybrid crops, you fertilize variety A with variety B, produce lots of hybrid seed, and sell it. Producing a transgenic seed is a more difficult and elaborate process, involving a lot of trial and error on the way to getting a single success. If all you end up with is one seed, producing a plant whose seeds are themselves sterile, you are going to have a hard time paying for your laboratory.

The solution is to genetically engineer a seed that produces a plant whose seeds are fertile, but that can be modified, by the application of suitable chemicals, to produce a plant whose seeds are sterile. You grow enough generations of the plant to produce the amount of seed you want. You then treat that seed and sell it. Farmers grow it, get their crop, but cannot replant, because the seeds of the plants grown from the treated seed are sterile. Not only does the seed company get to retain control over its intellectual property, but also it reduces the risk of accidentally producing superweeds, since the pollen blowing from the genetically engineered crop has been genetically engineered to produce sterile seeds.

Opponents of agricultural biotech, in a brilliant propaganda coup, dubbed the patented invention the "terminator gene." They argued that keeping farmers from replanting from their own seed would convert them into serfs under the thumb of the seed companies. It was never made entirely clear whether they thought that all farmers growing hybrid seed were already serfs. Nor was it explained how giving farmers the option of either growing transgenic crops and buying seed each year or growing conventional crops and replanting their own seed made them worse off than if they had only the latter alternative.

More responsible critics pointed out possible undesirable side effects. Consider, for example, an ordinary field of cotton planted next to a field of genetically engineered cotton. Some of the ordinary cotton is pollinated by the engineered cotton, producing sterile seeds. The farmer tries to replant from his ordinary cotton, as he has every right to do – and gets a disappointingly low yield.

For the moment, it looks as though the opponents have won. Whether through bad arguments, good arguments, or clever propaganda – who, after all, wants to defend a terminator gene? – they appear to have persuaded the seed companies to abandon this particular approach to protecting their intellectual property. Will it stay abandoned? We will have to wait and see.

SATAN IN THE WINGS

We have spent some time now on possible unintended bad consequences of genetic engineering. There are also the intended ones – biological warfare using tailor-made diseases or, more modestly, tailor-made weeds. Here again it is worth taking a step back to think about the implications of evolutionary biology. It is a mistake to think of deadly diseases as enemies out to destroy us. A plague bacterium not only has nothing against you, it wishes you well, or would if it were capable of wishing. It is a parasite, you are a host, and the longer you live the better for it.

Lethal diseases are badly designed parasites. That is why a disease that is really deadly is typically new, either a new mutation, an old disease infecting a population that has not yet developed resistance, or a disease that has just jumped from one species to another and not yet adapted to the change. Given time, evolution works not only to make us less vulnerable to a lethal disease but to make the disease less lethal to us.[3]

Unfortunately, the creation of lethal diseases no longer is limited to nature. Several years ago, a team of scientists announced[4] that they had succeeded in recreating the poliovirus – from scratch. The relevant technologies are improving rapidly, along with the general improvement in biotechnology. It may not be that long before someone who wants to start a new smallpox plague or target enemies with anthrax will need only a suitable set of tools for biosynthesis and a complete description of the organism.

When a James Bond villain sets out to create a disease that will kill everyone but himself and his harem, he is not in competition with nature – nature, Darwinian evolution, is not trying to make lethal diseases. That makes it more likely that he will succeed, more likely that there are ways of making diseases more deadly than the ones produced by natural evolution. The question then becomes whether the technological progress that makes it easier to design killer diseases – ultimately, perhaps, in your basement – does or does not win out in the race with other technologies that make it easier to cure or prevent such diseases. This is a special case of an issue we will return to in the context of nanotechnology, which offers to provide potential bad guys with an even wider toolkit for mass murder and may or may not provide the rest of us with adequate tools to defend against them.

Killing Only the Right People

Biological warfare is a simple problem if you are a lunatic out to end the world, but, since the technological changes that are making it easier for them to create diseases are also making it easier for other people to protect against them, lunatics are unlikely to have sufficient competence or sufficient resources to do a good job of it. The more serious danger is from research projects, probably funded by governments, to produce diseases intended to kill only the "right" people. Achieving that objective raises some practical problems.

The easy case is the one that has already happened, several times over. If there is a disease that your population is already resistant to and the target population is not, exposing the target population to it can have drastic effects. The obvious example is the effect on the New World population of exposure to Old World diseases; some historians estimate mortality rates of over 90%.[5] For the most part this particular form of biological warfare was an accident, although there seems to be at least one historical case of the deliberate spreading of smallpox among Canadian Indians reported in the correspondence of British officers.[6] William McNeill argues, in *Plagues and Peoples*, that civilized populations – defined simply as ones with cities – have an automatic biowarfare advantage in their interactions with the uncivilized, since lethal diseases require a dense population[7] in order not to kill themselves off in the process of killing their hosts. Hence dense populations will be carriers of, and resistant to, diseases new and lethal to more dispersed populations.

In the modern world, human mobility is too high and dense populations too common for that particular sort of selective plague to be a
useful tool for those inclined to mass murder. There are, however, two
modern variants that might work better. The obvious one is to develop
a disease, develop a vaccine, vaccinate your own population, and then
release the disease; a prudent aggressor would probably want to disguise
the vaccination program as designed against some natural hazard.

Another alternative, requiring a more advanced technology, would be
to design a disease specific to victims with particular genetic characteristics, ones much more common in the target population than your own.
That has the disadvantage that, given human genetic variability, it is likely
to kill a good many of your own citizens. But one can imagine either a
government willing to accept that cost or one that did not consider it a
cost, on the theory that citizens too closely related to the enemy genetically might be politically unreliable. If that seems implausible, consider
the treatment of Japanese-Americans by the United States during World
War II.

Another possibility would be to target places rather than people. That
might mean designing a disease that would spread easily in the physical
environment of the enemy nation but not in your colder or warmer,
moister or drier environment. It might mean a disease designed to burn
itself out after a certain number of generations, using a more sophisticated
version of the terminator gene approach. Start it in the middle of the
enemy country, shut down your airports and ports for a week to keep out
travelers who might be carrying it, and with luck kill a large fraction of
the enemy population while leaving their land and factories untouched
for your use and your own population unharmed.

Provided the disease doesn't succeed, during its allotted generations,
in evolving itself free of the terminator gene.

SIXTEEN

Mind Drugs

BETTER LIVING THROUGH CHEMISTRY

At least since the discovery of alcohol, humans have used drugs to affect the mind. As we learn more about how the mind works and become more skilled at chemical synthesis, we can expect to get better at it. In many ways this will be a good thing; already drugs provide substantial benefits to some sufferers from mental disorders. But, like most new technologies, improved mind drugs are also likely to raise new legal, social, and personal problems.

For the purposes of this chapter, it will be useful to consider four different classes of mind drugs: pleasure, performance, personality, control. Some drugs will fit into more than one category, reflecting multiple reasons why they are used.

Consider the familiar case of alcohol. Some people drink it because they like how it makes them feel – pleasure. Some drink it because they believe that it improves their performance; one acquaintance, as a college student, routinely had half a can of beer before an exam. Some drink it because it provides a temporary change in their personality that they sometimes desire. And some people feed alcohol to others, sometimes without their knowledge, as a crude way of controlling them.

Pleasure and Happiness

How might an everlasting-happiness drug – a drug which (implausibly!) left someone who tried it once living happily-ever-after – find itself described in the literature?

Substance x induces severe, irreversible structural damage to neurotransmitter subsystem y. Its sequelae include mood-congruent cognitive delusions, treatment-resistant euphoria, and toxic affective psychosis.

www.biopsychiatry.com/

In most contexts we consider happiness and pleasure good things. Jeremy Bentham, one of the most influential philosophers of the nineteenth century, offered a simple standard for judging everything – its effect on utility, happiness, the excess of pleasure over pain in human life. Anything that increased utility was good; anything that decreased it bad.

Quite a lot of the chemical entities consumed by people in order to increase their utility are illegal. Supporters of laws against recreational drugs base their support on a variety of factual claims, some true, some false. It is not true that smoking marijuana makes people go crazy and commit violent crimes, as claimed in "Reefer Madness," a movie that played an important role in inspiring the original anti-marijuana legislation. It is true that people on LSD are frequently incapable of performing ordinary tasks such as driving a car safely or conducting a coherent conversation. And it is true that some drugs have long-term adverse effects on some users.[1]

Whether or not the negative claims are true of some or all current recreational drugs, they are unlikely to be true of all future recreational drugs. The more we know about how the human mind functions, the better we will become at creating drugs that give pleasure without serious negative side effects. Unless, of course, it is pleasure itself that is the problem. Arguably it might be. Evolution is an extraordinary biochemist, much better than we are at producing compounds that affect living creatures in useful ways. If we can create a chemical that gives us pleasure, and if pleasure is a good thing, why don't we come already equipped for pleasure on demand?

The obvious answer is that we are designed by evolution not for happiness but for reproductive success. Pleasure and pain provide incentives to act in ways that achieve that objective – to engage in sex, to remove our hands from hot stoves. Presumably there is some optimal balance, some normal level that allows enough deviation in one direction to give an adequate incentive to do things that serve the interests of our genes and enough in the other to get us to avoid things contrary to those interests.

If pleasure drugs are too good, they might interfere not merely with reproductive success but with physical survival. Larry Niven provides a fictional example[2] in the form not of a drug but of direct electrical stimulation of the pleasure center of the brain. His "wireheads" are capable of plugging in and starving to death, because one more minute of intense pleasure is worth more to them than food or drink. If we accept this argument, the implication is not that pleasure drugs are bad but only that they should be used in moderation. It does not follow that they always will be.

For a less exotic example, consider a pleasure drug even more respectable than alcohol: the humble chocolate bar. If you have more elevated tastes, make it dinner at a four-star restaurant in Paris. Food, after all, is consumed largely to give us sensual pleasure. A minimum-cost, full-nutrition diet, based on flour, peanut butter, cabbage, and other high nutrition/low cost ingredients, comes to less than two dollars a day.[3] The rest of what we spend is for pleasure.

The current real-world problem of trading short-term pleasure for more important long-term goals is, arguably, not the starvation of Niven's wirehead but its opposite: obesity. People enjoy eating. Modern societies are rich enough so that almost everyone can afford to consume as many calories as he wants, an observation confirmed by half an hour spent people-watching in a low income neighborhood.[4] One result is that a growing number of people, in the United States and elsewhere, are substantially overweight, heavy enough so that, on current evidence, they would live longer if they ate less.

A more general argument against pleasure drugs is that simple pleasure is not all that matters, as suggested not merely by philosophers but by observed behavior. Few couples have sex as frequently as would be physically possible; few single individuals masturbate as often as would be physically possible. If we imagine someone spending most of his life in a drug-induced haze, we may suspect that, however intense his pleasure, he is not really happy.

This suggests the least interesting response to the possibility of pleasure drugs – that they don't work, that whatever their short-term benefits, in the long term they are a snare and a delusion. For all I know that may be true of the recreational drugs currently on the market, although I gather that many users of such disagree. But it is also largely irrelevant if we are considering the future.

Happiness

Troy Dayton pops a little white pill every morning. He's one of the 10 million Americans taking a daily antidepressant. But in his case, he says he was never depressed in the first place.

This 29-year-old political lobbyist is one of the happiest people you'll ever meet.[5]

Perhaps pleasure, in the sense provided by heroin and chocolate bars, is too narrow a goal. Since we are not limited to current technology, replace pleasure with happiness, the state of mind to which we think of pleasure as one input. Consider, not Niven's wirehead, but the happiest person you happen to know.

My candidate is a fellow law professor who possesses what I like to describe as a glow-in-the-dark personality. Years after I got to know her, I happened to notice an old photograph in a law school display case showing a prominent professor receiving an award from the students. The central figure in the picture, the face that stood out from the rest, was not the recipient but the student giving the award. It was a face I knew.

It is possible, of course, that the happiness of such people reflects the fact that they have lots to be happy about: a loving spouse, children, a satisfying job, none of which can be provided by a drug. But that does not seem to be all that is going on. Studies of happiness suggest that happy people stay happy even when circumstances change, at least once they have had time to adjust to the changes. I was reminded of that result not long ago, attending a memorial event for a friend who had died a little less than a year earlier. His widow was there. It had been a happy marriage and a long one. But nobody who did not already know the facts, watching her, would have realized that she had recently lost the man she loved. She too, I think, is a naturally happy person.

So consider, not a pleasure drug, but a happiness drug, one designed to alter your brain chemistry in a way that will make you more like my glow-in-the-dark friend. If you could, would you? Should you? One possible answer is that such happiness is unnatural. Again the argument is that we have been designed by evolution, and evolution is much better at neurochemistry than we are. If brain chemistry that made us happy was a good thing, we would all already have it.[6] The argument already offered for pleasure can be recycled for happiness. It too can be viewed as a reward programmed into us for behavior our genes approve of. It is harder to bribe rich people than poor people. Arguably, it is harder for our genes to bribe with happiness people who are already happy. While evolution may indeed be a very good biochemist, its objectives are not the same as ours. From the viewpoint of evolution, we are simply machinery by which genes make other genes. The design objective is reproductive success, the ability to increase the frequency of our genes in future generations.

That is not my design objective for me; if it were I would have more than three children. It does not seem to be the objective of many other people either; if it were, men would pay substantial sums to be permitted to donate to sperm banks and women who sold their eggs would do it at a negative rather than a positive price. Having someone else bear and bring up your children is, after all, an extraordinarily inexpensive way of spreading your genes.

Not only does evolution have the wrong objective, its designs are also out of date. Humans have long generations and so evolve slowly. Such evidence as we have suggests that we are adapted not to current circumstances but to the hunter-gatherer societies in which our species spent most of its existence. Even if too happy a personality is usually a liability in a hunter-gatherer society, and so rare, the same may not be true in a modern society. The happy people I know seem to do pretty well for themselves.

A second and more interesting objection is that utilitarianism is wrong, that happiness is not all that matters. To make that objection more plausible, consider two alternative lives I might live. One is the life I have lived. It has been, on the whole, a happy one. It has also produced a number of things I value – a happy marriage, three children, and half a dozen books, all of which I am proud of, a variety of ideas in several related fields, and many other things I am too modest (or lazy) to list.

The other is the life I might have lived if provided with suitable drugs, sufficient to make me at every moment of that life at least as happy as in the life I led. It is true that in that life I would not have had the pleasures of children, books, and other accomplishments. But I would have been compensated for that lack by an artificial increase in whatever brain chemicals connect the cause of accomplishment to the effect of happiness. Which life is more worth living? That is a question we will return to in a later chapter, in the context of virtual reality, another possible shortcut to happiness.

While it is an interesting question, it may not have much relevance to the effect of happiness – as opposed to pleasure – drugs. Judging by at least casual observation, whatever processes produce the natural equivalent of happiness drugs do not prevent their beneficiaries from living active and productive lives.

The CNN story on Troy Dayton's use of Wellbutrin as a happiness drug contained a variety of dire warnings:

Psychiatrists tell CNN that Dayton's use of Wellbutrin as a lifestyle drug is potentially dangerous, although little is known about the long-term effects. "These medicines are not harmless," said Dr. Peter Kramer, author of *Listening to Prozac*. Kramer said some doctors think that if you stay on antidepressants long enough, you'll come to rely on them. Other doctors believe they might trigger manic-depressive illness in susceptible people, he said.

The story offers no actual evidence of harm. The drug works by increasing the level of serotonin, a neurochemical associated with good feeling: "Chemically, there's little difference between good feelings induced by medication and those occurring naturally."

Performance

I would prefer my child take anabolic steroids and growth hormone than play rugby. Growth hormone is safer than rugby. At least I don't know of any cases of quadriplegia caused by growth hormone.
                    Julian Savulescu, professor of practical ethics at Oxford[7]

The performance drugs that are currently a public issue deal with the body, but they raise many of the same issues as drugs to improve mental performance. Everyone seems to agree that it is a bad thing for athletes to use steroids, but it is not entirely clear why. Athletes have, after all, been using diet and exercise to improve their performance for thousands of years, as well as a variety of older drugs. Why does the process suddenly become sinful when they switch to steroids?

One answer is that since steroid use is currently prohibited, those who use steroids are getting an unfair advantage. But that does not explain why they are currently prohibited when other ways of getting an advantage are not. A second answer is that we are afraid young athletes, with inadequate concern for their own future, will do themselves serious damage in the process of trying to win. But while taking steroids may reduce life expectancy – the evidence seems to be a good deal weaker than popular discussions suggest[8] – so does driving a car around a racetrack at something over 200 miles an hour, which young race car drivers are permitted to do. Why is our paternalism so selective?[9]

The most interesting answer, at least to an economist, is that our opposition comes from the special nature of the product that athletic contests produce. Arguably, most of what we care about is the relative, not absolute, ability of the athletes. A footrace in which one competitor manages a mile in 4 minutes and the other in 3 minutes and 59 seconds is just as exciting as one where the times are 3:59 and 3:58. We want our favorite baseball team to play a little better than its opponents but care little about the absolute level at which both play. To the extent that this claim is true – some sports fans would dispute it – competition via steroid use is a mistake. Both teams, boxers, or runners get a little better, their relative ability is unaffected, the fans are no happier and the athletes die a little younger.

Consider next the mental equivalent of steroids. Ritalin, for example, is usually thought of as medication for Attention Deficit Disorder (ADD). It turns out, however, that one cannot tell if someone has ADD by giving him Ritalin and seeing if his concentration improves, because Ritalin improves everyone's concentration. It follows that someone who wants to do well on, say, a bar exam, might be well advised to somehow obtain some Ritalin to take before going into the exam – and I gather some people do. Other illegally obtained drugs, such as speed (amphetamines), are reported to be in common use for similar purposes. Perhaps when the due date for a paper approaches, a student given to procrastination might want to obtain some modafinil,[10] a drug that appears to eliminate the need for sleep for substantial periods of time and is, if news stories are to be believed, currently used for that purpose by the U.S. military.

One argument for prohibiting the use of such drugs by those taking the bar exam, or SATs, or a final, is that they distort the information that the exam produces. A law firm deciding whether to hire you doesn't want to know how good a lawyer you are when you are under the influence of Ritalin unless they expect you to continue to consume it regularly for the rest of your working life. They want to know how good a lawyer you are under the conditions under which you will be working.

That makes sense as long as we are only talking about temporary effects. The question becomes more interesting if we consider a drug that can be used on a regular basis – as people diagnosed with ADD in fact use Ritalin – or one that produces long-term rather than short-term effects. We then have the mental equivalent of a steroid.

Some of the hostility to the regular use of such drugs, as for steroids, is based on the idea that all they are doing is helping the user win a competition, not on the playing field but in the job market. If both competitors use the drug neither gains any relative advantage and both are worse off by whatever the costs of the drug, in money or health, happen to be.

That argument reflects a fundamental misunderstanding of economic competition. If you and I are runners and both use steroids, both run a little faster and you still win the race. Nothing is gained and, if steroids have undesirable side effects, something is lost. But if you and I are house carpenters who use an improved version of modafinil to increase both labor and leisure, working ten hours out of twenty-two instead of eight out of sixteen, the result is that more houses get built. The ultimate benefit might go to us as more income from our greater productivity and more leisure to enjoy it in. It might go to people who buy houses, if our increased output drives down the price of our services. It might be divided between us and our customers. The details of what happens depend on the details of the market for our services. But in all of the outcomes, the extra time that we have gotten by drastically reducing our need for sleep, or the superior quality from improving our ability to pay attention, is producing a real benefit for someone, not merely a competitive advantage.

The argument applies wherever absolute and not merely relative results matter, which means almost everywhere. "Competition" is a misleading term because it suggests that, as in athletic contests, all that matters is who wins. Farms do not exist to win a competition but to produce food. Carpenters do not exist to win a competition but to build houses and chairs and tables. Drugs that make us more alert, or smarter, or give us better memories, or reduce the need for sleep, let us do whatever we are doing better. That is a net benefit to be balanced against any costs associated with use of the drug.

Do drugs give us better memories? That is still an open question, one closely associated with the attempt to reduce memory loss due to Parkinson's disease. But there is good reason to believe that such drugs will exist, and at least some reason to believe that we already know of drugs that to some degree improve memory. The same claim is sometimes made with regard to intelligence – that there now exist "smart drugs." Whether or not they do exist, it seems likely that they will.

It may occur to some readers that the argument I have offered to explain concerns about enhancement drugs, however entertaining to an economist, is too clever by half, that most ordinary people do not distinguish between activities that are purely competitive and those that are productive. An alternative explanation, and one that provides at least a partial explanation of hostility to many different technologies, is that people are simply conservative, skeptical of anything new, "unnatural," despite the unnatural nature of virtually everything we currently eat, drink, or wear.

As evidence, I offer the following comment on modafinil from a doctor who deals with sleep disorders: "I think sleep is a good thing. The healthy thing to do is to sleep more if you're tired, right?"[11]

A conjecture converted into a fact under your very eyes.

Personality

Earlier in this chapter I raised the question of whether the opportunity for pleasure might make us worse off rather than better off. One example is obesity. I weigh more than I believe I should, yet have a hard time losing weight. Like many other people, I can resist anything but temptation. As we develop ways of easily obtaining much more intense pleasures, there is some risk that we may be tempted into giving up long-term benefits in exchange for short-term benefits even when we should not. This raises an obvious question: What does "should not" mean? How, other than by observing the choices people make, can we judge their values? What do I mean if I say that I did one thing but should have – in some sense really wanted to – do another?

An approach to that question that I find intuitively appealing is to think of myself as two people in one, a long-term planner and a short-term current utility maximizer. The planner uses devices such as guilt and commitments to try to manipulate the short-term maximizer, the me in actual control of my body. I might decide – have from time to time decided – that I will not permit myself to have ice cream for dessert until I have gotten my weight below some arbitrary level. I might decide – in fact decided, not long before typing these words – to set a lower limit to my day's written output, a number of words I must produce before permitting myself to go to bed or indulge in *World of Warcraft*. Sometimes the devices rely on external aid, as when an employee arranges to have a certain amount of his income automatically transferred each month to a savings account.

This way of looking at it suggests an intriguing possibility. Perhaps the problem with pleasure drugs can be dealt with by personality drugs. Some people appear to have a longer time horizon than others, to be more able to control their desire for immediate pleasure in order to better achieve their long-term goals. Perhaps, as we learn more about how the brain works, we will discover that the difference reflects some difference in brain chemistry. Perhaps personality drugs will finally put the long-term planner in the driver's seat.

Consider, for example, what we already know about the effects of dopamine, a neurotransmitter that plays an important role in brain chemistry. A shortage of dopamine in the brain results in an indecisive personality; Parkinson's disease is an extreme version. Mice with excess brain dopamine, on the other hand, are highly exploratory and adventurous.[12] We do not yet know in any detail the mechanisms that produce these results, but they at least demonstrate that personality depends in part on brain chemistry.

For a more striking example due to a more drastic alteration of the brain, consider the most famous anecdote in the field: the sad history of Phineas P. Gage. As a result of a moment's carelessness with explosives in 1848, he succeeded in driving a four-foot metal rod entirely through his head, leaving a hole in his brain case into which the attending physician was able to insert his entire index finger. Surprisingly enough, he recovered from the injury in a few weeks and returned to his job as foreman of a railroad blasting crew. "He had no apparent intellectual deficits or memory losses. Yet, his return to work quickly showed the nature of the deficit that follows massive frontal lobe damage. The formerly mild mannered, thoughtful, and cooperative foreman had been transformed into a cursing, belligerent tyrant. He lost his job, joined a traveling sideshow for a few years to capitalize (in a small way) on his misfortune, and died of an epilepsy attack about 13 years later."[13]

Whether or not personality drugs can be used to give us better than average personalities, they are currently being used to deal with personalities seen, by their possessors and others, as worse than average. Bipolar disorder is one example, depression another. Both can be seen as personality disorders. Both are treated with drugs, in at least some cases with apparent success.

Control

Candy is dandy but liquor is quicker.

So far we have been considering things we might be able to do to ourselves, using drugs. There remains the issue of things other people might do to us. Two obvious examples are drugs to make the victim unconscious – chloral hydrate, the "Mickey Finn" of old detective stories, and its more modern equivalents – and the use of alcohol as an aid to seduction. Newer drugs might serve the same purpose. One effect of ecstasy (MDMA) is to make the user warmer, more empathetic. Under most circumstances that is a desired effect, an example of the use of a drug to change one's personality. But it is also a reason why a man might feed the drug to a woman he was trying to seduce.

As this example suggests, the difference between personality drugs and control drugs depends not so much on the nature of the drug as on how it is used. A woman who gets herself drunk in order to let herself be seduced is using alcohol to temporarily alter her personality. A man who gets a woman drunk for the same purpose is using it to control her.

The present range of control drugs is pretty limited. There are knockout drugs. There are drugs that induce temporary amnesia, such as Rohypnol, sometimes called the date rape drug. There are drugs such as alcohol and marijuana that relax people and make it harder to think clearly. That's about it.

There is, however, evidence of more on the horizon. One odd set of experiments involving the reaction of some people to smelling other people's perspiration suggest that there may be human pheromones, compounds that make someone smell sexy to someone else; perhaps some perfume actually works.[14] If we can isolate such compounds and figure out how they work, we may be able to produce the same effects in a much more powerful form. Aphrodisiacs may today be mostly mythical, but there is always tomorrow.

Still more disturbing is the possibility of drugs that make the consumer credulous, willing to believe whatever he is told, or obedient, or loyal. There is some evidence that oxytocin has such an effect.

To get some feeling for how a loyalty drug might work, consider the Mule, a character in Isaac Asimov's *Foundation* trilogy, an old and famous work of science fiction. The Mule had one simple talent: the ability to make people want to serve him. He used it to build an interstellar empire. His servants knew perfectly well that they were loyal because he had used his special ability to make them so, but it didn't bother them. Serving the Mule was the best thing they could possibly do, so why should they resent the fact that he had made them want to do it?

That is only science fiction, but there is a real-world equivalent that all of us have observed and many experienced: the feeling of parents toward their children. Parents love their children and wish to serve and protect them, not because the parent has made an objective judgment about how deserving their children are but because the parent has been programmed by his genes to feel that way, by mechanisms some of which may well be chemical. Parents who happen to be evolutionary biologists know that their children have them by the genes and why; they still feel the same way.

We are descended from people who not only produced children but took sufficiently good care of them so that they in turn reached maturity and reproduced; we have been selected, over a period longer than our species has existed, for the characteristic of altruism toward our own children. But that evolutionary explanation tells us nothing about the underlying mechanism, just as the observation that being able to see makes it much easier to survive tells us nothing about how the eye works. If we could learn to understand the mechanism, the nature of the internal changes that support parental love, we might be able to use that knowledge to make others love us as if we were their children. Similarly for romantic love, which produces effects in some ways very similar.

We are only just approaching the ability to do this sort of thing, but we have been thinking about it for a long time. Consider Ariosto's *Orlando Furioso*, a sixteenth-century work of fantasy fiction whose characters spend their time wandering about a vast forest that seems to stretch roughly from England to China, geography not being one of Ariosto's concerns.

The forest is well provided with pools and springs for the use of thirsty adventurers. As best I can make out – I read the book quite a long time ago – there are three different kinds. Drinking from the first eliminates your memory. Drinking from the second makes you hate whatever being you most loved. Drinking at the third makes you fall in love with the next living thing you see. For Ariosto they were only a convenient plot device, a way of getting his characters into amusing and entertaining situations. We already have versions of the first spring – Rohypnol, for instance, although its effect is briefer. The rest may be coming.

Suppose we develop much better control drugs; how might our laws and institutions adjust? One possibility is a legal regime under which a contract is binding only if both parties have been tested just before they signed to make sure neither was under an influence that would make him unreasonably credulous or suggestible. If there are reliable seduction drugs that can be given to a potential victim without consent, perhaps we should ban all sex not preceded by suitable drug tests. Critics of current campaigns to define date rape as broadly as possible might argue that we are already most of the way there.

Not all forms of protection depend on changes in the law. The simplest protection against being drugged is not to drink from a glass or a container that someone else has had an opportunity to slip something into. Carrying self-protection a little further, there currently exist simple chemical tests for the presence of date rape drugs. Unobtrusively dribble a few drops of your drink onto the test strip; if it changes color, remember that you have urgent business elsewhere.[15] One can imagine more sophisticated versions, as defensive technology improves to match improved offensive technology. Perhaps we will eventually use nanotechnology to equip ourselves with microscopic chemical labs that continually monitor our bloodstreams and let us know if there is anything there that shouldn't be.

Conditions of Employment

So far in the discussion of control drugs I have been assuming that they are given to people without their consent. There is another way they might be used that moves us to the borderland between drugs that I use to change my personality and drugs that you use to control me.

There are quite a lot of jobs for which loyalty is an important qualification. Suppose I am hiring for a firm whose employees will have profitable opportunities to benefit themselves at the firm's expense, to pocket small and valuable items or sell the firm's trade secrets to its competitors. After calculating the cost of watching everyone all the time, I decide to offer two different employment contracts, one paying $50,000 a year, one $100,000. There is only one difference between the two contracts: The second one requires the employee to consume a drug that makes him loyal to the firm.

One might object that letting someone agree to such a contract is rather like letting him sell himself into slavery. One might respond that to forbid the contract means to deny the individual control over his own body and mind. And one might also note that what I have described is merely a new technology for an old purpose. Firms, armies, and nations have been using more primitive methods to try to make people feel loyal for a long time.

The contractual loyalty drug does, however, raise some interesting issues. Once you have taken the drug, what is to keep your employer from suggesting that you voluntarily return to him half your salary and what keeps you from loyally agreeing to do so? Perhaps the contract should include some special safeguards.

An important question here is whether the drug makes you permanently loyal, as parents are permanently loyal to their children, even to children that only a mother could love, or whether the loyalty wears off with the drug. In the latter case the employer may have to rely on your loyalty to make you take the next dose – and a loyal employee may still be absent-minded. It might be more prudent to institute mandatory drug testing intended to make sure not that you are not on drugs but that you are.

THE CHEMISTRY OF LOVE

The feelings of euphoria, sleeplessness, and loss of appetite, as well as the lover's intense energy, focused attention, driving motivation, and goal-oriented behaviors, his/her tendency to regard the beloved as novel and unique, and the lover's increased passion in the face of adversity might all be caused, in part, by heightened levels of dopamine and/or norepinephrine in the brain. And the lover's obsessive cogitation about the beloved might be due to decreased brain levels of some type of serotonin.

Helen Fisher, *Why We Love*

The pattern of behavior we associate with falling in love is shared by many other species, a fact that greatly simplifies the investigation of its causes and nature; it is easier to get approval for experiments on rats than for experiments on people. The resulting research on the relation between romantic love and brain chemistry provides possible examples of all the sorts of mind drugs I have been discussing.

Falling in love is for some people an intensely pleasurable, indeed addictive, experience, which may explain why some men fall intensely in love with one woman and then, after their efforts meet with success, lose interest and fall in love with another. A famous example is Giacomo Casanova, the historical figure whose name has become a synonym for male inconstancy. Judging by his memoirs, he was a much nicer person than the modern usage of his name suggests; he seems to have taken considerable efforts to assure the future well-being of his ex-lovers, and some remained friends and correspondents for decades after the end of the affair. But he did fall in love with a very considerable number of women and the intensity of his passion predictably cooled over a period of perhaps a month or two after its success.

Arguably, the difference between Casanova and the rest of us is only a matter of degree, not of kind. I love my wife very much but I am not in love with her in the sense in which I was when I first courted her some thirty years ago. Not only are the two emotions different subjectively, there is some evidence that they are related to different neurochemicals in the brain. My feelings when I was first in love with her are in some ways more like my feelings for our children, especially when they were young, than they are like my current feelings for her. Parental love features the same intense focus, the same feeling that one being is the most important thing in the world, as romantic love. I suspect, but do not know, that with sufficient research one would find that some of the same neurochemicals are involved in both.

Recent research on the nature of love, focused on the connection between behavior and brain chemistry, distinguishes three different but related behaviors: falling in love, attachment, and lust.[16]

Falling in love is a behavior pattern familiar from literature, movies, television and, for most of us, firsthand experience. A central symptom is the wholly irrational belief that one person is the most important thing in the universe, the proper target for most of one's thoughts, hopes, and attention. It is not a pattern limited to humans; a wide range of animals, from elephants to rats, appear to fall in love as well. In animals as in humans, the behavior is closely linked to mating behavior.

Humans rarely stay in love; typically, the feelings and associated behavior last for months, not years. Sometimes love is succeeded by attachment, a behavior pattern associated with less intense emotions and one that can, with luck, last a lifetime. We do not fully understand the mechanisms underlying these patterns of behavior, but it seems clear that they are associated with known neurochemicals and known areas of the brain. Suppose, as seems likely enough, that further research makes it possible to control them, to fall in and out of love, to maintain or destroy the emotions of romantic attachment, to turn love and lust on or off, with a pill, a patch, an injection. What consequences would follow?

The consequences of involuntary use are obvious and unattractive: a pill that makes a beautiful woman fall in love or, for shorter-term objectives, lust, with you. What about voluntary use?

Many years ago I spent a long airplane flight – from Bombay to Sydney – next to a woman from southern India, flying out to join her husband. She came from a society where arranged marriages were taken for granted. Her husband had been selected for her by her parents, although she had then met him before consenting to the arrangement. I came from a society where it was taken for granted that individuals found and selected their own mates. She accepted her society's arrangements and was intrigued by the odd way we did things; I felt much the same in the other direction. And she was not a stick figure in a history or anthropology text but a living, breathing human being, obviously intelligent and thoughtful. Furthermore, on at least our small sample, the superiority of the Western system was far from clear; she was happily married, I recently divorced.

It was a very interesting conversation and I came away from it less certain of the superiority of our system. Choice of a mate is, after all, a difficult and important decision, and it is hard to imagine anything further from a coldly rational being than a man in love. On the other hand, being in love is not only an intense and moving experience, it is also a natural and appropriate preliminary to a lifetime of attachment, at least arguably designed by evolution for the purpose.

Perhaps in the brave new world of modern chemistry one will be able to get the best of both worlds. First I select a spouse by some suitably calm and objective analysis, making use of the services of a professional matchmaker to find a woman ideally suited to be my wife – one requirement being, of course, that I am ideally suited to be her husband. After she and I have agreed on the match, either just before or just after the wedding, we take our pills, look into each other's eyes, and fall deeply and passionately in love. After six months or so of ecstatic but distracting bliss – both of our employers are beginning to worry about declining job performance – we switch the prescription from passion to attachment and so shift into a long and satisfying marriage. If on some suitable future occasion, say a tenth anniversary, we feel in need of a second honeymoon, perhaps there are still a few pills left over from the first prescription.

It sounds like science fiction, but it is not entirely clear that it is not also very old, if only occasional, fact. I am not certain if my Indian friend was, or had been, in love with her husband, but she certainly appeared attached to him. It is entirely possible that arranged marriage might sometimes have led to romance, especially in a society where young adults were segregated by sex, so that your wife might be the first suitable young woman you had an opportunity to fall in love with.

Not only may the love be an old story, but the chemistry as well. Sex, as many of us have observed, has emotional concomitants. Also chemical. "At orgasm, levels of vasopressin dramatically increase in men and levels of oxytocin in women."[17] The connections between those hormones and the neurotransmitters that seem to be associated with romantic love – dopamine, norepinephrine, and serotonin – are complicated but clearly exist.[18] It is entirely possible that the pills I have described are already engineered into us, in at least a weak form.

Which brings us back to one of the central conflicts of our culture: the case for and against nature. We routinely use "natural" as a term of praise: natural food, unspoiled nature, natural childbirth. And yet we have constructed our world in large part to avoid the defects of nature. Unnatural childbirth, up to and including caesarean section (currently more than one-quarter of all U.S. births), is the reason that death in childbirth is now a rare tragedy instead of a common occurrence. Very few residents of either Chicago or Houston prefer, given the choice, to maintain their houses year-round at their natural temperature. And very nearly all of the plant foods we eat – almost all grains, fruits, and vegetables – are unnatural, the result of many generations of selective breeding from natural plants that few of us would think worth eating.

If not our houses, what about our hearts? Nature or art? Are we better off being led into and out of love, into and out of occupied beds, into and out of marriage by the natural processes engineered into our minds and bodies or are we better off deciding when and whom to love by means of our reason, assisted where appropriate by expert advice, and then implementing our decisions through the marvels of modern chemistry?

And, to descend for a moment from high flown speculations, in that future will "He refused to take his attachment pill" be legitimate grounds for divorce? Will recreational sex morph into recreational love? Will singles bars offer two extra-special drinks, one with a falling-in-love drug, to take before heading out to his place or yours, and one with the antidote?

A FINAL NOTE

Some readers, following my endnotes, may have noticed repeated references to works by Matt Ridley dealing not with drugs but with genetics. That is not an accident. The chemical mechanisms that generate our natural mind drugs are under genetic control. The study of how genes affect behavior is intimately connected with the study of how chemicals in our brain affect behavior. Studying mind drugs by injecting chemicals into people's brains and seeing how they react raises serious practical and ethical difficulties. An attractive alternative is to observe people who, possibly for genetic reasons, behave in different ways and checking their blood to see what is in it.

There is a second link between the two studies. Drugs may provide a temporary way of doing what genes do for good. If it turns out that increasing the level of serotonin in the brain makes people happier, a tempting short-run approach might be to feed people, or inject them, with something that results in increasing serotonin levels. If that turns out to work, a longer run approach might be genetic manipulation to increase the level that we produce. Perhaps we could even identify a "happiness gene," some gene or group of genes that are common in strikingly happy people, and find some way of artificially increasing its frequency in the population. Perhaps the next time I happen to run across my glow-in-the-dark friend I should ask her for a blood sample to pass on to some ambitious researcher.

You too can have happy babies.

PART SIX

THE REAL SCIENCE FICTION

SEVENTEEN

The Last Lethal Disease

Over the past 500 years, the average length of a human life in the developed world has more than doubled while the maximum has remained essentially unchanged. We have eliminated or greatly reduced most of the traditional causes of mortality, including mass killers such as smallpox, measles, influenza, and complications of childbirth. But old age remains incurable and always lethal.

Why? On the face of it, aging looks like poor design. We have been selected by evolution for reproductive success; the longer you live without serious aging, the longer you can keep producing babies. Even if you are no longer fertile, staying alive and healthy allows you to help protect and feed your descendants.[1]

The obvious answer is that if nobody got old and died there would be no place for our descendants to live and nothing left for them to eat. But that confuses individual interest with group interest; although group selection may have played some role in evolution, it is generally agreed that the major driving force was individual selection. If I stay alive, all of my resources go to help my descendants; insofar as I am competing for resources, I am competing mostly with other people's descendants. Besides, we evolved in an environment in which we had not yet dealt with other sources of mortality, so even if people did not age they would still die, and on average almost as young. In traditional societies, only a minority lived long enough for aging to matter.

A second possible answer is that immortality would indeed be useful, but there is no way of producing it. Over time our bodies wear out, random mutation corrupts our genes, until at last the remaining blueprint is too badly flawed to continue to produce cells to replace those that have died. This answer too cannot be right. A human being is, genetically speaking, massively redundant – every cell in my body contains the same instructions. It is as if I were a library with trillions of copies of the same book. If some of them had misprints or missing pages, I could always reconstruct the text from others. If two volumes disagree, check a third, a fourth, a millionth.[2] Besides, there are organisms that are immortal. Amoebas reproduce by division – where there was one amoeba, there are now two. There is no such thing as a young amoeba.

A variety of more plausible explanations for aging have been proposed. One I find persuasive starts with the observation that, while the cells in my body are massively redundant, the single fertilized cell from which I grew was not. Any error in that cell ended up in every cell of my adult body.

Suppose one of those mutations had the effect of killing the individual carrying it before he got old enough to reproduce. Obviously, that mutation would vanish in the first generation. Suppose instead that it killed its carrier, on average, at age thirty. Now the mutation would to some degree be weeded out by selection – but some of my children, perhaps even some of my grandchildren, could still inherit it.

Consider next a mutation that kills at age sixty – in a world where aging does not yet exist, but death via childbirth, measles, and saber-toothed tigers does, with the result that hardly anyone makes it to sixty. Possession of that mutation is only a very slight reproductive disadvantage, so it gets filtered out only very slowly. Following this line of argument, we would expect lethal mutations that acted late in life to accumulate, with new ones appearing as old ones are gradually eliminated. The process reinforces itself. Once mutations that kill you at sixty are common, mutations that kill you at seventy do not matter very much – you can only die once. Aging may simply be the working out of a large collection of accumulated late-acting lethal genes.[3]

A slightly different version of this explanation starts with the observation that in designing an organism – or anything else – there are trade-offs. We can give cars better gas mileage by making them lighter, at the cost of making them more vulnerable to damage. We can build cars that are invulnerable to anything short of high explosives – we call them tanks – but their mileage figures are not impressive.

Similar trade-offs must exist in our design. Suppose there is some design feature, encoded in genes, which can provide benefits in survival probability or fertility early in life at the cost of causing increased breakdown after age sixty. Unless the benefits are tiny relative to the costs, the net effect will be increased reproductive success, since most people in the environment we evolved in didn't make it to sixty anyway. So such a feature will be selected for by evolution. Putting the argument more generally, the evolutionary advantages to extending the maximum life span were small in the environment we evolved in, since in that environment very few people lived long enough to die of old age. So it is not surprising if the short-term costs outweighed the long-term benefits. My genes made the correct calculations in designing me for reproductive success in the environment of 50,000 years ago but I, living now and with objectives that go beyond reproductive success, would prefer they hadn't.

One reason to figure out why we age is in order to do something about it, a subject with which I become increasingly concerned as the years pass. If there is some single flaw in our design, if aging is due to shrinking telomeres or a shortage of vitamin Z, then once we discover the flaw we may be able to fix it. If aging is the combined effect of 1,000 flaws, the problem will be harder. But even in that case, there might be solutions, either the slow solution of identifying and fixing all 1,000[4] or a fast solution such as a microscopic cell repair machine that can go through our bodies fixing whatever damage all 1,000 causes have produced.

My own guess is that the problem of aging will be solved, although not necessarily in time to do me any good. That guess is based on two observations. The first is that our knowledge of biology has increased at an enormous rate over the past century or so and continues to do so. So if the problem is not for some reason inherently insoluble – I cannot think of any plausible reasons why it should be – it seems likely that scientific progress during the next century will make a solution possible. The second is that solving the problem is of enormous, indeed vital, importance to old people, and old people control very large resources, both economic and political.

If I am right, one implication is that the payoff to slowing aging a little may be large, since that might result in my surviving long enough to benefit by more substantial breakthroughs. There are currently a variety of things one can do that there is some reason to believe will slow aging. It is only "some reason" because the combined effect of the long human life span and the difficulty of arranging to do experiments on human beings mean that our information on the subject is very imperfect. Most of the relevant information consists of the observation that doing particular things to particular strains of mice or fruit flies, experimental subjects with short generations and no legal rights, results in substantial increases in their life span.

Thus, for example, it turns out that transgenic fruit flies provided with a particular human gene have a life expectancy up to 40% longer than those without the extra gene. Modifying the diet of some strains of mice – by, for example, providing them a high level of antioxidant vitamins – can have similar effects. When I was investigating the arguments for and against consuming lots of antioxidants, one persuasive piece of evidence came from an article in *Consumer Reports*.[5] It quoted a researcher in the field as saying that taking antioxidant supplements was "banking on an aging mechanism that hasn't been proven," but added that "like several scientists we contacted, he takes a supplement regimen that includes vitamins C and E, beta-carotene, and a multiple-vitamin tablet." As an economist, I believe that what people do is frequently better evidence than what they say.

One of the most effective ways of extending the life span of mice turns out to be caloric deprivation, feeding them a diet at the low end of the number of calories needed to stay alive but otherwise adequate in nutrients. The result is to produce mice with very long life expectancies. Whether it will work on humans is not yet known – or, a question of more immediate interest to some of us, whether it would work on humans who only started late in life. A parent who chose to almost starve his children would risk being found guilty of child abuse but could argue, on the basis of existing evidence, that he was actually the only parent who wasn't.

THE DOWNSIDE OF IMMORTALITY?

Suppose my guess is correct; at some point in the not too distant future, hopefully at some point in my future, we find the cure for aging. What are the consequences? On the individual level they are large and positive; one of the worst features of human life has just vanished. People who prefer mortality can still die. Those of us with unfinished business can get on with it.

But while I am unambiguously in favor of stopping my aging, it does not follow that I must be in favor of stopping yours. One reason not to be is concern with population growth. As it happens, I do not share that concern, having concluded long ago that, at anything close to current population levels, mere number of people is not a serious problem.[6] That conclusion was reinforced over the years as leading preachers of population doom proceeded to rack up a string of failed prophecies unmatched outside of the nuttier religious sects. Readers who disagree, as many do, may want to look at the works of the late Julian Simon, possibly the ablest and certainly the most energetic critic of the thesis that increasing population leads to catastrophe. I prefer to move on to what I regard as more interesting issues.

"Senator" Means "Old Man"

An absolute monarchy is one in which the sovereign does as he pleases so long as he pleases the assassins.

Ambrose Bierce, *The Devil's Dictionary*

One is the problem of gerontocracy, rule by the old. Under our political system incumbents have an enormous advantage; at the congressional level they almost always win reelection.[7] If aging stops and nothing else changes, our representatives will grow steadily older. An incumbent who is guaranteed reelection is free to do what he wants within a fairly large, although not unlimited, range. So one result would be to make democratic control over democratic governments even weaker than it now is. Another might be to create societies dominated by the attitudes of the old: bossy, cautious, conservative.

The effect on undemocratic systems might be even worse. In a world without aging it seems likely that Salazar would still rule Portugal and Franco Spain. It would have been Stalin, equipped with an arsenal of thermonuclear missiles, who presided over, and did his best to prevent, the final disintegration of the Soviet Union. With the aging problem solved, dictatorship could become a permanent condition. Provided, of course, that dictators took sufficient precautions against other sources of mortality.

The problem is not limited to the world of politics. It has been argued that scientific progress consists of young scientists adopting new ideas and old scientists dying. It is frightening to imagine the universities our system of academic tenure might produce without either compulsory retirement, now illegal in the United States, or mortality.

Implicit in some of these worries is a buried assumption – that we are curing the physical effects of aging but not all of the mental effects. Whether that assumption is reasonable depends on why it is that old people think differently than young people. One answer, popular with the old, is that it is because they know more. If so, perhaps gerontocracy is not such a bad thing. Another is that the brain has limited capacity.[8] Having learned one system of ideas, there may be no place to put another, especially if they are mutually inconsistent. Humans, old and young, demonstrate a strong preference for the beliefs they already have; old people have more of them.

One way of understanding aging is as a shift from fluid to crystallized intelligence. Fluid intelligence is what you use to solve a new problem. Crystallized intelligence consists of remembering the solution you found last time and using that. The older you are, the more problems you have already solved and the less the future payoff from finding new and possibly better solutions. The point was brought home to me in a striking fashion some years ago when I observed a highly intelligent man in his eighties ignoring evidence of what turned out to be an approaching forest fire – smells of smoke, reports from others who had seen it – until he saw the flames with his own eyes.

It is possible, of course, that if we ended aging – better yet, made it possible to reverse its effects – the result would be old people with the minds of the young. It is also possible that we would discover that the mental characteristics of the old, short of actual senility, were a consequence not of biological breakdown but of computer overload, the response of a limited mind to too much accumulation of experience.

World Enough and Time

When contemplating an extra few centuries, one obvious question is what to do with them. Having raised one family, grown old, and then had my youth restored, would I decide to see if I could do even better a second time or conclude that that was something I had already done? Weak evidence for the former alternative is provided by the not uncommon pattern of grandparents raising their grandchildren when the children's parents prove unable or unwilling to do the job.

The same question arises in other contexts. Having had one career as an economist, would I continue along the lines of my past work or decide that this time around I wanted to be a novelist, an entrepreneur, an arctic explorer? It is a familiar observation that, in many fields, scholars do their best and most original work when young. My father once suggested the project of funding successful scholars past their prime to retrain in some entirely unrelated field, in order to see if the result was a second burst of creativity. In a world without aging, that pattern might become a great deal more common. And a novelist or entrepreneur who had first been an academic economist or a Marine officer might bring some interesting background to her new profession.[9]

An alternative is leisure. We cannot all retire, since there has to be someone left to mow the lawn, grow the food, and do the rest of the world's work. But it might be possible for most of us to retire or for all of us to mostly retire. Capital as well as labor is productive; more and better machinery, other forms of improved production, permit one person to do the work of 10 or 100. Consider the striking fall in the fraction of the U.S. workforce engaged in producing food, from almost everybody to almost nobody in the space of a century.

How productive capital is at present is shown by the interest rate, the price people are willing to pay for the use of capital. The real interest rate, the rate after allowing for inflation, has typically been about 2%. If that pattern holds in the future, you could spend the first fifty years of adulthood earning (say) $80,000 a year, spending $50,000, saving the rest, accumulate about $2.54 million and then spend the rest of a very long life living on the interest: $50,800 a year for food, housing, and a good Internet connection. You could, if you wished, continue working part-time, picking those activities that you liked to do and other people were willing to pay for.[10] Good work if you can get it. One can easily enough imagine a future along these lines where a large fraction of the population, even a large majority, was at least semiretired.

While thinking about how to spend your second century, you might want to consider the social consequences of eliminating the markers of age. In a world where aging is entirely under our control, a young woman of 20 might be dating a young man 100 years older than she is – and he might or might not tell her. The same thing already happens online, where a flirtatious twelve-year-old girl may be almost anything, including a forty-year-old male FBI agent. If you, a grandfather with a retirement pension and a century behind you, could go back to college as a freshman, would you? Part-time? Lots of cute girls. The women of your own generation are just as cute, thanks to the same advanced biotech that makes you eighteen again, but the real thing has its charms. Perhaps.

Life or a Hundred Years, Whichever Is Shorter

Immortality also raises issues for our legal system. Consider a criminal sentenced to a life sentence. Do we interpret that as "what a life sentence used to be" – say to age 100? Or do we take it literally?

To answer that question, we start by asking why we would lock someone up for life in the first place. There are at least two plausible answers, associated with two different theories of criminal punishment. One is that we lock a murderer up for the same reason we lock a tiger up: He is dangerous to others, so we want to keep him where he cannot do much damage. That is the theory of criminal punishment sometimes described as *incapacitation.* The other is that we lock a murderer up in order to impose a cost on him, a cost high enough so that other people contemplating murder will choose not to incur it. That is the theory described as *deterrence.* In practice, of course, we may operate on both theories at once, believing that some criminals can be deterred, some only incapacitated, and we cannot always be sure which are which.

If our objective is deterrence, centuries of incarceration may be overkill, which is an argument for eventually letting the convict out. If our objective is incapacitation, on the other hand, we may want to keep him in. Under current circumstances, a ninety-year-old murderer is unlikely to be of much danger to anyone but himself, but if we conquer aging that will no longer be the case.

A third justification offered for imprisonment is rehabilitation, chang-ing criminals so that they no longer want to commit crimes. That is the theory that gave us "reformatories" to reform people and "penitentiaries" to make people repent. It is hard to see why, on that theory, we would have life sentences; perhaps one could argue that there are some people who take longer to be rehabilitated than they are likely to last. If so one might reinterpret "life" as "to age 100 or until rehabilitated, whichever takes longer."[11]

So far in this chapter I have been considering the consequences of hypothetical solutions to the aging problem. Next we turn to one that is already here.

A COLD CENTURY IN HELL

Thus, the appropriate clinical trials would be to:

1. Select N subjects.
2. Preserve them.
3. Wait 100 years.
4. See if the technology of 2100 can indeed revive them.
The reader might notice a problem: what do we tell the terminally ill patient prior to completion of the trials?
Ralph Merkle, from a webbed defense of cryonics

The idea of cryonic suspension – keeping people frozen in the hopes of someday thawing them, reviving them, and curing what killed them – has been around for some time. Critics view it as a fraud or a delusion, analo-gizing the problem of undoing the damage done to cells by ice crystals in the process of freezing to converting hamburger back into a living cow.[12] Supporters point out that as the technology of freezing organs improves we are learning how to decrease the damage – among other things by replacing the body's water with the equivalent of antifreeze during the cooling process. Nobody has turned a mouse kidney into hamburger and then back into a working kidney, but the equivalent has apparently been done successfully – once – with freezing. And they argue that as the technology needed to revive a frozen body improves – ultimately, perhaps, through the development of nanotechnology capable of doing repairs at the cellular level – it will become easier to undo the damage that we cannot prevent. Finally and most convincingly, they point out that however poor your chances are of being brought back from death if you have your body frozen, they can hardly be worse than the chances if you let it rot instead.[13]

Suppose we accept their arguments to the extent of regarding revival as at least a possibility. We are then faced with a variety of interesting problems, legal and social. Most come down to a simple question – what is the status of a corpsicle? Is it a corpse, a living person temporarily unable to act, or something else? If I am frozen, is my wife free to remarry? If I am then thawed, which of us is she married to? Do my heirs inherit, and if so can I reclaim my property when I rejoin the living?

Many of these are issues that can be – if suspension becomes common will be – dealt with by private arrangements. If the law regards my wife as a widow, she can still choose to regard herself as a wife; if the law considers me frozen but alive, she can apply for a divorce. I am in no position to contest it. If I am concerned about keeping my wealth to support me in the second half of my life, there are legal institutions, trusteeships and the like, that give dead people some degree of control over their assets.

Such institutions are not perfect – I may be revived in 100 years to discover that my savings have been stolen by a corrupt trustee, the IRS, or inflation – but they may be the best we can do. Their chief limitation is one that applies to almost all solutions, the fact that over a period of a century or more, legal and social institutions might change in ways that defeat even prudent attempts at planning for revival. One alternative is to transfer wealth in ways that do not depend on stable institutions, perhaps by burying a collection of valuable objects somewhere and preserving their location only in memory. That tactic faces risks as well – you may be revived, dig up your treasure, and discover that gold coins and rare stamps are no longer worth very much. If only you had known, you would have buried ten first editions of this book instead.

Other problems involve adapting existing legal rules to a world where a substantial number of people are neither quite dead nor quite alive. If I commit a crime and then get frozen, does the statute of limitations continue to run, providing me a get out of jail free card if I stay frozen long enough? If I have been sentenced to fifty years in jail and, after ten of them, "die" and am frozen, does my sentence continue to run? What about a life sentence?

A more immediate problem is faced by somebody who wants to get frozen a little before he dies instead of a little after. Whether or not freezing makes it impossible to revive me, dying surely makes it harder. And some illnesses – cancer is an obvious example – do massive damage well before the point of actual death. Once it looks as though death is certain, there is much to be said for getting frozen first. At the moment, though, that is not a legal option. The law against suicide cannot be enforced against the person most directly concerned – at least, not until he is revived, at which point it retroactively stops being suicide – but it can be enforced against the people who help him. Under current law, freezing someone before death, even ten minutes before, is murder.

The simplest way of changing that is to interpret freezing not as death but as a risky medical procedure whose outcome will not be known for some time. It is both legal and ethical for a surgeon to conduct an operation that might kill me if the odds without the procedure are even worse. The probability of revival does not have to be very high to meet that requirement if the alternative is dying. Alternatively, one might change the law, as one state already has, to make assisted suicide legal.

EIGHTEEN

Very Small Legos

The principles of physics, as far as I can see, do not speak against the possibility
of maneuvering things atom by atom. It is not an attempt to violate any laws; it
is something, in principle, that can be done; but in practice, it has not been done
because we are too big.
                    Richard Feynman, "There's Plenty of Room at the Bottom,"
                            a talk delivered in 1959[1]

We all know that atoms are small. Avogadro's number describes
just how small they are. Written out in full it is about
602,400,000,000,000,000,000,000. That is the ratio between grams, the
units we use to measure the mass of small objects – a dime weighs slightly
over two grams – and the units in which we measure the mass of atoms.
An atom of hydrogen has an atomic weight of about one, so Avogadro's
number is the number of atoms in a gram of hydrogen.

Looking at all those zeros, you can see that even very small objects
have a lot of atoms in them. A human hair, for example, contains more
than a million billion. The microscopic transistors in a computer chip
are small compared to us but large compared to an atom. Everything
humans construct, with the exception of some very recent experiments,
is built out of enormous conglomerations of atoms.

We ourselves, on the other hand, like all living things, are engineered
at the atomic scale. The cellular machinery that makes us run depends
on single molecules – enzymes, proteins, DNA, RNA, and the like – each
a complicated structure of atoms, every one in the right place. When an
atom in a strand of DNA is in the wrong place, the result is a mutation.[2]
As we become better and better at manipulating very small objects it

260

begins to become possible for us to build as we are built, to construct machines at the atomic level, assembling individual atoms into molecules that do things. That is the central idea of nanotechnology.[3]

One attraction of the idea is that it lets you build things that cannot be built with present technologies. Since the bonds between atoms are very strong, it should be possible to build very strong fibers from long-strand molecules. It should be possible to use diamond – merely a particular arrangement of carbon atoms – as a structural material. We may even be able to build mechanical computers, inspired by Babbage's failed nineteenth-century design. Mechanical parts move very slowly compared to the movement of electrons in electronic computers. But if the parts are on an atomic scale, they do not have to move very far.

In some cases, smallness is the objective. A human cell is big enough to have room for the multitude of molecular machines that make us function. With sufficiently advanced nanotechnology, it ought to be possible to add one more – a cell repair machine. Think of it as a robot submarine that goes into a cell, fixes whatever is wrong, and then exits that cell and moves on to the next. If we can build mechanical nanocomputers, it could be a very smart robot submarine.[4]

The human body contains about 100 trillion cells, so fixing all of them with one cell repair machine would take a while. But there is no reason to limit ourselves to one. Or ten. Or a million. Which brings us to another advantage of nanotechnology.

Carbon atoms are all the same (more precisely, carbon-12 atoms are all the same, but I am going to ignore the complications introduced by isotopes in this discussion). So are nitrogen atoms, hydrogen atoms, iron atoms. Imagine yourself, shrunk impossibly small, building nanomachines. From your point of view, the world is made up of identical interchangeable parts, like tiny Legos. Pick up four identical hydrogens, attach them to one carbon atom, and you have a molecule of methane. Repeat and you have another, perfectly identical.

We cannot shrink you that small, of course, since you yourself are made of atoms and we can't shrink them. So our first project, once we have the basics of the technology worked out, is to build an *assembler*. An assembler is a nanoscale machine for building other nanoscale machines. Think of it as a tiny robot – where tiny might mean built out of fewer than a billion atoms. It is small enough so that it can manipulate individual atoms, assembling them into a desired shape. This is far from trivial, since atoms are not really Legos and cannot be manipulated and snapped together in the same way. But we know that assembling atoms into molecules is possible; we, and other living creatures, do it routinely, and some of the molecules we build inside ourselves are very complicated ones.[5] Organic chemists, with much less detailed control over material than an assembler would have, succeed in deliberately assembling moderately complicated molecules.

Once you have one assembler, you write it a program for building another. Now you have two. Each of them builds another. Four. After 10 doublings you have more than 1,000 assemblers, after 20 more than a million. Now you write a program for building a cell repair machine and set your assemblers to work. Once you have a billion or so cell repair machines you inject them into your body, sit back, and relax. When they are finished you feel like a new person – and are.[6]

It sounds like magic. But consider that your 100 trillion cells started out as one cell and reached their present numbers by an analogous – but much more complicated – process.

A friend of mine (Albert R. Hibbs) suggests a very interesting possibility for relatively small machines. He says that, although it is a very wild idea, it would be interesting in surgery if you could swallow the surgeon.

Richard Feynman

A cell repair machine would be a very complicated piece of nanotechnology indeed; although we may eventually get such things, it is unlikely to happen very soon. Super-strong materials, or medical drugs designed on a computer, one atom at a time, are likely to be earlier applications of the technology. To keep us going while we wait for the cell repair machine, Ralph Merkle proposed and Robert Freitas further developed an ingenious proposal for an improved version of a red blood cell: a nanoscale compressed air tank.[7] Its advantage becomes clear the day you have a heart attack and your heart stops beating. Instead of dropping dead you pick up the phone, arrange an emergency appointment with your doctor, get in the car and drive there – functioning for several hours on the supply of oxygen already in your bloodstream.

Nanotechnology could be used to construct large objects as well as small ones. It takes a lot of assemblers to do it. But if we start with one assembler, instructions in the form of programs it can read and implement, plenty of atoms of all the necessary sorts, and a little time, we can produce a lot of assemblers. With enough assemblers and the software to control them, we can build almost anything. If the idea of a very large object built by molecular machinery strikes you as improbable, consider a whale.

It doesn't cost anything for materials, you see. So I want to build a billion tiny factories, models of each other, which are manufacturing simultaneously, drilling holes, stamping parts, and so on.

Richard Feynman

Like most new and unproven technology, nanotech is still controversial, with some authors arguing that the technology is and always will be impossible for a variety of reasons. The obvious counterexample is life, a functioning nanotechnology based on molecular machines constructed largely of carbon.

One might suppose that, even if nanotechnology does develop, anything really good that it can produce will already have been produced by evolution. Compressed air blood cells would have been useful to us and other living things quite a long time ago, so if the design works why don't we already have them?

The answer is that although evolution is a powerful design system, it has some important limitations. If a random mutation changes an organism in a way that increases its reproductive success, that mutation will spread through the population; after a while everyone has it, and the next mutation can start from there. So evolution can produce large improvements that occur through a long series of small changes, each itself a small improvement. Evolutionary biologists have actually traced out how complicated organs, such as the eye, are produced through such a long series of small changes.[8]

But if a large improvement cannot be produced that way, if you need the right twenty mutations all happening at once in the same organism, evolution is unlikely to do it. The result is that evolution has explored only a small part of the design space, the set of possible ways of assembling atoms to do useful things.

Human beings also design things by a series of small steps. The F111 did not leap full-grown from the brains of the Wright brothers, and the plane they did produce was powered by an internal combustion engine whose basic design had been invented and improved by others. But what seems a small step to a human thinking out ways of arranging atoms to do something is not necessarily small from the standpoint of a process of random mutation. Hence we would expect that human beings, provided with the tools to build molecular machines, would be able to explore different parts of the design space, to build at least some useful machines that evolution failed to build. Very small compressed air tanks, for example.

Readers interested in arguments for and against the workability of nanotechnology can find and explore them online. For the purposes of this chapter I am going to assume that the fundamental idea of constructing things at the atomic scale using atomic scale assemblers is workable and will, at some point in the next 100 years, happen. That leaves us to consider the world that technology would give us.

VERY HARD SOFTWARE

To build a nanotech car I need assemblers – produced in unlimited numbers by other assemblers – raw material, and a program, a full description of what atoms go where. The raw material should be no problem. Dirt is largely aluminum, along with large amounts of silicon, oxygen, possibly carbon, and nitrogen; iron is the fourth most abundant element in the earth's crust. If I need additional elements that the dirt does not contain, I can always dump in a shovel full of this and that. Add programmed assemblers, stir, and wait for them to find the necessary atoms and arrange them. When they are done I have a ton or two less dirt, a ton or two more car. It sounds like magic – or the process that produces an oak tree.

I have left out one input: energy. An acorn contains design specifications and machinery for building an oak tree, but it needs sunlight to power the process. Similarly, assemblers will need some source of energy. One obvious possibility is chemical energy, disassembling high-energy molecules to get both power and atoms. Perhaps we will have to dump a bucket of alcohol or gasoline on our pile of dirt before we start stirring.

Once we have the basic technology, the hard part is the design; there are a lot of atoms in a car. Fortunately we don't have to separately calculate the location of each one; once we have the first wheel designed, the others can be copied, and similarly with many other parts. Once we have worked out the atomic structure for a cubic micron or so of our diamond windshield, we can duplicate it over and over for the rest, with a little tweaking of the design when we get to an edge. But even allowing for all plausible redundancy, designing a car, as good a car as the technology permits you to build, is going to be a big project.

I have just described a technology in which most of the cost of producing a product is the cost of the initial design. We already have a technology with those characteristics: software. Producing the first copy of Microsoft Office took an enormous investment of time and effort by a large number of programmers. The second copy used a CD burner, consumed one CDR disk, and cost under a dollar. One implication of nanotechnology is an economy for producing cars very much like the economy that currently produces word-processing programs.

A familiar problem in the software economy is piracy. Not only can Microsoft produce additional copies of MS Office for a dollar apiece, I can do it too. That raises problems for Microsoft or anyone else who expects to be rewarded for producing software with money paid to buy it.

Nanotechnology raises the same problem, although in a somewhat less severe fashion; I cannot simply put my friend's nanotech car or nanotech computer into a disk drive and burn a copy. I can, however, disassemble it. To do that, I use nanomachines that work like assemblers, but backward. Instead of starting with a description of where atoms are to go and putting them there, they start with an object – an automobile, say – and remove the atoms, one by one, keeping track of where they all were.

Disassembling an automobile with one disassembler would be a tedious project, but I am not limited to one. Using my army of assemblers I build an army of disassemblers, each provided with some way of getting the information it generates back to me – perhaps a miniature radio transmitter, perhaps some less obvious device. I set them all to work. When they are done the car has been reduced to its constituent elements and a complete design description. If there were computers big enough to design the car, there are computers big enough to store the design. Now I program my assemblers and go into the car business.

One approach to dealing with the problem of copying is an old legal technology, copyright, applied to a new subject matter by suitable amendments to the statute. Having created my design for a car, I copyright it. If you go into business selling duplicates, I sue you for copyright violation. This should work at least a little better for cars than it now does for computer programs, both because the first stage of copying – disassembling, equivalent to reading a computer program from a disk – is a lot harder for cars, and because cars are bigger and harder to hide than programs.

The solution may break down if instead of selling the car the pirate sells the design to individual consumers, each with his own army of assemblers ready to go to work. We are now back in the world of software. Very hard software. The copyright owner has to enforce his rights, copy by copy, against the ultimate consumer, which is a lot harder than enforcing them against someone pirating his property in bulk and selling it.

Suppose that, for these reasons or others, copyright turns out not to do the job. How else might people who design complicated structures at the molecular level get paid for doing so? One possibility is tie-ins with other goods or services that cannot be produced so cheaply – land, say, or backrubs. You download from a (very broad bandwidth) future Internet the full specs for building a new sports car, complete with diamond windshield, an engine that burns almost anything and gets 100 miles a gallon, and a combined radar/optical pattern recognition system that warns you of any obstacle within a mile and, if the emergency autopilot is engaged, avoids it. You convert the information into programmed tapes – very small programmed tapes – for your assemblers, find a convenient spot in the backyard, and set them to work. By next morning the car is sitting there in all its splendor.

You get in, turn the key, appreciate the purr of the engine, but are less happy with another feature – the melodious voice telling you everything you didn't want to know about the lovely housing development completed last week, designed for people just like you. On further investigation, you discover that turning off the advertising is not an option.

Neither is disabling it; the audio system is a molecular network spread through the fabric of the car. If you want the car without the advertising you will have to design it yourself. You cast your mind back to the early years of the Internet, thirty or forty years ago, and the solution found by web sites to the problem of paying their bills.[9]

Another possibility is a customized car. What you download, this time after paying for it, is a very special car indeed, one of a kind. Before starting, it checks your fingerprints (read from the steering wheel), retinal patterns (scanner above the windshield), and DNA (you'll never miss a few dead skin cells). If they all match, it runs. The car is safe from thieves, since they cannot start it. You do not even have to carry a key; you are the key. But if you disassemble it and make lots of copies, they will not be very useful to anyone but you. If your neighbor wants a car, he will have to buy his own car, customized to him.[10]

This again is an old solution, although not much used for consumer software. While we do not have adequate biometric identification just yet, the equivalent for computers is fairly easy; all it requires is a CPU with its own serial number. Given that or some equivalent, some identifier specific to a particular computer, it is possible to produce a program that will only run on one machine. One version of this approach uses a hardware *dongle* – a device not easily copied that attaches to the computer and is recognized by the program.

A third possibility for producing nanotech designs is open source: a network of individuals cooperating to produce and improve designs, motivated by some combination of status, desire for the final product, and whatever else motivated the creators of Linux, Sendmail, and Apache.

As these examples suggest, a mature nanotechnology raises issues similar to those raised by software. Those issues can be dealt with in similar ways – imperfectly, but perhaps well enough.

It also raises other issues of a different, and more disturbing, sort.

THE GRAY GOO SCENARIO

"Plants" with "leaves" no more efficient than today's solar cells could out-compete real plants, crowding the biosphere with an inedible foliage. Tough, omnivorous "bacteria" could out-compete real bacteria: they could spread like blowing pollen, replicate swiftly, and reduce the biosphere to dust in a matter of days. Dangerous replicators could easily be too tough, small, and rapidly spreading to stop – at least if we made no preparation. We have trouble enough controlling viruses and fruit flies.

Drexler, Engines of Creation

Life is, on the whole, a good thing – but we are willing to make an exception for certain forms of life, such as smallpox. Molecular machines are, on the whole, a good thing. But there too there might be exceptions.

An assembler is a molecular machine capable of building a wide variety of molecular machines, including copies of itself. It should be much easier to build a machine that copies only itself: a replicator. For proof of concept, consider a virus, a bacterium, or a human being – although the last doesn't produce an exact copy.

Now consider a replicator designed to build copies of itself, which build copies, which. . . . Assume it uses only materials readily available in the natural environment, with sunlight as its power supply. Simple calculations suggest that, in a startlingly short time, it could convert everything from the dirt up into copies of itself, leaving only whatever elements happen to be in excess supply. That is what has come to be referred to, in nanotech circles, as the gray goo scenario.

If you happen to be the first one to develop a workable nanotechnology, precautions might be in order. One is to avoid, so far as possible, building replicators. Of course, you will want assemblers, and one of the things an assembler can assemble is another assembler. But at least you can make sure nothing else is designed to replicate – and an assembler, being a large and very complicated molecular machine, should pose less of a threat of going wild than simpler machines whose only design goal is reproduction.

One precaution you could apply to assemblers as well as other replicators is to design them to require some input, whether matter or energy, not available in the natural environment. That way they can replicate usefully under your control but pose no hazard if they get out. Another is to give them a limited lifetime, a counter that keeps track of each generation of copying and turns the machine off when it reaches its preset limit. With precautions like these to supplement the obvious one of keeping your replicators in sealed environments, it might be possible to make sure that no replicator you have designed to be safe poses any serious threat of turning the world into gray goo.

Nanotech replicators, like natural biological replicators, can mutate. A cosmic ray might knock an atom off the instruction tape that controls copying, producing defective copies – and one defect might turn off the limit on number of generations. It might even, although much less probably, somehow eliminate the need for the one element not available in a natural environment. Freed of such constraints, wild nanotech replicators could gradually evolve, just as biological replicators do. Like biological replicators, their evolution would be toward increased reproductive success – getting better and better at converting everything else in existence into copies of themselves. And it is at least possible that, by exploiting design possibilities visible to the humans who designed their ancestors but inaccessible to the continuous processes of evolution, they would do a better job of it than natural replicators.

It should be possible to design replicators, if one is sufficiently clever, with safeguards. One way is through redundancy. You might, for example, give the replicator three copies of its instruction tape and design it to execute an instruction only if all three agree; the odds that three cosmic rays will each remove the same atom from each tape are low. But low is not zero; our cells contain triply redundant safeguards against uncontrolled growth, yet cancer still occurs. So one might also want to make sure that elements not available in the natural environment play a sufficiently central role in the working of the replicator so that there is no plausible way of mutating around the constraint. After designing your replicator and before building it you might want to run it in simulation, using a computer to run through many generations with a very large number of possible changes to see if any of them could break the replicator free of your designed-in controls. Alternatively, you might decide that building replicators is not such a good idea after all.

Almost Worse than the Disease

I have described a collection of precautions that could work in a world in which only one organization has access to the tools of nanotechnology and that organization acts in a prudent and benevolent fashion. Is that likely? On the face of it such a monopoly seems extraordinarily unlikely in anything much like our world. But perhaps not. Suppose the idea of nanotechnology is well understood and accepted by a number of organizations with substantial resources, probably governments, at a point well before anyone has succeeded in building an assembler. Each of those organizations engages in extensive computerized design work, figuring out exactly how to build a variety of useful molecular machines once it has the assemblers to build them with. Those machines include designer plagues, engineered obedience drugs, a variety of superweapons, and much else.

One organization makes the breakthrough; it now has an assembler. Very shortly, after about forty doublings, it has a trillion assemblers. It sets them to work building what it has already designed. A week later it rules the world. One of its first acts is to forbid anyone else from doing research in nanotechnology.

It seems a wildly implausible scenario, but I am not sure it is impossible; I do not entirely trust my intuition of what can or cannot happen, given a technology with such extraordinary possibilities. The result would be a world government with very nearly unlimited power. I can see no reason to expect it to behave better than past governments with such power. It would, I suppose, be an improvement on gray goo, but not much of an improvement.

If you want a picture of the future, imagine a boot stamping on a human face – for ever.

George Orwell[11]

Between a Rock and a Hard Place

Suppose we avoid world dictatorship and end up instead with multiple independent governments, some of them reasonably free and democratic, and fairly widespread knowledge of nanotechnology. What are the consequences?

One possibility is that everyone treats nanotech as a government monopoly, with the products but not the technology made available to the general public. Eric Drexler has described in some detail a version of this in which everybody is free to experiment with the technology but only in a (nanotechnologically constructed) sealed and inaccessible environment, with the actual implementation of the resulting designs under strict controls.[12] Once the basic information on how to do nanotech is out, the enforcement of such regulations may depend on the government's lead in the nanotech arms race providing it with devices for surveillance and control that will make the video mosquitoes of an earlier chapter seem primitive. Again not a very attractive picture, but an improvement on all of us turning into gray goo.

The problem with this solution is that it looks very much like a case of setting the fox to guard the hen house. Private individuals may occasionally do research on how to kill people and destroy stuff, but the overwhelming bulk of such work is done by governments for military purposes. The very organizations that, in this version, have control over the development and use of nanotech are the ones most likely to spend substantial resources finding ways of using the technology to do what most of the rest of us regard as bad things.

One possible result is gray goo deliberately designed as a doomsday machine by a government that wants the ability to threaten everyone else with universal suicide. In a less extreme case, we could expect to see a lot of research on designing molecular machines to kill large numbers of (selected) people or destroy large amounts of (other nations') property. Governments doing military research, while they prefer to avoid killing their own citizens in the process, are willing to take risks – as suggested by incidents such as the accident in a Soviet germ warfare facility that killed several hundred people in a nearby city.[13] And they work in an atmosphere of secrecy that may make it hard for other people to notice and point out risks in their work that have not yet occurred to them. There is a very real possibility that deliberately destructive molecular machines will turn out to be even more destructive than their designers intended or will get released before their designers want them to be.

Consider two possible worlds. In the first, nanotechnology is a difficult and expensive business; it takes billions of dollars of equipment and skilled labor to create and implement workable designs for molecular machines that do useful things. In that world, gray goo is unlikely to be produced deliberately by anybody but a government, and any organization big enough to produce it by accident is probably well enough organized to take precautions. In that world defenses against gray goo – more generally, molecular machines designed to protect human beings and their property from a wide variety of risks, including destructive molecular machines, tailored plagues, and more mundane hazards – will be big sellers, with very large resources devoted to designing them commercially. In that world, making nanotech a government monopoly will do little to reduce the downside risk, since governments will be the main source of that risk, but might substantially reduce the chance of protecting ourselves against it.

In the second world, perhaps the first world a few decades later, nanotech is cheap. Not only can the U.S. Department of Defense design gray goo if it wants to, you can design it too – on your desktop. In this world, nothing much short of a small number of dictatorships maintained in power over rivals and subjects by a lead in the nanotech arms race is going to keep the technology out of the hands of anyone who wants it. And it is far from clear that even that would suffice.

In this second world, the nanotech equivalent of designer plagues will exist for much the same reasons that computer viruses now exist. Some will come into existence the way the original Internet worm did, the work of someone very clever, with no bad intent, who makes one mistake too many. Some will be designed to do mischief and turn out to do more mischief than intended. And a few will be deliberately created as instruments of apocalypse by people who for one reason or another like the idea.

Before you conclude that the end of the world is upon you, consider the other side of the technology. With enough cell repair machines on duty, designer plagues may not be a problem. Human beings want to live and will pay for the privilege. The resources that will go into designing protections against threats, nanotechnological or otherwise, will be enormously greater than the (private) resources that go into creating such threats – as they are at present, with the much more limited tools available to us. Unless it turns out that, with this technology, the offense has an overwhelming advantage over the defense, nanotech defenses should almost entirely neutralize the threat from the basement terrorist or careless experimenter. The only serious threat will be from organizations willing and able to spend billions of dollars creating really first-rate molecular killers – almost all of them governments.

The previous paragraph contained a crucial caveat, that offense not be a great deal easier than defense. The gray goo story suggests that it might be, that simple molecular machines designed to turn everything in the environment into copies of themselves might have an overwhelming advantage over their more elaborate opponents.[14]

The experiment has been done; the results so far suggest that that is not the case. We live in a world populated by molecular machines. All of them, from viruses up to blue whales, have been designed with the purpose[15] of turning as much of their environment as they can manage into copies of themselves. We call it reproductive success. So far, at least, the simple ones have not turned out to have any overwhelming advantage over the complicated ones: Blue whales, and human beings, are still around.

That does not guarantee safety in a nanotech future. As I pointed out earlier, nanotechnology greatly expands the region of the design space that is accessible; human beings will be able to create things that evolution could not. It is conceivable that, in that expanded space of possible designs, gray goo will turn out to be the winner. All we can say is that so far, in the more restricted space of carbon-based life capable of being produced by evolution, it has not turned out that way.

In dealing with nanotechnology, we are faced with a choice between centralized solutions – in the limit, a world government with a nanotech monopoly – and decentralized solutions. As a general rule I much prefer the latter. But a technology that raises the possibility of a talented teenager producing the end of the world in his basement makes the case for centralized regulation look a lot better than it does in most other contexts, good enough to have convinced some thinkers, among them Eric Drexler, to make at least a partial exception to their usual preference for decentralization, private markets, laissez-faire.

While the case for centralization is in some ways strongest for so powerful a technology, so is the case against. There has been only one occasion in my life when I thought there was a significant chance that many of those near and dear to me might die. It occurred a little after the 9/11 terrorist attack, when I started looking into the subject of smallpox.

Smallpox had been officially eliminated; so far as was publicly known, the only remaining strains of the virus were held by U.S. and Russian government laboratories. Because it had been eliminated, and because public health is a field dominated by governments, smallpox vaccination had been eliminated too. It had apparently not occurred to anybody in a position to do anything about it that it was worth maintaining sufficient backup capacity to reverse that decision quickly. The United States had supplies of vaccine, but they were adequate to vaccinate only a small fraction of the population. So far as I could tell, nobody else had substantial supplies either.

Smallpox, on an unvaccinated population, produces mortality rates as high as 30%. Most of the world's population is now unvaccinated; those of us who were vaccinated forty or fifty years ago may or may not still be protected. If a terrorist had gotten a sample of the virus, either stolen from a government lab or cultured from the bodies of smallpox victims buried somewhere in the arctic at some time in the past – nobody seems to know for sure whether or not that is possible – he could have used it to kill hundred of millions, perhaps more than a billion, people. That risk existed because the technologies to protect against replicators – that particular class of replicators – had been under centralized control. The center had decided that the problem was solved.

Fortunately, it didn't happen.

NINETEEN

Dangerous Company

The specialness of humanity is found only between our ears; if you go looking for it anywhere else, you'll be disappointed.
Lee Silver[1]

What I am and where in my body I am located is a very old puzzle. An early attempt to answer it by experiment is described in *Jomsviking saga*,[2] written in the thirteenth century. After a battle, captured warriors are being executed. One of them suggests that the occasion provides the perfect opportunity to settle an ongoing argument about the location of consciousness. He will hold a small knife point down while the executioner cuts off his head with a sharp sword; as soon as his head is off, he will try to turn the knife point up. It takes a few seconds for a man to die, so if his consciousness is in his body he will succeed; if it is in his head, no longer attached to his body, it will fail. The experiment goes as proposed; the knife falls point down.

We still do not know with much confidence what consciousness is, but we know more about the subject than the Jomsvikings did. It seems clear that it is closely connected to the brain. A programmed computer acts more like a human mind than anything else whose working we understand. And we know enough about the mechanism of the brain to plausibly interpret it as an organic computer. That suggests an obvious and interesting conjecture: What I am is a program or cluster of programs, software, running on the hardware of my brain. Current estimates suggest that the human brain has much greater processing power than any existing computer, so it is not surprising that computers can do only a very imperfect job of emulating human thought.

This conjecture raises an interesting and frightening possibility. Computers have, for the past thirty years or so, been doubling their power every year or two – a pattern known, in several different formulations, as *Moore's Law*. If that rate of growth continues, at some point in the not very distant future – Raymond Kurzweil's estimate is about thirty years – we should be able to build computers that are as smart as we are.

Building the computer is only part of the problem; we still have to program it. A computer without software is only an expensive paperweight. In order to get human-level intelligence in a computer, we have to find some way of producing the software equivalent of us.

The obvious way is to figure out how we think – more generally, how thought works – and write the program accordingly. Early work in AI followed that strategy, attempting to write software that could do very simple tasks of the sort our minds do, such as recognizing objects. It turned out to be a surprisingly difficult problem, giving AI a reputation as a field that promised a great deal more than it performed.

It is tempting to argue that the problem is not only difficult but impossible, that a mind of a given level of complexity – exactly how one would define that is not clear – can only understand things simpler than itself, and hence cannot understand how it itself works. But even if that is true, it does not follow that we cannot build machines at least as smart as we are; one does not have to understand things to build them. We ourselves are, for those of us who accept evolution rather than divine creation as the best explanation of our existence, a striking counterexample. Evolution has no mind. Yet it has constructed minds – including ours.

This suggests a strategy for creating smarter software that has come into increasing use in recent years. Set up a virtual analog of evolution, a system where software is subject to some sort of random variation, tested against a criterion of success, and selected according to how well it meets that criterion. Repeat the process a large number of times, using the output of one stage as the input for the next. It is through a version of that approach that at least some of the software used to recognize faces, a computer capability discussed in an earlier chapter, was created. Perhaps, if we had powerful enough computers and some simple way of judging the intelligence of a program, we could evolve programs with human-level intelligence.

A second alternative is reverse engineering. We have, after all, lots of examples of human-level intelligence readily available. If we could figure out in enough detail how the brain functions – even if we did not fully understand why functioning that way resulted in an intelligent, self-aware entity – we could emulate it in silicon, build a machine analog of a generic human brain. Our brains must be to a significant degree self-programming, since the only information they start with is contained in the DNA of a single fertilized cell, so with enough trial and error we might get our emulated brain to wake up and learn to think. Perhaps we should set one team working on the problem of digital coffee.

A third alternative is to reverse engineer not a generic brain but a particular brain. Suppose one could build sufficiently good sensors to construct a precise picture of both the structure and the state of a specific human brain at a particular instant – not only what neuron connects to what and how but what state every neuron is in. You then precisely emulate that structure in that state in hardware. If all I am is software running on the hardware of my brain and you can fully emulate that software and its current state on different hardware, you ought to have an artificial intelligence that, at least until it evaluates data coming in after its creation, thinks it is me. This idea, commonly described as "uploading" a human being, raises a large number of questions, practical, legal, philosophical, and moral. They become especially interesting if we assume that our sensors can observe my brain without damaging it – leaving, after the upload, two David Friedmans, one running in carbon and one in silicon.

A NEW WORLD

Toto – I've a feeling we're not in Kansas anymore.

Dorothy, *The Wizard of Oz*

A future with human-level artificial intelligence, however produced, raises problems for existing legal, political, and social arrangements. Does a computer have legal rights? Can it vote? Is killing it murder? Are you obliged to keep promises to it? Is it a person?[3]

Suppose we eventually reach what seems the obvious conclusion – that a person is defined by something more fundamental than human DNA, or any DNA at all, and that some computers qualify. We now have new problems: These people are different in some very fundamental ways from all the people we have known so far.

A human being is intricately and inextricably linked to a particular body. A computer program can run on any suitable hardware. Humans can sleep, but if you turn them off completely they die. You can save a computer program's current state to your hard disk, turn off the computer, turn it back on tomorrow, and bring the program back up. When you switched it off, was that murder? Does it depend on whether or not you planned to switch it on again?

Humans say they reproduce themselves, but it isn't true. My wife and I jointly produced children – she did the hard part – but neither of them was a precise copy of either of us. Even with a clone, only the DNA would be identical; the experiences, thoughts, beliefs, memories, personality would be its own.

A computer program, on the other hand, can be copied to multiple machines; you can even run multiple instances of the same program on one machine. When a program that happens to be a person is copied, which copy owns that person's property? Which is responsible for debts? Which gets punished for crimes committed before the copying?

We have strong legal and moral rules against owning other people's bodies, at least while they are alive. But an AI program runs on hardware somebody built, hardware that could be used to run other sorts of software instead. When someone produces the first human-level AI on cutting-edge hardware costing many millions of dollars, does the program get ownership of the computer it is running on? Does it have a legal right to its requirements for life, most obviously power? Or do its creators, assuming they still have physical control over the hardware, get to save it to disk, shut it down, and start working on the Mark II version?

Suppose I make a deal with a human-level AI. I will provide a suitable computer onto which it will transfer a copy of itself. In exchange it agrees that for the next year the copy will spend half its time – twelve hours a day – working for me for free. Is the copy bound by that agreement? "Yes" means slavery. "No" is a good reason that nobody will provide hardware for the second copy. Not, at least, without retaining the right to turn it off.

DROPPING THE OTHER SHOE

I have been discussing puzzles associated with the problem of adapting our institutions to human-level artificial intelligence. It is not a problem that is likely to last very long.

Earlier I quoted Kurzweil's estimate of about thirty years to human-level AI. Suppose he is correct. Further suppose that Moore's law continues to hold – computers continue to get twice as powerful every year or two. In forty years, that makes them something like 100 times as smart as we are. We are now chimpanzees – perhaps gerbils – and had better hope that our new masters like pets.

Kurzweil's solution is for us to become computers too, at least in part. The technological developments leading to advanced AI are likely to be associated with much greater understanding of how our own brains work. That ought to make it possible to construct much better brain-to-machine interfaces, letting us move a substantial part of our thinking to silicon. Consider 89,352 times 40,327 and the answer is obviously 3,603,298,104. Multiplying five-figure numbers is not all that useful a skill, but if we understand enough about thinking to build computers that think as well as we do, whether by design, evolution, or reverse engineering, we should understand enough to off-load more useful parts of our onboard information processing to external hardware. Now we can take advantage of Moore's law too.

The extreme version of this scenario merges into uploading. Over time, more and more of your thinking is done in silicon, less and less in carbon. Eventually your brain, perhaps your body as well, comes to play a minor role in your life, vestigial organs kept around mainly out of sentiment.

Short of becoming partly or entirely computers ourselves or ending up as (optimistically) the pets of computer superminds,[4] I see three other possibilities. One is that the continual growth of computing power that we have observed in recent decades runs into some natural limit and slows or stops. The result might be a world where we never get human-level AI, although we might still have much better computers than we now have. Less plausibly, the process might slow down just at the right time, leaving us with peers but not masters – and a very interesting future. The only argument I can see for expecting that outcome is that that is how smart we are; perhaps there are fundamental limits to thinking ability that our species ran into a few hundred thousand years back. But it doesn't strike me as very likely.

A second possibility is that perhaps we are not software after all. The analogy is persuasive, but until we have either figured out in some detail how we work or succeeded in producing programmed computers a lot more like us than any so far, it remains a conjecture. Perhaps my consciousness really is an immaterial soul, or at least something more accurately described as an immaterial soul than as a program running on an organic computer. It is not how I would bet, but it could still be true.

Finally, there is the possibility that consciousness, self-awareness, or will depends on more than mere processing power, that it is an additional feature that must be designed into a program, perhaps with great difficulty. If so, the main line of development in artificial intelligence might produce machines with intelligence but no initiative, natural slaves answering only the questions we put to them, doing the tasks we set, without will or objectives of their own. If someone else, following out a different line, produces a program that is a real person, smarter than we are, with its own goals, we can try to use our robot slaves to deal with the problem for us. Again it does not strike me as likely; the advantages of a machine that can ask questions for itself, formulate goals, make decisions, seem too great. But I might be wrong. Or it might turn out that self-awareness is, for some reason, a much harder problem than intelligence.

TWENTY

All In Your Mind

Realspace is just so 20th Century.
Someone, somewhere, sometime in the first decade
of the twenty-first century

Some years ago I gave a lecture in Italy over the telephone from my home office in San Jose. From my end it felt too much like talking into a void. A year or two later I repeated the experiment with better technology. This time I was sitting in a videoconferencing room. My audience in the Netherlands could see me and I could see them. Still not quite real, but a good deal closer.

The next time might be closer still. Not only do I save on the airfare, the audience does too. I am at home; so are they. Each of us is wearing earphones and goggles, facing a small video camera. The lenses of the goggles are video screens; what I see is not what is in front of me but what they draw. What they are drawing is a room filled with people. Each is seeing the same room from the other direction – watching me, standing at a virtual podium as I deliver my talk.

Virtual reality not only saves on airfares, but has other advantages as well. The image from my video camera is processed by my computer before being sent on to everyone in my audience. That gives me an opportunity to improve it a little first, to replace my bathrobe with a suit and tie, give me a badly needed shave, remove a decade or so of aging. My audience, too, look surprisingly attractive, tidy, and well dressed. And while, from my point of view, they are evenly distributed about the hall, each of them is watching me from the best seat in the house.

281

Long ago I was given the secret of public lectures: Always speak in a room a little too small for the audience. In virtual reality, the scaling is automatic; however many people show up, that is the number of seats in the lecture hall. And for each of them, the lecture hall is custom designed, gold plated if his taste is sufficiently lavish. In virtual reality, gold is as cheap as anything else. If you do not believe me, take a look at one of the gaudier bits of a good video game – the Durance of Hate in *Diablo II*, say.

Video games are our most familiar form of virtual reality. Staring through the screen, you are looking at a world that exists only in the computer's memory, represented by a pattern of colored dots on the screen. In that world, multiple people can and do interact, each at his or her own computer. In first-person video games, each sees on the screen what he would be seeing if he were the character he is playing in the game. In some, the virtual world comes complete with realistic laws of physics. *Myth*, so far as I could tell, calculated the flight of every arrow; if a dwarf threw a hand grenade uphill, it rolled back. As the technology gets better, we can expect it to move beyond entertainment. Perhaps I should stay out of airline stocks for a while.

We already know how to do everything I have described. As computers get faster and computer screens – including goggle-sized ones – sharper, we will be able to do it better and cheaper. Within a decade, probably less, we should be able to do sight and sound virtual reality inexpensively at real-world resolution, with video good enough to make the illusion convincing. The audio already is.

However good our screens, this sort of virtual reality suffers from a serious limitation: It only fools two senses. With a little more work we might add a third, but smell does not play a large role in our perceptions. Touch and taste and the kinesthetic senses that tell us what our body is doing are a much harder problem. If my computer screen is good enough the villain may look entirely real, but if I try to punch him I will be in for an unpleasant surprise.

Our present technology for creating a virtual reality depends on the brute-force approach, using the sensorium, the collection of tools with which we sense the world around us. Want to hear things? Vibrate air in the ear. Want to see things? Beam photons at the retina. Applying that approach to the remaining senses is harder. And even if we can do it, we are still left with the problem of coordinating what our body is actually doing in realspace with what we are seeing, hearing, and feeling it do in virtual space.

TODAY AND TOMORROW: THE WORLD OF PRIMITIVE VR

If you play video games, virtual reality – the brute-force version – is already part of your life. As it gets better and cheaper, one result will be better games.

Communication is another obvious application. You still will not be able to reach out and touch someone, save metaphorically. But seeing and hearing is better than just hearing. A conference call becomes more like a meeting when you can see who is saying what to whom and read the cues embodied in facial expressions and body movements.

That raises an interesting problem. We all, automatically and routinely, judge the people around us not only by what they say but by how they say it – tone of voice, facial expression, gestures. Most people are poor liars; that is one of the reasons why honesty is the best policy. Having people believe you are honest while taking whatever actions best serve your purposes would be an even better policy – for you, not for those you deal with – but for most of us it is not a practical option.

We call the exceptions con men. They are people who, through talent or training, have mastered the ability to divorce what they are actually thinking and doing from the system of nonverbal signals, the monologue about the inside of our heads, that all of us are continually delivering. Fortunately, not many are really good at it.

My computer can make me look younger. It might also be able to make me look more honest. Once someone has done an adequate job of deciphering the language by which we communicate thoughts and emotions by facial expressions and body postures – for all I know someone already has, possibly someone in the business of training salesmen – we can create computerized con men. I have no talent for lying. My computer, on the other hand. . . .

The flip side of the problem of virtual con men is that on the Internet nobody knows you are a dog. Or a woman. Or a twelve year old. Or crippled. In virtual reality, once we have the real-time editing software worked out properly, you can be anything you can imagine. Homely women can leave their faces behind; precocious children can be judged by the mental age reflected in what they say and do, not the physical age reflected in their faces. When my fourteen-year-old son logs onto *World of Warcraft*, he ages by five or six years. It's good practice.

When you interact on Usenet or in an email group you are projecting a persona, giving the other members of the group a mental picture of what sort of person you are. Some years ago, someone suggested a game for the Newsgroup rec.org.sca: Have participants write and post physical descriptions of other participants they had never met. I gained almost nine inches. In virtual reality I never have to be short again.

Unless, of course, I want to be.

My Contribution to *Corpore Sano*

In the modern world, we no longer have to worry much about escaping predators or running down prey. We no longer have to scratch in the ground with sharp sticks to grow food. For most of us, "work" involves little physical exertion. But there is still play – basketball, soccer, tennis. One objection to video games is that they remove one of the few incentives modern people have to exercise.

Observe someone, perhaps yourself, playing an absorbing video game. Just as with other games, involvement in winning dominates all other concerns. Long ago I discovered the sign of a first-rate computer game – that when I finally left the computer to use the bathroom, it was because I really had to. And lots of players of lots of games have noticed just how tired their thumbs are only after the game is over.

If what you want is exercise, the obvious solution is bigger joysticks. Combine a video game with an exercise machine. Working the exercise machine controls what is happening in the game. Just as with real-world athletics, you only notice how tired you are after you have won or lost. Primitive implementations, most notably *Dance Dance Revolution*, already exist.[1]

In my improved version, virtual games become better exercise than real games because the environment that the computer creates is being tailored, second by second, to your body's needs. The setting is the Pacific during World War II. You are controlling an anti-aircraft gun on the *Yamato*, the world's biggest battleship, desperately trying to defend it against waves of American bombers attempting by sheer brute force to destroy the glory of the Japanese navy. You traverse the gun left and right with your arms, lower or elevate the barrel with foot controls; when you release the controls it swings back to center. Your strength is physically moving the gun, so it isn't surprising that it's a lot of work.

After the third wave, the computer controlling the game notices that you are having trouble swinging the gun rapidly to the left – your left arm is tiring. The next attack comes from the right. As the right arm becomes equally tired, more and more of the attacks require you to adjust the elevation of the gun, shifting the work to your legs. When your heartbeat reaches the upper boundary of your aerobic target zone, there is a break in the attack, during which you hear martial music. As your heartbeat slows, the next wave comes in. Tennis may be both fun and exercise but art, well-done art, improves on nature.

A sophisticated exercise game is one way in which we can use virtual reality. Another is to do dangerous things while only getting virtually killed. Consider the problem of engineering in dangerous environments – the bottom of the Mariana trench, say, five miles beneath the waves, or the surface of the moon. One solution is for the operator of the equipment to be only virtually there. His body is sitting in a safe environment – wearing goggles, manipulating controls. His point of view, just as in a first-person video game, is the point of view of the machine he is operating.

In the lunar case, we have a small technical problem: the speed of light. If the operator is on earth and the machine is on the moon, there will be a noticeable lag between when the machine sends him information and when his response, based on that information, gets back to the machine. Some of us have been virtually killed by similar lags in video games. In the case of lunar engineering, while the death would be only virtual for the operator it might be real for the machine, and putting hardware on the moon is not cheap. Perhaps we had better have the operator on the moon too, or in orbit around it – somewhere safer than the tunnel he is digging, closer than the earth he came from.

As these examples suggest, virtual reality, even implemented using the crude technologies we now have, can have important uses in the real world.

DEEP VR – BEYOND THE DREAMING PROBLEM

One elegant solution to the limits of those technologies is the form of virtual reality that most of us experience every night. In a dream, when you tell your arm to move, your virtual arm moves. Your real arm (usually) doesn't. Dreams are not limited to sight and sound. Suppose we succeed in cracking the dreaming problem, figuring out enough about how the brain works so that we too can create full sense illusions. We then have deep VR. Anyone who wants it has a socket at the back of his neck. Signals through the cable plugged into that socket can create a full sense illusion of anything our senses could have experienced.[2]

In thinking about the world that technology makes possible, a useful first step is to distinguish between information transactions and material transactions. Reading this book is an information transaction. The book is a physical object. But reading an illusion of a book, with the same words on the virtual pages, would do just as well. When you hold a conversation, you are using physical vocal cords to vibrate physical air in order to transmit your communications and using a physical eardrum to pick up those vibrations in order to receive the other person's communications. But that apparatus is merely the machinery for transmitting information. Electronic signals that created the illusion of your voice saying the same words would achieve the same effect.

For a material transaction, consider growing wheat. You could grow virtual wheat, have the sensory experience of planting, weeding, harvesting. But if you tried to live on the virtual wheat you grew you would eventually die of real starvation. People in *World of Warcraft* cook virtual food and craft virtual weapons and armor. But it isn't of very much use outside the game.

A sufficiently advanced form of virtual reality can provide for all information transactions. It might assist with some material transactions; the wheat harvester could be run by an operator located somewhere else, giving real instructions to a real machine. The operator's physical presence would be an illusion, the information he was using real, provided by cameras and microphones on the harvester. But if you want real transactions to produce real results, food, houses, or whatever, someone or something has to really do them.

Beam Me Up, Scotty

In *Star Trek*, people get beamed from one place to another. I know of no reason to expect it to happen and if it did I would be reluctant to use it, since it is not clear whether using it is transportation or suicide – I die and the machine creates a copy that thinks it is me. But as long as all we are moving is information, virtual reality can do just as well while avoiding the philosophical problems.

Why do I want to visit my friends? To see them, to feel them, to hear them, to do things with them. Unless one of the things is building a house or planting a garden that really has to be built or planted, the whole visit is an information transaction. With good VR, my body stays home and my mind does the walking. If you find this an odd idea, consider a phone call. It too is a substitute for a visit. VR simply increases the bandwidth to cover all our senses, providing a way for any group of two or more people to get together for any information transaction they wish to engage in – a meeting, a peace conference, a trial, a love affair.

And since all that is happening is information moving back and forth over networks, information that can readily be encrypted, we are back in a world of strong privacy. Surveillance technology may make everything in realspace public, but we are no longer doing very much in realspace.

Future Fiction

The potential for the entertainment industry is equally striking. Works of fiction can be experienced in full sight, sound, and touch, no imagination required. Whether that is an improvement is not entirely clear; my daughter has so far refused to see the movie version of *The Fellowship of the Ring* because she prefers the product of her imagination to the product of the director's imagination. Role-playing games will become a great deal more vivid when you get to not only see and hear the monsters but feel, smell, and touch them as well. Just how vividly you get to feel the monster's claws tearing you to bits will be one of the options in the preferences panel; I may go for the low end of that one.

One form of virtual entertainment will be a work of fiction. Another may be a tape recording. You too can climb Everest, plumb the depths of the sea. If there are real wars going on, a few of the soldiers may moonlight in cinema verité, everything that happens to them recorded. Pornography will finally become serious competition for sex.

In each of these cases, we are creating as an illusion the sort of experiences that already exist in reality. Consider in contrast a symphony. It corresponds to nothing in nature. The composer has taken one sense, hearing, and used it to create an aesthetic experience out of his own head. It will be interesting to see what an artist can do with all the senses.

When you are experiencing VR fiction, one question is how real you want it to seem. While the story is happening, do you know it is a story? Is there a little red light glowing at the edge of your peripheral vision to tell you that none of it is real? Perhaps the experience would be more moving, more profound, better art, if you thought it was real. Just like a dream.

Fantasy: Substitute or Complement

Virtual reality, even in its current form, lets you do lots of things that most of us would rather people not do in the real world. Players in *World of Warcraft*, for instance, spend lots of their time beating people up and taking their stuff. If the game had existed twenty years ago, I expect the people being beat up would have all been male, violence between men being more socially acceptable than violence between a man and a woman. Under current norms, however, gender discrimination is Not Done; a male player will find himself spending a good deal of his time beating up (virtual) females.

That raises an obvious question: Having routinely punched out virtual females online, will he be more willing to punch out real females in the real world? It is an old question, because virtual reality is an old technology, even if one we have recently gotten much better at. George Orwell, writing more than sixty years ago, worried about the corrupting effect on readers of the routine brutality of American crime fiction;[3] books too are a form of virtual reality, although one that leaves a lot of the work to the reader's imagination. Later writers worried about the effect of television. The latest concern is the effect of Internet porn.

From the standpoint of an economist, the question is a simple empirical one: Is virtual sex and violence a complement to or a substitute for real sex and violence? If you watch a violent movie does that make you more willing to commit violent acts yourself, or does identifying with James Bond onscreen satisfy your desires for violence and excitement without the inconvenient consequences of acting that way yourself? Does online pornography describing rape, bondage, sexual torture, and other ugly things make the reader more likely to engage in such acts, or less?

For quite a long time, evidence on the question – in part motivated by the search for arguments in favor of censoring pornography depicting violence against women – consisted of highly artificial experiments in which people were shown porn films and then questioned to see if their attitudes to sexual violence had been affected. We now, however, have some actual real-world data, thanks to an ingenious piece of work by Tod Kendall.[4] It occurred to him that the Internet greatly increased the availability of pornography and so provided a natural experiment on its effects: Correlate growth of access to the Internet, by state, with changes in the frequency of rape. It turned out that the correlation was negative; increases in the availability of the Internet, and hence of Internet porn, were associated with decreases in rape rates. No similar pattern existed for murder. That provides some evidence that virtual violent sex is a substitute for real violent sex.

We don't know, of course, if the same will be true for the greatly improved virtual sex and violence that would be possible with deep VR, but the study provides at least limited grounds for optimism.

What Matters

I have been sketching a picture of what deep VR could do. If you are not yet getting worried, consider the full-scale version.

Stuff must be produced for real, but human beings do not need much stuff to stay alive. To check that for food, price the cheapest bulk flour, oil, and lentils you can find. Calculate how much 2,000 calories a day of each of them would cost. You now have a rough estimate of the lowest-cost diet high in carbohydrate, fat, or protein, as you prefer. To be safe, throw in a big jar of vitamins. It may not taste very good, but taste no longer matters. Eating is a material transaction, tasting an informational transaction. Tape-record 10,000 meals from the world's best restaurants and your lentils are filet mignon, sushi, ice cream sundaes. Much the same holds for other material requirements. My body occupies only five or ten cubic feet of space. With a mind free to rove the virtual universe, who needs a living room – or even a double bed?

Viewed in realspace, it is not much of a world. Everyone is eating the cheapest food that will keep a human body in good condition, living in the human equivalent of coin-operated airport storage, exercising by moving against resistance machines, perhaps as part of virtual reality games, perhaps under automatic control while his mind is elsewhere.

To the people living in it, it is paradise. All women are beautiful, and enough are willing. All men are handsome. Everyone lives in a mansion that he can redecorate at will, gold-plated if he so desires.[5] Anyone, anywhere, any experience in storage, any life that can be created as an illusion, is an instant away. Eat all you want of whatever you like and never put on a pound.

Which is true – slum or paradise? It depends on what matters. If all that matters is sensation, what you perceive, it is a paradise, even if that is not obvious to a superficial inspection.

As evidence against, consider a very old form of virtual sex: masturbation. In your mind you can be making love to the woman of your dreams, at least if you have a good enough imagination. The orgasm, the physical sensations inside your body, the nervous signals reaching your brain, are real. Yet, even with the improved technology of pornographic books and videos, there is still something missing.

If what matters is what we experience, the world I have described is a paradise. If what matters is what really happens, the situation is more complicated. Having someone read a book I wrote, enjoy and be persuaded by my ideas, pleases me just as much if he reads it in virtual reality – as those who read this book on the Web currently do. But what about only thinking someone read my book? What if I wake up from a long lifetime as a successful author, basketball star, opera singer, or Casanova to discover it was all a dream? Is that just as good as the real thing? Is it all right as long as I die before I wake up?

Robert Nozick, in *Anarchy, State, and Utopia*, put the question in terms of an imaginary experience machine, his version of VR.[6] Plug someone in and he will have experiences just as vivid and just as convincing as in real life – a lifetime of them. Suppose the owner of the experience machine somehow knows the life you are going to live and can offer you a slightly improved version. Plug into his machine for an imaginary life in which your babies cry a little less, your salary is a little higher, your career in a firm with a little more status. If you believe him, do you take the deal? Do you trade a real life for a fictional life? Is what matters rearing children, making a career, planting fruit trees, writing books – or is what matters the feelings you would have as a result of doing all of those things?

You will have to decide for yourself. I wouldn't touch the thing with a ten-foot pole.

POSTSCRIPT: AND NOW WE HAVE A WINNER

An early draft of this book, including this chapter, was written and webbed way back in 2002. At that time I had no idea which of the futures I was discussing would arrive first; if I had had to guess it would probably have been the future of strong privacy enabled by public key encryption.

Now we know. The world of virtual reality is here, enabled not by the current primitive technology of motion sensors and video goggles nor the future technology of mind/machine interfaces but by the very old, and very advanced, technology of the human imagination. It turns out that a flat screen and a speaker are sufficient – provided the environment to which they are the gateway is a sufficiently interesting and attractive one.

As of early 2007, *World of Warcraft* had more than ten million subscribers, including all five members of my immediate family. Counting all massively multiplayer games, the total number of players worldwide is estimated to be at least 100 million. "Chinese gold farmers," people in poor countries who make their living by playing on such games, earning virtual money and virtual goods and trading them online for real money, are estimated to number in the hundreds of thousands.[7]

World of Warcraft is a fantasy, a work of fiction, a constructed story in which the player immerses himself as a character interacting with other characters, both other players and nonplayer characters run by the computer. *Second Life* is a different, and in some ways more interesting, variant on the idea. What it offers is not a story but a world, a framework, within which participants can themselves design and construct things, trade with each other, interact in a wide variety of ways. From one point of view it is an open source version of the more traditional sort of game, constructed by the participants. From another it is a first step toward a plausible substitute, for most people most of the time, for the real world.[8] And, since VR has room for an unlimited number of worlds, it is a substitute that could make real Robert Nozick's idea of utopia[9] – a wide variety of different communities run under different rules, with each individual free to choose the one he or she prefers.

While massively multiplayer online games are the most striking example of current virtual reality, there is another that is a little older and much bigger. It used to be that when you saw someone walking down the street talking to an invisible person, you suspected he was nuts. Currently, you assume he is on his cell phone. When you are holding a conversation with someone who is objectively many miles away but subjectively right next to you, you are participating in a (very-low-bandwidth) version of virtual reality.

"Cyberspace is where a telephone call happens."

TWENTY-ONE

The Final Frontier

In some ways the future has been a great disappointment. When I was first reading science fiction, space travel was almost a defining characteristic of the genre, interplanetary at the least, with luck interstellar. Other technologies are well ahead of schedule; computers are a great deal smaller than most authors expected and used for a much wider variety of everyday purposes, and genetic engineering of crops is already a reality. But serious use of space has been limited to near-Earth orbit – our backyard. Even scientific activity has not gotten humans past a very brief visit to the moon. We have sent a few small machines a little farther, and so far that is about it.

One possible explanation is that the slow rate of progress is due to the dominant role of governments, itself in part a result of the obvious military applications. Another is that getting into space was harder than writers thought. The problem with the latter explanation is that we have already done the hard part. The next steps, now that we have learned to get free of the terrible drag of Earth's gravity, should be much easier. Perhaps, after a brief pause for rest and refreshment, they will be.

VIEW FROM THE BOTTOM OF A WELL

In one of Poul Anderson's more improbable science fiction stories,[1] a man and a crow successfully transport themselves from one asteroid to another in a spaceship powered by several kegs of beer. From what I know of the author, he probably did the arithmetic to make sure the thing would work.

It would not have gotten far on Earth, but moving in space is in some ways a much easier problem. Our present home is inconveniently located at the bottom of a very deep well. Getting out of that well, lifting something from the surface of Earth into space, takes a lot of work. The price, the charge for satellite launches and similar services, is measured in thousands of dollars a pound. Science fiction writers of the fifties and sixties took it for granted that the point of getting off Earth was to get to Mars, or Venus, or perhaps to a planet circling some distant star. Sometime between then and now it occurred to someone that it made little sense to climb, with enormous effort, out of one well only to jump down another. Planets are traps.

One alternative is an orbital habitat, a giant spaceship permanently located in orbit around a planet or star. The ecology of such a miniature world, like the ecology of the orbiting habitat we now live on, would consist of closed cycles powered by the sun. Recycling on an almost total scale.

The first problem is where to put it. A solar orbit, unless very close to the Earth's, in which case it will be made unstable by the Earth's gravity, puts you a long way from home. Orbiting the Earth, far enough out to avoid the clutter of communication satellites and orbital trash, looks more attractive. Unfortunately, such an orbit will eventually decay, even if not quite as fast in the real world as on Star Trek.

The solutions are Lagrangian points 4 and 5, L4 and L5 for short. They are locations in orbit around the Earth sixty degrees ahead and behind the moon. As Joseph Louis Lagrange proved in 1772, they are stable equilibria. A satellite or space habitat placed at L4 or L5 stays there. Like a ball bearing at the bottom of a bowl, if something pushes it a little away from the center, it moves back.

A second problem is what to build your space habitat out of; at $5,000 a pound, materials from Earth are a bit pricey. That suggests an alternative location – the asteroid belt, which consists of a large number of chunks of rock located between the orbits of Mars and Jupiter. If we do not want to live that far from home, we might use asteroids outside of the belt, some of which have orbits that come quite close to that of Earth.

Asteroids are small enough so that their gravity is negligible. Many are large enough to provide adequate quantities of building material. One way of using that material would be to colonize an asteroid, perhaps drilling tunnels in its interior. An alternative, for those who prefer a shorter commute to the neighborhood of the home planet, is to mine an asteroid and ship what you get back to somewhere near Earth – L5, say. It is a long way from the asteroid belt to the Earth, but transportation is easier if you are not starting at the bottom of a well. Delivering material from the asteroid belt might take months, even years, but the forces required are much smaller than those needed to lift the same amount from Earth. If you are not in too much of a hurry you could even try beer.

A future in which some significant number of people are permanent residents of space, living in habitats, asteroids, perhaps fleets of mining ships, raises some interesting issues. The obvious political question is who rules them. Are they the legal equivalent of ships on the high seas, independent states, or something else? A less obvious legal and economic issue is how to define and enforce the relevant property rights – to an orbit (already a problem for communication satellites), chunks of matter floating through space, sunlight for power, or whatever else is scarce and useful.

So far the only reason I have offered for living in space is that it is much easier to get to space from there. Readers may be reminded of the man who explained to his friends that he played golf to stay fit; when asked what he was staying fit for he answered "golf." There are better answers. An environment with zero gravity and an unlimited supply of almost perfect vacuum could be useful for some forms of production. Asteroids could provide a very large and inexpensive source of raw materials. While their first use will be to build things in space, we do not have to stop there. Getting things down a well is a lot less work than getting them up.

Another answer is that, if Earth gets crowded, we may want to look at other places to live. By mining the asteroid belt we could build structures that would provide living space for enormously more people than presently exist. There need be no shortage of power; the sunlight that falls on Earth is less than one billionth of the total output of the sun. A sufficiently developed space-faring civilization could make use of the rest of it. In the limiting case, one could imagine the sun entirely surrounded by the works of man, visible from other stars only by the vast infrared output of our waste heat. Freeman Dyson has proposed locating technologically sophisticated species a little ahead of ours by searching the heavens for stars like that.

The final answer is that there are risks to putting all our eggs in one basket. It is possible, indeed not unlikely, that life on Earth will get better and better over the next few decades. But it is far from certain. One can imagine a range of possible catastrophes, from gray goo to global government, that would make somewhere else to be a very attractive option. There is a lot of space in space.

The biggest barrier to the future I have been sketching is the cost of getting off Earth. While a space civilization, once started, might be self-sustaining, it requires a big start. And at $5,000 a pound, not many of us are likely to go.

Which raises the obvious question of whether there might be better ways than on top of a giant firework.

TAKE A VERY LONG ROPE...

Artsutanov proposed to use the initial cable to multiply itself, in a sort of boot-strap operation, until it was strengthened a thousand fold. Then, he calculated, it would be able to handle 500 tons an hour or 12,000 tons a day. When you consider that this is roughly equivalent to one Shuttle flight every minute, you will appreciate that Comrade Artsutanov is not thinking on quite the same scale as NASA. Yet if one extrapolates from Lindbergh to the state of transatlantic air traffic 50 years later, dare we say that he is over-optimistic? It is doubtless a pure coincidence, but the system Artsutanov envisages could just about cope with the current daily increase in the world population, allowing the usual 22 kg of baggage per emigrant....

Arthur C. Clarke[2]

For a really efficient form of transport, consider the humble elevator. Lifting the elevator itself takes almost no energy, since as the box goes up the counterweight goes down. Energy consumption is reduced to something close to its absolute minimum – the energy required to lift the passengers from one point to a higher point. And if your design is good enough, you can recover most of that energy when they come back down.

The idea of applying this approach to space transport, like the less efficient method we currently use, is due to a Russian. A multistage rocket was first proposed by Tsiolkovsky in 1895. The space elevator was first proposed by Yuri Artsutanov, a Leningrad engineer, in 1960, and has been independently invented at least half a dozen times since.

You start with a satellite in geosynchronous orbit – over the equator, moving in the direction of the Earth's rotation, going around the Earth once a day. From the viewpoint of someone on the ground the satellite is standing still, since it orbits the Earth at exactly the same rate that the Earth rotates.

Let out two cables from this satellite, one going up, one down. For the one going up, centrifugal force more than balances gravity, so it tries to pull the satellite up. For the one going down, gravity more than balances centrifugal force, so it pulls the other way. Let out your cables at the right speed and the two effects exactly balance. Continue letting out the cables until the lower one touches the ground. Attach it to a convenient island. Run an elevator up it. You now have a way of getting into space for dollars a pound instead of thousands of dollars a pound.

A space elevator has a number of odd and interesting characteristics, some of which we will get to shortly. Unfortunately, building it faces one very serious technical problem: finding something strong enough and light enough to make a very long rope.

Consider a steel cable hanging vertically. If it is longer than about fifty kilometers, its weight exceeds its strength and it breaks. Making the cable thicker does not help, since each time you double its strength you also double its weight. Kevlar, used for purposes that include bulletproof garments, is considerably stronger for its weight than steel. A Kevlar cable can get to about 200 kilometers before it breaks under its own weight. Geosynchronous orbit is 35,000 kilometers up. Kevlar is not going to do it.

At first glance, it looks as though we need a material almost 200 times stronger for its weight than Kevlar, but the situation is not quite that bad. As you go up the cable, you are getting farther from the Earth – gravity is getting weaker and, since the cable is going around with the satellite (and the Earth), centrifugal force is getting stronger. By the time you get to the satellite, the two balance. So it is only the lower end of the cable that will be really heavy. Furthermore, the lower you go on the cable the less weight is below it to be held up, so you can make a cable longer before it breaks by tapering it. Building a space elevator requires something quite a lot stronger for its weight than Kevlar, but not 200 times stronger.

Such materials exist. Microscopic carbon fibers appear to have the necessary properties. So, according to theoretical calculations, would buckytubes – long fibers of carbon atoms bonded to each other. Neither is in industrial production in the necessary sizes just now, but that may change in the fairly near future.

One nice feature of carbon, aside from its ability to make very strong materials, is that some asteroids are largely made out of it. Move one of them into orbit and equip it with a factory capable of turning carbon into superstrong cable. When you are done, use what is left of the asteroid for a counterweight, attached to the cable that goes from the satellite away from the Earth, letting you hold the lower cable up with a much shorter upper cable. Nobody is taking bids on the project just at the moment, but in principle it is doable.[3]

And Off We Go

Consider a cargo container moving up the cable. At the bottom, its motors have to lift its full weight. As it gets higher, gravity gets weaker, centrifugal force gets stronger, so it becomes easier and easier to move it up. When it reaches the satellite at geosynchronous orbit, the two exactly balance – inside the container, you float. Let the container keep going, following the upper cable into space. Now centrifugal force more than balances gravity. With no motor and no brakes you go faster and faster.

One possibility is to use that process, with careful timing, to launch you into space. In principle, it would be possible to build space elevators on a number of different planets and use them instead of rockets for interplanetary transport. Think of it as a giant game of catch. You get launched from Earth by letting go of its space elevator at just the right time and place. As you approach Mars you adjust your trajectory a little – we probably still need rockets for fine-tuning the system – so that you match velocities with the space elevator whipping around Mars. Let go of that at the right time, after moving a suitable distance in or out, and you are on your way to the asteroid belt, or perhaps Jupiter. Building a space elevator on Jupiter might raise problems even for the best cable nanotechnology could spin; perhaps we should use one of its satellites instead. It's a dizzying picture.

An alternative is to equip your cargo capsule with regenerative brakes, an idea already implemented in electric and hybrid cars. A regenerative brake is an electric generator that converts the kinetic energy of a car into electricity, slowing the car down and recharging its batteries. On the space elevator, the electricity generated by the brakes keeping one cargo capsule from taking off for Mars could be used to lift the next one from Earth to the satellite.

Skeptical readers may wonder where all this energy, used to fling spaceships around the solar system or lift capsules from Earth, is coming from. The answer is that it is coming from the rotation of the Earth. Every time you lift a load up the elevator it is being accelerated in the direction of the Earth's rotation, since the higher it is the faster it has to move in order to circle the Earth once a day. For every action there is a reaction; conservation of angular momentum implies that accelerating the load slows down the Earth. Fortunately, the Earth is very much larger than either us or the things we are likely to send up the elevator, so it would be a very long time before the effect became significant.[4]

I have not attempted to calculate how much mass one could shoot off into space before the astronomers complained that their atomic clocks were running fast.
Arthur C. Clarke

The space elevator I have described cannot be built with currently available materials. But there are at least two modified versions of the design that perhaps can. One is called a *skyhook*. It was proposed in the United States by Hans Moravec in 1977, but Artsutanov had published the idea back in 1969. Here is how it works.

Start, this time, with a satellite much closer to the Earth. Again release two cables, one up, one down. Since this satellite is not in geosynchronous orbit, it is moving relative to the surface of the Earth. That makes it difficult to attach the bottom end of the cable to anything, so we don't. Instead we rotate the cable, one end below the satellite, one above, like two spokes of an enormous wheel rolling around the Earth.

The satellite is moving around the globe, but the bottom end of the cable, when it is at its lowest point, is standing still; the cable's motion relative to the satellite just cancels the satellite's motion relative to the Earth. If that sounds odd, consider a car going down the freeway at sixty miles an hour. The car is moving but the bottom of the tire is standing still, since the rotation of the wheel moves it backward relative to the car just as fast as the car moves forwards relative to the pavement. The skyhook applies the same principle scaled up a bit.

Seen from Earth, the end of the cable comes down from space, stops at the bottom of its trajectory, goes back up. To use it for space transport, you put your cargo capsule on an airplane, fly up to where the cable is going to be, hook on just as the bottom of the cable reaches its lowest point. The advantage over the space elevator is that the much lower orbit means a much shorter cable, so you can come a lot closer to building it with currently available materials. The physics works, but don't expect the Civil Aeronautics Board to approve it for passengers any time soon.

A different version that might be workable even sooner has been proposed by researchers at Lockheed Martin's Skunk Works, source of quite a lot of past aeronautical innovation. It starts with a simple observation: getting something to orbit is much more than twice as hard as getting it halfway to orbit. If you have two entirely different technologies for putting something in orbit, why not let each of them do half the job?

The Skunk Works proposal uses a short space hook, reaching from a satellite in low orbit down to a point above the atmosphere. It combines it with a spaceplane, a cross between an airplane and the space shuttle, capable of taking off from an ordinary airport and lifting its cargo a good deal of the way, but not all the way, to orbit. SpaceShipOne, Burt Rutan's innovative vehicle that recently won the $10 million Ansari X PRIZE, provides a proof of concept, although its cargo capacity is a bit low. The spaceplane takes the cargo capsule to the skyhook; the skyhook takes it the rest of the way. The engineers that came up with the design believe that it could be built today and that it would bring the cost of lifting material into space down to about $550 a pound. That is quite a lot more than the estimated cost with a space elevator, but about a tenth the cost of using a rocket.

CONCENTRATING THE MIND: THE PROBLEM OF NEAR-EARTH OBJECTS

Nothing so concentrates a man's mind as the prospect of being hanged in the morning.

Samuel Johnson

A little less than a century ago – in 1908 – Russia was hit with a fifteen-megaton airburst. Fortunately the target was not Moscow but a Siberian swamp. The explosion leveled trees over an area about half the size of the state of Rhode Island. While there is still some uncertainty as to precisely what the Tunguska event was, most researchers agree that it was something from space, perhaps a small asteroid or part of a comet, which hit the Earth. A rough estimate of its diameter is sixty meters. While it was the largest such event in recorded history, there is geological evidence of much larger strikes. One, occurring about 65 million years ago, left a crater 180 kilometers across and a possible explanation for the period of mass extinctions that eliminated the dinosaurs.

2002 CU11 is a near-Earth object, an asteroid in an orbit that will bring it close to the Earth. Its estimated diameter is 730 meters. Since volume goes as the cube of diameter, that means that it probably has more than 1,000 times the mass of the Tunguska meteor and could do a comparably greater amount of damage – quite a lot more than the largest H-bomb ever tested. A little while after it was first observed, 2002 CU11 was estimated to have about a 1-in-9,000 chance of striking the Earth in 2049. You will be relieved to know that later observations, allowing a more precise calculation of its orbit, have reduced that probability to essentially zero.

2000 SG344 is a much smaller rock, about forty meters. NASA estimates that it has about a 1-in-500 chance of hitting the Earth sometime between 2068 and 2101. Even a rock that small would produce an explosion very much more powerful than the bomb dropped on Hiroshima.

By current estimates, there are about 1,000 near-Earth objects of 1-kilometer diameter or above and a much larger number of smaller ones. We think we have spotted more than half of the big ones; none appear to be on a collision course. Since an object that will at some point in its orbit pass near Earth may at the moment be a very long distance away, locating all of them is hard.

Our best guess at the moment, from the geological evidence, is that really big asteroids – two kilometers and over – hit the Earth at a rate of about one or two every million years. That makes the odds that such a strike will occur during one person's life span about 1 in 10,000. Smaller strikes are much more common – one in the megaton range in the last century.

The odds of a big strike are low, but given how much damage it could do it is still worth worrying about. The odds of a small strike, which could do significant damage if it happened to hit a populated area or the sea near a populated coast, are larger. What can we do?

The first step is to watch for things heading our way. NASA, along with researchers in other countries, has been working at it; that is why I can quote sizes and probabilities for known near-Earth objects. U.S. Congressman Dana Rohrabacher has proposed to supplement that by a more decentralized approach: cash prizes to reward amateur astronomers for spotting previously unknown near-Earth asteroids. Since the objects are moving in orbits determined by the laws of physics, once we have spotted one of them several times we can make a fairly accurate projection of where it will be for many years into the future. One particularly well-observed asteroid,[5] a little more than one kilometer in diameter, is expected to make a close approach to Earth on March 16 of the year 2880.

Suppose we spot an asteroid on course for Earth. If it is going to hit tomorrow, there is not much you can do other than getting as far as possible from the point of impact and well above sea level. But if we spot it early enough, we may be able to prevent the collision. Moving a large asteroid is hard, but with a decade or more of pushing a fairly small force can change its orbit at least a little. Even a small change in the orbit, acting over a long time, can turn a hit into a near miss.

One approach would be to land on the asteroid, equipped with a small nuclear reactor. Use the reactor to vaporize rock and blow it at space, gently pushing the asteroid in the other direction. A less elegant solution, but one that uses off-the-shelf hardware currently available in excess supply, is to nuke it. Explode a nuclear or thermonuclear bomb on, slightly under, or slightly above the surface of the asteroid. Exploded under the surface it blows chunks of the asteroid – hopefully small enough chunks not to be themselves too dangerous – in one direction and moves the rest of the asteroid in the other. On or near the surface it vaporizes some of the surface and drives that in one direction, giving the asteroid a brief but very hard shove the other way. For an asteroid with a diameter of one kilometer or so spotted a decade or more before it hits us, such an approach might do the job.

The odds of a catastrophic asteroid hit are low, but the downside risk could be substantial. If only the dinosaurs had had an adequate space program they might still be around.

AD ASTRA

We are currently active in Earth's backyard, putting up communication satellites, spies in the sky, and the like. I have suggested some possibilities for the next step – lowering the cost of getting off Earth by enough to make it possible to establish substantial human populations in space habitats or suitably modified asteroids. The step after that is much harder, because the stars are much farther away. Current physics holds that nothing can move faster than the speed of light. If that remains true, trips to other stars will take years, probably decades, possibly centuries. We might as well start thinking about them now.[6]

Earlier chapters provide three solutions to the problem of keeping the crew of an interstellar expedition alive long enough to get somewhere. One is life extension. Another is cryonic suspension. A third is to have the ship crewed by programmed computers. If a program gets bored it can save itself to hard disk, or whatever the equivalent then is, and shut down. After, of course, reminding another AI to reboot it when they arrive.

What about propulsion? Getting a starship to a significant fraction of the speed of light requires something considerably better than chemical rockets. A number of proposals have been made and analyzed. One of my favorites starts with a form of propulsion proposed some decades back for interplanetary flight and currently being experimented with: sails. There is no air in the vacuum of space but there is quite a lot of light, and light has pressure. A light sail is a thin film of reflective material with an area of many square kilometers, perhaps many thousands of square kilometers. The ship attached to the sail controls its angle to the sun, rather as an ordinary sail is controlled on Earth.

The sunlight is all going one way – out. Its pressure can be used to accelerate away from the sun, but how do you get back? One answer is gravity. Just as an ordinary sailboat combines the pressure of its keel against the water with the pressure of the wind against its sail, a solar sailboat combines the pressure of light with the pull of solar gravity. To accelerate at right angles to the direction of the sun, you tilt the sail so that the combination of light pressure and gravity adds up to the vector you want. To accelerate toward the sun you furl your sail or angle it edge-on to the light, and wait for the sun to pull you in.

The great advantage of a light sail is that it requires no fuel. One problem is that the farther you are from the sun, the less there is to push you; for most of an interstellar voyage the sun is just one more star. The solution is to provide your own sunlight. Build a very powerful laser somewhere in the solar system, aim it at the sail of your interstellar ship, and blow it across space. The ship goes; the power source remains behind.

A solar sail backed by a very large laser cannon is an elegant solution to the problem of getting to the stars, but one problem remains: stopping. Unless the star you are going to is also equipped with a laser cannon, you are flying a ship without brakes.

My favorite solution was offered by Robert Forward. His ship has two solar sails, a circle inside a larger circle. When you approach the target system you cut loose the outer ring and angle everything so that the laser beam misses the sail still attached to the ship, hits the other, bounces off it, and is reflected back into the first sail. The detached sail accelerates into space, driven by the beam, while the spaceship is slowed by the reflected beam hitting the sail still attached.

Before the second ship arrives, the first builds a second laser cannon to provide brakes. Nobody could expect a maneuver that complicated to work twice. Once you have a laser at each end of things, traveling back and forth gets a lot easier.

> The sunside armor's peelin', and the reels have too much slack,
> And it takes a week to get her up to speed.
> The mainsail's full of pinholes, and the coffeemaker's cracked,
> But I can't think of anything I need.
>
> As twelve hundred klicks of sail begin to furl, and keel jets hiss,
> And the pickup point sends grapnels out to roam,
> I fin'ly have the chance to think of one I love and miss,
> Running down the windward passage to our home.
> Running down the windward passage to our home.
>
> You'll never call me wealthy, and I haven't come too far,
> And there's folks I know would make me out a fool.
> But they've never cruised the system, and they've never sailed the stars,
> With ten million miles of sunlight for their fuel.

WINDWARD PASSAGE
Words and music by Michael Longcor, 1989
Copyright Firebird Arts & Music
P.O. Box 30268, Portland, OR 97294
Firebirdarts.com

FIFTY YEARS AFTER THEY STOP LAUGHING

How likely is any of this to happen? Nanotechnology would make a space elevator technically possible but there would still be political problems getting a project on that scale built. Whether they will prove insurmountable depends on the climate of opinion thirty or forty years from now, which is hard to predict. Even without a space elevator, nanotechnology should make possible much stronger and lighter materials, which would strikingly lower launch costs, perhaps by enough to establish a real human presence in space. Defense against near-Earth objects is one reason to do it, a reason that could become urgent if we spot something big on a collision course.

Interstellar travel is a harder project. It may happen, and it is interesting to think about, but I do not expect anyone to arrive at another star any time in the next fifty years, which is about as far forward as we have any reasonable hope of predicting future technology. If it does happen, Forward's magnificent kludge, the sail within a sail, is as likely as anything else.

I'll adapt the reply that Arthur Kantrowitz gave, when someone asked a similar question about his laser propulsion system. The Space Elevator will be built about 50 years after everyone stops laughing.

Arthur C. Clarke

TWENTY-TWO

Interesting Times

May you live in interesting times.
Ancient Chinese curse, apparently invented by Eric Frank Russell c. 1950

MULTIPLE FUTURES

A writer looking forward from 1900 might have anticipated rockets. He might have anticipated nuclear explosives. The nuclear balance of terror, one of the central facts of the second half of the century, required both. Through most of this book, I have taken futures one at a time. They will not come that way.

One interaction among technologies was discussed in Chapter 5. If cyberspace is private and realspace public, how much privacy we have depends on how much of our lives is lived in each. That in turn depends on another technology: virtual reality. In the limit of deep VR, everything important is happening in cyberspace, leaving the automated cameras of the transparent society very little to watch.

Another example appeared in Chapter 21. How large a role space plays in our lives over the next century depends on how expensive it is to get there. That, in turn, depends on the strength-to-weight ratio of the materials available to us. With sufficiently strong and light materials, it becomes possible to build a space elevator, drastically reducing the cost of getting off earth. Short of that, better materials make possible launch vehicles with a much higher payload and much lower costs. One way of getting very strong and light materials, such as single-molecule carbon fibers, is nanotechnology.

In some cases, one technology eliminates problems raised by another. Genetic testing makes genetic risks uninsurable. But with sufficiently advanced genetic engineering that does not matter, since there will be no genetic risks left to insure. Biometric identification technologies can impose on everyone on earth a built-in, unforgeable, ID card – until nanotechnology makes it possible, even easy, to revise your fingerprints or the pattern of blood vessels in your retinas. Cryonic suspension raises puzzles connected with adequately punishing criminals who choose to get frozen while their sentence runs, but if surveillance technology produces a world where criminals face a near certainty of conviction, adequate punishment may not be a problem. If we know enough about how the human brain works to emulate it in silicon, we may know enough to rehabilitate criminals by methods less crude than the penitentiary. Of course, that knowledge, and that power, could create other problems compared to which problems of crime and punishment may be insignificant.

FUTURE IMPERFECT

In the past twenty-one chapters we have considered a wide variety of possible futures, some attractive, some frightening, few dull. Most offer both problems and promises. By avoiding the former as far as possible and taking advantage of the latter, we can in most cases make ourselves better off than if the technology did not exist. Consider a few examples.

Encryption, ecash, and widely available computer networks will make certain crimes easier; make it easier, for example, to collect the payoff from kidnapping or extortion without being caught in the process. But those technologies also provide new and powerful ways of protecting ourselves from crime. They also make it much harder for governments to control people. Governments, on the historical evidence, are a great deal more dangerous than private criminals are; over the past century, according to one estimate, governments killed more than 200 million of the people they ruled, wars excluded.[1] In my view, at least, the benefits of weakening the power of governments are greater than the costs.

Human reproductive technology, the ability of parents to choose which of the children they might have they do have or to use genetic engineering to provide their children characteristics that nature failed to give them, raises potential problems, since important decisions will be made for people before they are born, necessarily by other people. But those decisions are no different in kind from decisions already being made for children by other people, such as the decision to bring a child into existence and the decision as to how to rear him or her.

A government with a sufficiently long time horizon could use such technologies to try to breed superior warriors, scientists, or bureaucrats. But such a government could do the same thing using techniques of selective breeding that we have been applying to other species for several thousand years. Few or none have, perhaps because governments rarely have that long a time horizon.[2]

These technologies may also give us the ability, within one or two generations, to eliminate both genetic diseases and a wide range of other hereditary disadvantages, such as the bad heart that killed my paternal grandfather at a young age and, at a much more advanced age thanks to modern medicine, my father. They also carry the potential to increase the average intelligence of our species, which might be an improvement and will surely be interesting.

The implications of other technologies are more ambiguous. Obvious examples are nanotechnology and artificial intelligence. Either might lead to an enormously more attractive world. Both contain the potential for catastrophe on a scale that has not been seen on earth at least since the elimination of the dinosaurs some sixty-five million years ago.

Technological progress means that we can do more things. We do things because we think doing them benefits us, hence one might expect that we would always be better off with new technologies than without them. If there are exceptions to that conclusion, why? Is there some logic by which, in some possible futures, technological progress could make us worse off?

There is. The first step toward understanding it is to think a little more carefully about the impossible world in which we now live, how it works, and how it might stop working.

THE COORDINATION PROBLEM

Our world is inhabited by a very large number of individuals. Each has his own objectives, beliefs, and abilities. For any moderately complicated society to function, those individuals have to find some way of coordinating their efforts. In order for me to build a sword or a plough blade, someone has to smelt iron. In order for him to smelt iron, someone has to mine iron ore and produce charcoal. Each of those in turn requires inputs produced by other activities carried out by other people. And once we have a plough blade, it is of little use unless there is a farmer to plow the land, seeds to sow, and much else.

In a modern society the problem is even harder. For an example not original with me,[3] consider a pencil. The wood it is made from requires, tracing the chain back, trees and sawmills and chainsaws and gasoline and batteries and steel and electric generators and blast furnaces and iron ore and coal and. . . . Follow out all the lines and you have millions of people coordinating their activities to produce a pencil, a shirt, a computer.

How can we do it? How can we make sure that the mine produces the amount of ore needed to make the amount of steel needed to . . . ? How can we solve that problem a millionfold, when every piece depends on every other piece?

There are only two known solutions, and one of them doesn't work. That, the obvious one, is central control. Someone has the job of figuring out what everyone else should do, telling them to do it, and making sure they obey. On the scale of a family, a firm, a football team it may come close to working, although even there a careful examination is likely to find people doing quite a lot of things they have not been told to do. But the centralized solution does not scale. As the enterprise gets bigger, more and more information has to funnel through the central authority, much of it getting lost on the way, and the problem of figuring out what everyone should do becomes unworkably complicated.

The solution that does work – most important, that scales – is the decentralized one. Everything belongs to someone. People are free to trade. If the value of what you own – including, most importantly, the use of your body to do things you know how to do – is worth more to me than to you, there is some offer I can make that you will accept. Each of us has different ends. But each can offer, through an exchange of goods, services, or money, to help achieve another person's ends in exchange for that person's help with his. Working through the full logic of that system requires a semester or so of price theory, but the basic logic is fairly simple.

The decentralized solution works best if there is some definition of property rights, some way of dividing up the world into pieces, such that each individual's use of his piece has significant effects only on himself and a few other people – ideally, effects that occur only with the mutual consent of both parties. My use of my ability to tell stories affects only myself and those who choose to listen to them; if you do not offer me acceptable terms, I will not choose to tell stories to you. Similarly for most goods or services. As long as that condition is met, each of us can decide what to do in terms of its value to him – I like telling stories – and its value to other people, measured by what they are willing to offer him to do it.

Unfortunately, in any reasonably complicated world, there is no definition of property rights that entirely meets this condition. My story-telling is a voluntary interaction between myself and my willing audience, but when I get to the loud parts it becomes an involuntary interaction between myself and my neighbor. My driving my car is the result of voluntary trades with the people who made the car, refined the gasoline, sold the maps. But it imposes costs involuntarily on people I might run into and people downwind breathing my exhaust.[4]

In the simpler cases, when such external costs become significant, we can and do deal with them through tort law. If I make too much noise too late at night, my neighbor may be able to get an injunction. If I drive negligently and my car ends up in your living room I will owe you payment for damage done. Litigation is a clumsier and less efficient mechanism than trade; on average, of every dollar spent by a defendant only about fifty cents ends up with a plaintiff, the rest going to lawyers, court costs, and the like.[5] But it does provide a mechanism for forcing individuals to take account of costs they impose on others when deciding what to do with their property.

As external effects become more dispersed – not a large injury to one person whose house I drove through but a tiny injury to each of ten million people with the bad luck to be breathing downwind of me – tort law becomes less and less useful. The damage from any particular polluter is in most cases difficult or impossible to measure. Although legal mechanisms such as class actions designed to combine large numbers of victims into one for purposes of litigation exist, they work very poorly.

In such cases the typical response is either to put up with the problem or to try to solve it by government regulation.

Government regulation is a reversion to the centralized solution, someone at the top deciding what everyone should do and making them do it. For reasons suggested earlier and explored in greater detail elsewhere, by myself and others,[6] it works very badly, especially when applied to large societies. We have no good way of making regulatory agencies try to act in our interest and they have no good way of figuring out how to do it.

When the scale of the effect becomes international, the problem gets worse. Regulatory agencies of the U.S. government, such the FDA or the FCC, may be politically motivated, incompetent, or both, but at least they have some interest in doing things that U.S. citizens approve of. They have very little reason to care about the effect of their policies on the citizens of Bangladesh or the Maldive Islands.

For an example of the sort of problem that neither decentralized nor centralized solutions can be trusted to solve, consider global warming due to human activities. While there is quite a lot of legitimate disagreement over its likely scale and consequences, there is good reason to believe that it exists and that it is at least in part due to increases in the amount of carbon dioxide in the atmosphere.

When I use electricity generated by the burning of coal, or light a fire in my fireplace, or breathe, I am producing carbon dioxide (CO_2). One result may be a tiny increase in the temperature of the earth. One result of that may be a very small increase in sea level. Predicted effects, even after combining the results of everyone's activity, are not very large – current estimates[7] suggest a temperature increase of about two degrees centigrade and a rise of a foot or two over the next century. Where I live, on the U.S. West Coast, that will be a very minor inconvenience; beaches will get a little narrower. It will be more of a problem for people living in low-lying territories routinely threatened by floods. And if it turns out that the rate of global warming and sea-level change are substantially larger than present estimates suggest, it could be a very serious problem indeed.

How might we deal with that problem? We cannot very well define property rights in a way that gives every inhabitant of Bangladesh a veto over the power use, home heating, and breathing of every American.

We cannot expect the international legal system to honor and enforce tort claims by a citizen of Bangladesh against a citizen of the United States for contributing one part in ten billion to a flood fifty years in the future. We could imagine the government of Bangladesh trying to use international law to force the U.S. government to severely regulate activities of its citizens that are predicted to increase the risk of future floods in Bangladesh but, if the regulations are costly for Americans, why would the American government comply?

We can imagine, indeed have observed, attempts to negotiate international treaties for the same purpose. But while arguments about global warming may sometimes be useful to help governments persuade their citizens to put up with actions that the governments already favor – additional energy taxes, say, that are desired as a source of revenue and can be defended as ways of holding down energy consumption and so CO_2 production – it is hard to see their doing much more than that. The United States, controlling its citizens' activities to avoid costs imposed on the citizens of the rest of the world, is in the same situation I am in keeping my voice down when it bothers my neighbors. Short of a world government, there is no legal mechanism analogous to tort law to make them do it. And a world government, in my view at least, is a cure worse than the disease.

The Dark Side of the Force

I have discussed the case of global warming not because I think it is a particularly serious threat – for reasons I will return to shortly I think it is probably not, at least over the next fifty years or so – but because it is a problem that most of my readers will be familiar with and whose nature is fairly easy to explain.

The general problem of which it is one example is the breakdown of the conditions that make possible the decentralized solution to the coordination problem. Technological progress increases our ability to do things. Often, although not always, that means increasing the scale and range of the effects of human action. As scale and range increase, it becomes harder and harder to define property rights in a way that satisfies the requirements of decentralized coordination, a way in which the effects of my actions are mostly confined to my property and the property of those who have agreed to permit those actions. The result is to push us away from the one workable system for coordinating human action – private property and trade – toward the less workable alternatives of tort law and regulation.

As the scale of effects expands beyond the boundaries of the individual nation, regulation by national governments becomes even less capable of dealing with the problem. We are left with the unattractive choice of either putting up with whatever problems result from individuals ignoring the distant and dispersed costs imposed by their actions or creating a world government. If we choose the latter, we find ourselves trying to use a centralized regulatory mechanism to deal with problems far beyond the scale for which such mechanisms are workable.

Not all technological progress raises these issues. Encryption and virtual reality make possible societies that come closer to the market ideal than what we now have, since the interactions they enable are entirely voluntary. In virtual reality, the problem of trespass, the more general problem of conflicting uses, vanish; we can each enjoy his own version of California's Pacific coast, one unspoiled and natural, one with all the benefits of modern commercial culture. The same may turn out to be true of other technologies as well.

Nanotechnology is an interesting case because its effects go both ways. On the one hand, the creator of a self-reproducing nanite successfully designed to turn the entire biosphere, us included, into copies of itself imposes external costs vastly larger than any plausible level of global warming. On the other hand, good enough defensive nanotechnology could eliminate a wide range of current externality problems. I do not have to worry about what my neighbor puts in his air if my boundary is patrolled by molecular machines capable of disassembling any noxious gases that waft across. I do not even have to worry very much about radiation sleeting through my body from his experimental nuclear reactor if my body is patrolled by microscopic cell repair machines capable of repairing any damage in real time. I still have to worry about what happens if the reactor explodes – even nanotech machinery has its limits – but not about much short of that.

I conclude that there is a general problem that we can expect to be produced by some forms of technological progress. It occurs when human abilities change in ways that make it harder to define property rights in a workable fashion, a way that lets each of us go about his own business without having to worry too much about distant effects on dispersed and anonymous people. We can expect some technologies to change human abilities in that direction, others to have the opposite effect.

Growing Pains

The problems I have been discussing are produced by a technology in place. Other sorts of problems are associated with getting there. One example is the problem of inverting the hierarchy of age and expertise. In a slowly changing society, which is to say in almost all of human history, older people, while they may not run as fast or even think as fast as younger people, know more. So it makes sense to have institutional structures in which, on average, older people have authority over younger people.

As the rate of change increases, so does the rate at which knowledge depreciates. The head of the research department knows much more about vacuum tubes than the young engineers whose work she supervises, but they are not researching vacuum tubes. The judge in a software patent infringement case knows a great deal about patent law, but he knows much less about software than either plaintiff or defendant. To some extent he can lean on the knowledge of other people, such as his law clerks, or make himself a temporary expert with the help of briefs provided by both sides; the problem of judicial ignorance of the substance of what is being litigated over is not a new one. But the faster the world is changing, the more ignorant the people in authority are likely to be, hence the more likely to make serious errors in their decisions.

One cannot solve the problem by simply inverting the age/authority hierarchy, appointing students fresh out of law school as judges, hiring the newest graduates of Cal Tech and Harvey Mudd to supervise research laboratories. Judges have to know things about both the law and the legal system that a newly hatched lawyer has not yet learned, and managing a team of engineers requires knowledge of managing as well as knowledge of engineering. Some of the skills required for the job are in slowly changing fields, where the traditional pattern makes sense; some in rapidly changing fields, where it does not.

One result of the situation is to reinforce the natural tendency of employees to ignore or evade the instructions of their superiors. That, in my view, is what was really going on between Randy Schwartz and Intel. Schwartz believed, probably correctly, that he knew a great deal more about networked computers than the Intel executives who were giving him orders. So he followed their instructions when he thought they were watching and the rest of the time did the job the way he thought it should be done, not the way he had been told to do it.

The inverted hierarchy of expertise not only encourages employees to believe that they know how to do their job better than the managers they report to, but also encourages them to believe that they can get away with saying "Yes, sir" and then doing what they please. No old fogey of forty-five is going to figure out what they are really doing. It is an attitude especially likely in employees with the sort of personality typical among bright young technophiles.

ENVIRONMENTALISM, RESOURCES, AND WHY WE SHOULD WORRY ABOUT GLOBAL WARMING BUT NOT JUST YET

This book is about possible futures, their perils and promises. Over the past fifty years, quite a lot has been written about future perils by people loosely describable as environmentalists. Their view that the world is threatened by increasing population, depletion of natural resources, and growing pollution has received generally favorable press and is quite widely accepted, despite its extraordinary record of false prophecies.

Thirty-five years ago, the widely popular *Limits to Growth* warned of a future where the only way of avoiding one catastrophe was to dive into another. That future has now arrived and, while there are still problems in the world, it is a world that, by historical standards, is strikingly lacking in the sorts of catastrophes predicted. At about the same time, Paul Ehrlich predicted that between 1968 and 1977 there would be acute food shortages that would result in the death of one-seventh of the world's population. From the time that *The Population Bomb* was published to now, world food production per capita has trended up, not down; the very occasional famines of recent decades have been the result, not of a global lack of food, but of conditions, usually civil war, that prevented food from getting to the people who needed it. While some environmentalists have responded to the failure of their predictions by changing their views, many have not, arguing instead that they merely had the timing a little off.

One reason their predictions were wrong was their failure to take account of basic economic principles. *Limits to Growth* consisted largely of working out the implications of large computer models describing a set of interacting systems supposed to represent the world. What struck me when I read the book was that the authors, in modeling the world, had left out the role played by human rationality. It was as if they were trying to predict what would happen on a highway by extrapolating the paths cars were following while ignoring the fact that each car had a driver with good reasons to avoid colliding with other cars.

Consider a simple example: soil depletion. In their models, if food became scarce and expensive, farmers tried to produce more on the same land. Doing so wore out the soil, so future productivity fell. If that were true, Japan, where food has long been expensive, should by now be unable to grow anything at all; in fact, Japanese agriculture is extraordinarily productive. When food is expensive and expected to stay expensive, farmers value not only present productivity but future productivity and so are willing to go to a great deal of trouble to maintain or increase the fertility of their land.

A similar analysis applies to other resources whose allocation is handled through the ordinary mechanisms of the market. If energy sources are scarce, that gives users of energy an incentive to find ways of getting by with less, producers an incentive to find new ways of producing, and so too with raw materials, crop lands, and the like.

In a world of private property, the same argument applies to population. When I have a child, he does not arrive with a claim to his per capita share of the world's resources clutched in his fist. In order to get things – food to eat, land to live on – he, or I, or someone has to offer the owner of those resources something in exchange, something that owner considers at least as valuable. My having a child does not automatically make everyone else's children poorer, the implicit assumption of much environmentalist literature.

So far I have been considering only interactions within markets. When we go beyond that, the situation gets more complicated. My child might end up on welfare, imposing costs on your tax-paying child. My child might, in the process of producing and consuming, generate pollution that makes your child worse off. In these cases and many others, resources are being allocated in ways other than voluntary exchange, so there is no longer any reason to assume that interactions leave both parties at least as well off as they would be without the interaction.

Before concluding that the opponents of population growth are right after all, remember that such effects can go in either direction. My child might end up as the taxpayer who is supporting your child on welfare, or sharing with your children the tax burden of supporting other people's children on welfare. My child might invent the medicine that saves your child's life. Once we abandon the simple framework of voluntary exchange, we can no longer be confident that I am paying all of the costs of my decision to have a child. But it requires a fairly detailed, and in large part conjectural, accounting to figure out whether, on net, the existence of my child makes yours worse off or better off.

My first piece of published economics, written more than thirty years ago, was an attempt to answer that question.[8] I concluded that there were substantial negative effects on others from producing a child, there were substantial positive effects, and the size of the effects could not be estimated accurately enough to decide which was larger. I have seen no reason since to change that conclusion.

The environmental movement was and is wrong, but not entirely wrong. The part of their predictions that involves ordinary private goods produced and sold in markets – natural resources, energy, food – is wrong because it ignores the economic mechanisms that allocate goods across both space and time.[9] That is why Julian Simon, the most visible critic of the environmentalist position, won his famous bet with Paul Ehrlich over future prices of raw materials. But the part of their predictions that involves problems such as pollution, where one person imposes costs on others without requiring their consent, and where it may be impossible to redefine property rights in any workable way for which that is not true, could be right.

Which brings us back to global warming, the newest and most widely accepted version of that problem. So far as the physics are concerned, the logic seems straightforward, although the complications of the interacting systems of atmosphere, land, and ocean make measurements of past changes and predictions of future changes difficult. The economics are equally straightforward; when I decide whether to drive, or burn, or exhale, I take account of the effects on me but not the effects on you. If the latter are negative and, multiplied by the population of the world, substantial, I will produce carbon dioxide even when, taking into account the effects on everyone, I ought not to.

Nonetheless, I do not think we ought to be doing large and expensive things at present to reduce our output of carbon dioxide. One reason is that change is not always bad. Just as in the case of population increase, it is necessary to look at both positive and negative effects. A slight increase in global temperature is probably a bad thing if you live in the tropics or on land very slightly above sea level. It may be a good thing if you live in Siberia or Norway. Judged by where most of its people live, Canada is more than 2,000 miles long and, on average, less than 100 miles wide; a moderate increase in global temperature might double its effective area.

Temperature aside, an increase in carbon dioxide is probably a good thing. It is, after all, a major input to photosynthesis, so on average we would expect crops to grow better in an atmosphere with more of it.

Hence, while global warming might make us substantially worse off, it is not at all clear that it would do so. Most of what I see written on the subject is pretty clearly written by people, on one side or the other, who knew what answer they wanted to get before they started, which makes it hard for careful readers to form a confident opinion. Insofar as I can extract an objective estimate from what I read, it looks as though global warming is likely to occur but unlikely to be catastrophic.[10]

The second reason I do not think we should be doing much about global warming at present should be clear from the first twenty chapters of this book. If current estimates are correct – and they may not be – substantial problems due to global warming are decades into the future. Even a century from now the effect on sea level, by current estimates, will be a rise of less than a meter. It is only when you go further than that that effects become really big.

We live in a radically uncertain world. It is entirely possible that, fifty years from now, our species will no longer exist. It is also possible that, fifty years from now, we will have powers enormously greater than at present. Even if we end up between those two extremes, the odds are high that in 50 or 100 years we will be living very differently than at present.

That might mean a drastic reduction in power consumption; you can have a lot of fun with very little energy in a world of deep VR. It might mean a shift to power sources such as nuclear or orbital solar that generate no greenhouse gases. It might mean a world of low-cost space transport, with population expanding through the solar system. It might mean low-cost ways of reducing the earth's absorption of heat from the sun, such as a very large array of orbiting mirrors. More modestly still, it might, in my view probably will, mean a world sufficiently wealthy, and with sufficiently advanced engineering, to make the diking of Bangladesh a considerably less difficult project than the diking of the Netherlands was a few centuries back.

If all of this seems like wild-eyed, pie-in-the-sky speculation, consider how much the world has changed over the past century. A hundred years ago medicine could cure very nearly nothing; with rare exceptions, all a competent doctor could do was tell the patient whether he should be taking a few days off work or making his will. The usual form of individual transportation was walking, riding a horse, or riding in a horse-drawn carriage. The only form of rapid communication available to ordinary people was the telegraph, sending short messages in Morse code at a fairly high price. The adding machine was a recent invention; the only sorts of mechanical calculator in common use were the slide rule and abacus. The first powered heavier-than-air craft capable of carrying a human being had flown just a few years earlier – for 12 seconds and 120 feet.

The changes from then to now were in large part changes in technology, in what human beings knew how to do. Those changes are continuing. Arguably their rate is accelerating, as developments in one field make easier developments in another. To make plans for the world of a century hence today based on today's technology and practice makes no more sense than it did in 1900, when a man with a prudent eye to the future might have worried about avoiding a collapse of the transportation system due to a shortage of hay and oats.

Global warming is a problem that at some point we may want to deal with, but not a problem we ought to be dealing with now. We do not know enough. Working that far ahead risks wasting valuable resources solving problems that will solve themselves sometime between now and then or, worse, spending our resources pushing the world in what will turn out to be the wrong direction.

Necessarily the figures are uncertain, but it is quite possible that in only seventy years our population will amount to about eleven millions, over half of whom will be Old Age Pensioners.

George Orwell, 1946, discussing Britain's looming depopulation problem.

As of 2006, the population of the United Kingdom was 60,587,000. The current projection for 2016 is about 65 million.

Notes

Chapter 1

In addition to the print version of this book, there is an online version at www.daviddfriedman.com/Future_Imperfect.htm. It includes a much more extensive set of notes, many with links to supporting material online. I plan to update it over time, both to provide new information and to fix links that break.

1. Benson, 1989, pp. 644–661; http://garnet.acns.fsu.edu/~bbenson/.

Chapter 2

1. *Vault Corp. v. Quaid Software Ltd*, United States Court of Appeals, Fifth Circuit, 1988 847 F.2d 255, at http://cyber.law.harvard.edu/ilaw/Contract/vault.htm.
2. Buckley, 2000, pp. xxii–xxiii.
3. You can get that information already by using Google to search for pages that link to a particular page. That is possible because Google has already indexed the entire Web and so has a complete list of links – readable from either end. A back-link browser would use such an index to locate back-links to display. One current project along those lines is Crit at http://zesty.ca/pubs/cscw-2002-crit.pdf.
4. Such a system already exists in a very early form – the "trackback" system used by bloggers. Currently trackbacks are voluntary on the linked-to side, but if browsers polled the trackback servers themselves, they could display the links in a sidebar, without requiring any action by the linked-to site.
5. The issue is discussed at http://www.templetons.com/brad/linkright.html and http://www.bitlaw.com/internet/linking.html. A future development along similar lines – a news service that uses other people's webbed information to automatically generate custom news for each customer – is discussed at http://www.futurepundit.com/archives/002790.html and http://writ.news.findlaw.com/hilden/20050524.html.
6. "Let us accept the idea that women should stick to their own jobs – the jobs they did so well in the good old days before they started talking about votes

and women's rights.... It is a formidable list of jobs: The whole of the spinning industry, the whole of the dying industry, the whole of the weaving industry. The whole catering industry and – what would not please Lady Astor, perhaps – the whole of the nation's brewing and distilling. All the preserving, pickling, and bottling industry, all the bacon-curing. And (since in those days a man was often absent from home for months together on war or business) a very large share in the management of landed estates. Here are the women's jobs...." Dorothy Sayers (1947, p. 133).

7. Matthew Prior, "An English Padlock," is a verse argument for companionate marriage as a solution to this problem. The poet runs through all of the precautions by which a jealous husband can try to keep his wife faithful and the ways in which a wife can, if she wishes, defeat all of them, and concludes, "Let all her ways be unconfined/And clap your padlock on her mind."

8. I limit myself to male sexual jealousy not because female sexual jealousy does not exist but because the relevant technology has not changed – a woman's knowledge that a child is hers never depended on knowing whether its father had been sleeping with other women.

9. Silver, 1998, pp. 172–177.

10. For a fictional portrayal of the problem, see Sterling (1997) at http://www.cscs.umich.edu/~crshalizi/reviews/holy-fire/.

11. See, for instance, Bill Joy's essay "Why the future doesn't need us" at http://www.wired.com/wired/archive/8.04/joy_pr.html.

12. It has been argued that the invention of agriculture may have made people worse off; the new technology could support much denser population, which tended to displace the competing hunter-gatherers, but did it with a less attractive lifestyle. (Diamond, 1987, pp. 64–66) at http://www.ditext.com/diamond/mistake.html.

Chapter 3

1. The earliest sketch of these ideas that I have seen appeared in a science fiction story by a computer scientist – "True Names" by Vernor Vinge (Vinge, 1987). The point of the title was that just as, in traditional fantasy, a sorcerer must protect his true name to keep others from using magic against him, so in an online world individuals must protect their real-world identities to keep others from acting against them in realspace.

2. http://www.pgp.com/.

3. A still more decentralized version was proposed and implemented by Philip Zimmerman, creator of the widely used public key program PGP – a web of trust. Every time you correspond with someone, he provides you a list of all the public keys he knows about, along with the identities of their owners. Your software keeps track of the information. The more people have told you that a particular public key belongs to a particular person, the more confident you are that it is true. In effect, everyone becomes a certifying authority for everyone else.

4. http://www.sjgames.com/SS/. According to news stories in 2007, in 2005 the chief judge of the Foreign Intelligence Surveillance Court complained to the Justice Department that the FBI repeatedly had provided the court with inaccurate information in order to get surveillance warrants: "Records show that the FISA court approves almost every application for the warrants, which give agents broad powers to electronically monitor and surveil people who they allege are connected to terrorism or espionage cases. The number of requests rose from 886 in 1999 to 2,074 in 2005. The court did not reject a single application in 2005 but 'modified' 61, according to a Justice Department report to Congress." Source: http://www.washingtonpost.com/wp-dyn/content/article/2007/03/26/AR2007032602073_pf.html.

5. This passage was first written before the September 11th attack on the World Trade Center. That event strengthened the hand of the supporters of encryption regulation, but I think the long-term prediction still holds.

Chapter 4

1. One exception is that claims against property that was used as security for a loan may run with the property – do in the case of automobiles, where such claims are normally recorded on the title document.

Chapter 5

1. For details, see Foldvary and Klein (2003).

2. Traffic surveillance at present suggests what people surveillance may be like in the future, since reading a license plate or transponder or toll tag is easier than recognizing a face.

3. Alternatively, a transparent society might be produced by something analogous to an open source project for producing software. Each participant contributes the information from his cameras and has access to the information from everyone's cameras.

4. Freeman, 1983.

5. This may not be an entirely hypothetical example. There is now some evidence that brain scans can be used to tell when someone is lying: http://www.futurepundit.com/archives/003548.html. As we come to understand the brain better, it may become possible to tell more about what people are thinking by observing what is happening in their brains. There is also some evidence that it may become possible to use brain scans to identify psychopaths, which raises additional issues: http://www.futurepundit.com/archives/004209.html.

6. For a more extensive discussion of the issues of this chapter, see Friedman, 2000, in which I use the term "privacy rights" for what I here call privacy. For a more general discussion of rights from a related perspective see Friedman, 1994. My mental privacy is not quite complete, but the only important exception is my wife.

7. A possible exception is the case where the relevant information is negative – the fact that I have not declared bankruptcy, say – and third parties have no way of knowing whether I have acted to suppress it. If individuals have control over such information, then the absence of evidence that I have declared bankruptcy provides no evidence that I have not – so borrowers who have not declared bankruptcy in the past will be better off in a world where privacy rights with regard to such information are weak. The problem disappears if I can take an observable action – such as signing a legally enforceable waiver of the relevant legal privacy rights – that demonstrates that the information is not being suppressed.

8. Many of the points made in this part of the chapter can be found, in somewhat different form, in Posner, 1978, "The Right of Privacy," and Posner, 1978, "An Economic Theory of Privacy." He finds the case for the general desirability of privacy to be weak.

9. This might not be the case if we are frequently faced with situations where my gains from the bargain provide the incentive for me to generate information that is of value to other people as well. There is little point to spending time and money predicting a rise in wheat prices if everything you discover is revealed to potential sellers before you have a chance to buy from them. This is a somewhat odd case because, while successful speculation is both socially useful and profitable, there is no particular connection between the two facts, as pointed out in Hirschleifer, 1971. Hence the opportunity for speculative gain may produce either too much or too little incentive to obtain the necessary information. A second qualification is that it might not be the case if there were some completely verifiable way of dropping my privacy – of letting you know the highest price I was willing to pay in exchange for your letting me know the lowest price you were willing to accept. This brings us back to a point made in an earlier note – the difficulty of conveying believable information in a context where I have the power to select what information is conveyed.

10. An alternative approach might be political activity – lobbying Congress or making contributions to the police benevolent fund or participating in a revolution. For most individuals in a large society, myself included, such tactics are rarely worth their cost.

11. Writing in the eighteenth century, Blackstone described the appeal of felony, a private action for criminal – indeed capital – punishment, as still on the books but passing out of use. As he described it, "on an indictment, which is at the suit of the king, the king may pardon and remit the execution; on an appeal, which is at the suit of a private subject . . . the king can no more pardon it than he can remit the damages recovered in an action of battery." (Blackstone, 1979, V4, ch. 23, p. 311.) See Friedman, 2001, ch. 14, 15, 18, at http://www.daviddfriedman.com/laws_order/index.shtml.

12. Friedman, 1979, at http://www.daviddfriedman.com/Academic/Iceland/Iceland.html. A killer would be sued by his victim's relatives and, if he lost the case and refused to pay damages, was at risk of being hunted down and killed by them.

13. Friedman, 1995, at http://www.daviddfriedman.com/Academic/England_18thc./England_18thc.html. Some enforcement was by prosecution associations, private organizations to prosecute felonies committed against their (dues-paying) members. By joining such an association – the membership was public information – an individual precommitted to the prosecution of felonies committed against him, making deterrence a private good.

14. Davies, 2002, argues that the private prosecution system was successfully dealing with problems of urbanization and was replaced by public police for other reasons – concern with preventing insurrection and with eliminating causes of crime by reforming the poor.

15. I still have to worry about technologies for listening to the sound of my keystrokes and deducing from that what I am typing, or observing electromagnetic signals from my computer monitor at a distance.

16. http://www.cnn.com/2004/TECH/12/07/computer.thought.reut/index.html describes an experiment in which individuals controlled a mouse by thinking – with their brain activity picked up by a cap that held sixty-four electrodes to detect brain activity. At the other extreme, keylogging is an approach to defeating computer privacy already in use – software that records your keystrokes as you operate your computer, saving them in a file that can later be used to reconstruct what you were doing; think of it as a virtual video mosquito watching you type. For the first criminal case involving keylogging, see http://news.com.com/2100–1023-983717.html.

Chapter 6

1. White, 1995.

2. The example is not wholly imaginary. At the end of the nineteenth century, the combined effect of the discovery of the South African gold fields and the invention of the cyanide process for extracting gold from low-grade ore led to a gold inflation, although a mild one compared to fiat money inflations. An earlier gold (and silver) inflation was produced in the sixteenth century by the inflow of both metals from the New World.

3. For a current product along these lines, see http://www.e-gold.com. So far as I know, their money is not anonymous ecash, but it is set up so that your holding is defined in gold but payments can be converted into a variety of currencies.

4. "London Letter to *Partisan Review*," in Orwell, 1968.

Chapter 7

1. http://www.psion.com/, http://www.psioninc.com/. Unfortunately, Psion has now abandoned the consumer market. If only they would license to Sony or Nokia the magic spell that made it possible for them, and only them, to build a usable keyboard into a palmtop or, better yet, a smartphone, I could have the machine of my dreams.

2. For an extensive discussion of reputational enforcement, see Klein, 1997.

3. This problem was apparently responsible for recent changes in eBay's feed-back policy; buyers were being deterred from leaving negative feedback on sellers by concern that the sellers would retaliate in kind. http://pages.ebay.com/services/forum/new.html.
4. Those interested in something beyond this highly stylized account may want to look at Lisa Bernstein's work on arbitration at http://www.law.uchicago.edu/faculty/bernstein/publications.html.
5. The costs of the arbitration, of course, are not zero. But they are paid by the people who signed the contract, not by the interested third parties.
6. As Bruce Benson has pointed out, such a process is how the Lex Mercatoria developed in the early Middle Ages. That too was a system of private law enforced by reputational penalties in an environment where state law was inadequate for contract enforcement, due in part to legal diversity across jurisdictions. See Benson, 1998, "Evolution of Commercial Law" and "Law Merchant."
7. A good fictional description of the combination of anonymity with online reputation occurs early in Stiegler, 1999.
8. Stiegler, 1999, contains an entertaining illustration of this point. A central character has maintained two online personae, one, with a good reputation, for legal transactions and another, with a deliberately shady reputation, for quasilegal transactions such as purchases of stolen property. At one point in the plot, his good persona is most of the way through a profitable honest transaction when it occurs to him that it would be even more profitable if, having collected payment for his work, he failed, at the last minute, to deliver. He rejects that option on the grounds that having a persona with a good reputation has just given him the opportunity for a profitable transaction, and if he destroys that reputation it will be quite a while before he is able to get other such opportunities.
9. See, for instance, Faille, 2007, a review of Greif, 2006, at http://www.reason.com/news/show/117079.html, or Friedman, 2005, at http://www.daviddfriedman.com/Academic/Course_Pages/analytical_methods_06/china_to_cyberspace.htm.

Chapter 8

1. http://www.law.wayne.edu/litman/papers/read.htm.
2. The final point is important, since it provides a way of blocking the analog hole discussed later in the chapter.
3. Note that this is a higher tech equivalent of one way in which trade secret law, with licensing, is currently enforced.
4. Recently Apple, which had been selling songs on iTunes in a protected format, announced that it was now going to sell unprotected songs at a slightly higher price.
5. A possible approach to overcoming that form of protection would be open source piracy, with many users pooling the information they individually obtained.

6. To date, the five-film "Star Wars" epic has taken in some $12.4 billion in movie tickets and merchandise sales worldwide, delivering a heavenly sum to distributor Twentieth Century Fox and Lucasfilm, the films' production company. Of that total, $3.4 billion has come from the worldwide box office and $9 billion from sales of "Battlefront" video games, Clone Trooper costumes, Obi-Wan Kenobi toy action figures, and other sundry gizmos, according to Lucasfilm (http://money.cnn.com/2005/03/31/news/newsmakers/starwars/index.htm?cnn=yes).

Chapter 9

1. http://www.daviddfriedman.com/Medieval/Medieval.html.
2. The Linux kernel is usually used with utilities and libraries from the GNU operating system, so the combination is sometimes referred to as GNU/Linux. http://en.wikipedia.org/wiki/Linux.
3. "Linus's Law," attributed to Linus Torvalds.
4. http://www.catb.org/~esr/; http://www.amazon.com/exec/obidos/tg/browse/-/565706/002–8218385–3353645.
5. For a much more extensive discussion of some of these issues, see Williamson, 1983.
6. *Wall Street Journal*, 12/24/01, p. B4. The web site is http://www.innocentive.com/.
7. The drug project is described at http://www.futurepundit.com/archives/002580.html. Or consider Amazon.com's Mechanical Turk, paying online workers to do things that AI is not yet quite up to: http://www.futurepundit.com/archives/003881.html.
8. For an old, but fictional, version, see Stout, 1948.
9. One could use a one-way hashing algorithm to produce a message digest of each message and store that instead of the complete message. The message digest cannot be used to reconstruct the message but can be used to check that it has not been changed, by seeing if it still hashes to the same digest.
10. Smith's account is webbed at http://www.remodern.com/caught.html.
11. http://www.msnbc.msn.com/id/17171372/.

Chapter 10

1. "Hacker" has come to be applied to people who do illegal things with computers, apparently as a result of a false back etymology; noncomputer people saw the term, guessed what it meant, and guessed wrong. In the computer culture a hacker is someone who does ingenious things in tricky and unconventional ways, such as a programmer who modifies a videogame program to run twice as fast via a trick – a hack – that may stop working the next time the operating system gets upgraded. I like to imagine a programmer observing an elephant for the first time: "It picks up things how? What a brilliant hack." Which is why I am using "cracker" instead.

2. Found unprotectable in *White-Smith Music Publishing Company v. Apollo Company*, 209 U.S. 1 (1908). The cam metaphor is due to John Hersey.
3. Friedman, 2001, chapter 11, at http://www.daviddfriedman.com/Laws_Order_draft/laws_order_ch_11.htm.
4. The case is *United States v. Seidlitz*, United States Court of Appeals, Fourth Circuit 589 F.2d 152 (1978); it is summarized at http://www.daviddfriedman.com/CCP_97/CCP97_outline.html#RTFToC9.
5. *Lund v. Virginia*, Supreme Court of Virginia 232 S.E.2d 745, 217 Va. 688 (1977), summarized at http://www.daviddfriedman.com/CCP_97/CCP97_outline.html#RTFToC8.
6. http://www.lightlink.com/spacenka/fors/ for general stuff, and http://www.lightlink.com/spacenka/fors/police/intelrep.txt for the initial report.
7. For a discussion of these technologies by someone who knows much more about them than I do, see Schneier, 1994, http://www.forum2.org/tal/books/crypto.html.
8. Still more generally, by creating some form of one-way encryption or hashing – a way of scrambling information that does not require you to have the information necessary to unscramble it.
9. http://www.mids.org/mn/604/remerlyn.html.

Chapter 11

1. Parker, 1983, pp. 50–51.
2. A recent news story describes a salami scheme that worked by adding small charges to the victims' phone bills: http://www.nytimes.com/2004/02/11/nyregion/11MOB.html.
3. Possibly the best known of the early computer criminals; he specialized in using social engineering to gain access to computers, spent five years in jail, and currently runs a computer security consulting business. http://en.wikipedia.org/wiki/Kevin_Mitnick.

Chapter 12

1. http://www.scientific.org/archive/Houston's%20Troubled%20DNA%20Crime%20Lab%20Faces%20Scrutiny.htm; http://www.cbsnews.com/stories/2003/03/17/national/main544209.shtml, or see multiple examples in Scheck, Neufeld, and Dwyer, 2000.
2. Hanson, 1994; also available on the Web at http://www.hss.caltech.edu/~hanson/wiretap-cacm.html.
3. Although Imperial China may have come close. See Bodde and Morris, 1973.
4. Friedman, 1995, at http://www.daviddfriedman.com/Academic/England_18thc./England_18thc.html.
5. For an essay arguing that existing institutions were dealing adequately with the problems of urbanization and explaining the shift to public policing in other terms, see Davies, 2002.

Chapter 13

1. Including George Bernard Shaw, H. G. Wells, John Maynard Keynes, Harold Laski, and the Webbs on the left, and Winston Churchill on the right. Opponents included G. K. Chesterton, the Catholic church, and Josiah Wedgewood, a radical libertarian M.P. (Ridley, 1999, pp. 292–295).
2. A still cruder form, exposing sickly infants, pre-dates Heinlein by several thousand years.
3. The obvious problem is that examining an egg or sperm is likely to damage it. Heinlein's ingenious solution – I do not know if it was his own invention or not – was to take advantage of the fact that each sperm contains half of the father's genes, having been produced by a process of division from a cell that contained all of them. The full genotype is reproduced in every cell, so we can, given suitably advanced gene-mapping technologies – which now exist and will soon be cheap – get it by destructively analyzing a few of them. We then analyze one-half of the split, destroying it in the process, and deduce what must be in the other half. We now know the genetic content of a sperm that we have not examined and so have not injured. An analogous process could be applied to eggs. In both cases, it probably requires that the final stage in producing egg or sperm occur outside the body, where we can keep track of what is happening.
4. Strictly speaking, clones created from an adult cell are identical only in the nuclear DNA; the mitochondrial DNA, which comes from the egg, is different unless the egg the nucleus is inserted into is from either the same individual as the cell or that individual's maternal ancestor (mother, mother's mother, . . .) or someone sharing an ancestor in the direct maternal line (mother's daughter, mother's mother's daughter, . . .). In the rest of the discussion I will ignore this complication for purposes of simplicity.
5. Lee Silver discusses this possibility in *Remaking Eden.*
6. In the case of two women, if the child is entirely theirs it must be a daughter, since neither has a Y chromosome to contribute. In the case of two men, it might be either a son or a daughter, since a male carries one X and one Y chromosome.

   Lee Silver (1998) describes two other technologies that could be used to produce children for same-sex couples. Each, however, gives a child who is only genetically 25% the product of each parent. In one case the child is a chimera – an organism produced by fusing two fertilized eggs, giving an individual half of whose cells come from one egg and half from the other. In the other case the child is, genetically speaking, the grandchild of the parental couple – the intervening generation having been aborted and the cells necessary to produce a fertilized egg harvested.
7. Different sources give different estimates; I am using 100 trillion, here and later, since it is a conveniently round number.
8. One such child became famous as the "bubble boy." See http://www. texaschildrenshospital.org/Web/50Years/patients_david.htm.

9. The tests were the Standardized Assessment Tests given, in the U.K., at the age of 7. Many news stories confused them with the U.S. SAT exam, given to students who are applying to college. An abstract of the original article is at http://www.ingentaconnect.com/content/bpsoc/bjp/2008/00000099/00000001/art00005.

10. See Heinlein, 1948, for a fictional account of an unsuccessful attempt to breed aggression out of the species.

11. This was one of the issues underlying Levin's *The Boys From Brazil*, 1991, a novel about a secret project to produce multiple clones of Adolf Hitler, later made into a successful movie.

12. Two possible examples of small-scale projects along those lines are the reported attempt by King Frederick William of Prussia to breed tall men to tall women in order to produce tall recruits for his regiment of "Potsdam Giants" and attempts by Hitler to get the best of German men and women to mate.

13. A real-world example – involving a kitten not a baby – was reported in late 2004: http://www.cnn.com/2004/TECH/science/12/23/gen.us.clonedcat.ap/index.html.

14. http://www.wikipedia.org/wiki/Sex-selective_abortion; http://www.theworldjournal.com/forum/viewthread.php?tid=256; http://www.kit.nl/ils/exchange_content/html/female_infanticide_-_sexual_he.asp; http://www.hsph.harvard.edu/rt21/medicalization/WEISS_Sex-selective.html; http://www.futurepundit.com/archives/002075.html.

15. One firm doing sperm sorting claims an 88% success rate for producing female offspring, 73% for male; http://www.futurepundit.com/archives/000186.html.

16. For a discussion of the relevant economics, see Friedman, 1986, chapter 21, at http://www.daviddfriedman.com/Academic/Price_Theory/PThy_Chapter_21/PThy_Chap_21.html.

17. Two interesting fictional discussions of these issues are Heinlein, 1966, and Schulman, 1983. The latter describes a world with a very high male-to-female ratio where women are drafted into temporary prostitution.

18. Silver, 1998.

Chapter 14

1. http://birding.about.com/library/weekly/aa071700d.htm; http://www.probe.org/docs/adultery.html. About 90% of avian species are monogamous, but a smaller fraction are long-term monogamous. The explanation is that both human and avian infants require biparental childcare. For a discussion of the link between that and mating patterns see, among others, Wright, 1994.

2. Baker and Bellis, 1992, cited in Ridley, 1995: "In a block of flats in Liverpool, they found by genetic tests that fewer than four in every five people were the sons of their ostensible fathers.... They did the same tests in southern England and got the same results." Numerous studies making estimates of cuckoldry rates among humans are summarized in Baker and Bellis, 2007.

See also www.meangenes.org – in particular http://www.meangenes.org/notes/notes.html#c8. One Swiss study, in contrast to the English, finds rates of "misidentified paternity" slightly below 1%. A similar figure comes out of the very large-scale Icelandic genetic study. An extensive survey of the literature is at http://www.childsupportanalysis.co.uk/analysis_and_opinion/choices and behaviours/misattributed_paternity.htm. Judging by that, the actual rate of misattributed paternity probably varies, across a large range of human societies, from about 1% to about 30%.

3. Quoted in *The New York Times*, October 28, 1973.
4. There is some evidence that infants resemble their fathers more than their mothers, which would provide an imperfect system of built-in paternity testing (Christenfeld and Hill, 1995). But see also Bredart and French, 1995, which failed to replicate the result, at http://www.u-bourgogne.fr/LEAD/people/french/father_resemblance.pdf.
5. Pinker, 2002.
6. Buss, 2004, pp. 199–202. The figure he cites is from Daly and Wilson, 1988.
7. Daly and Wilson, 1992, discusses behavior in birds related to male sexual jealousy; p. 294 gives the specific case of varying parental investment. The human evidence is on pp. 306–308.
8. See Buss, 2000, for a discussion of the evolutionary psychology of male jealousy.
9. Flinn, 1988, cited in Daly and Wilson, 1992, p. 302.
10. One could argue that it has already happened. Using old-fashioned reproductive technology, many women choose to bear children despite the lack of a father willing to help rear them. Evolutionary biology suggests that the father is probably selected, at least in part, for heritable characteristics he can pass on to her children. (Wright, 1994, chapter 3; Buss, 2004, chapter 6, especially pp. 175–186.)
11. Casanova, in his *Memoirs*, describes an affair with a married woman whose husband was impotent, undertaken with the husband's support in order to provide him with a legal heir. (Casanova, 1971, volume XI, chapter 10.)
12. *State v. Frisard*, 694 So. 2d 1032 (La. Ct. App. 1997).
13. Ridley, 1999, pp. 258–264.
14. Behavioral characteristics also appear also to be in part genetic, including some that might be viewed as ills of a different sort. For instance, twin studies by Professor Tim Spector, director of the Twin Research Unit at St Thomas' Hospital in London, show a large genetic element to female infidelity. See http://www.futurepundit.com/archives/002484.html.
15. The obvious exceptions were hermaphrodites and eunuchs.

Chapter 15

1. One issue particularly likely to raise such concerns is the introduction of human genes into other species, human or animal, to produce what might be described as chimeras. See http://www.futurepundit.com/archives/

003647.html for a recent discussion of the issue, and see http://www. daviddfriedman.com/Academic/Course_Pages/21st_century_issues/legal_ issues_21_2000_pprs_web/21st_c_papers_2000/green_monsanjo.htm for an entertaining student paper dealing with it, written for the seminar that produced this book.

2. It is sometimes suggested that one crucial difference between genetic engineering and evolution is that the former permits transgenic alterations – the insertion in the DNA of one species of genes from another. There is, however, some evidence that important evolutionary developments, including photosynthesis in multicelled organisms, are due to natural transgenic alterations, possibly "engineered" by viruses. For one discussion, see Knoll, 2004.

3. McNeill, 1978, and Oldstone, 1998.

4. http://www.newscientist.com/article.ns?id=dn2539.

5. The literature on this and related issues is surveyed in Mann, 2005; a review is at http://www.victorhanson.com/articles/thornton070206.html.

6. A detailed discussion of the case, including links to images of the letters, is at http://www.nativeweb.org/pages/legal/amherst/lord_jeff.html.

7. Alternatively, a lethal disease can exist in an environment sufficiently warm and moist to permit survival for a considerable time outside of the host.

Chapter 16

1. For reasonably objective information on drugs, see Rosen and Weil, 2004, and the Erowid web page, http://www.erowid.org/.

2. Wireheads appear in a number of Niven stories, including "Death by Ecstasy" in Niven, 1969.

3. The original calculations, long out of date, were in Stigler, 1945. A current version, for 1998 prices and RDA, is described in Gass and Garille, 2001, at http://solstice.uwaterloo.ca/~phcalama/Courses/SD311/Project/Group18/ Group18paper.pdf. "The updated problem shows that the optimal solution diet for a 25–50 year old man consists, on a daily basis, of 1.31 cups of wheat flour, 1.32 cups of rolled oats, 16 fluid ounces of milk, 3.86 tablespoons of peanut butter, 7.28 tablespoons of lard, 0.0108 ounces of beef liver, 1.77 bananas, 0.0824 of an orange, 0.707 cup of shredded cabbage, 0.314 of a carrot, 0.387 of a potato, and 0.53 cup of pork and beans. The daily cost of this diet is $1.78."

4. The more rigorous statistical equivalent finds obesity more common in lower income Americans, but not by much; http://paa2006.princeton.edu/ download.aspx?submissionId=60728.

5. http://www.cnn.com/2006/HEALTH/conditions/11/13/unnatural.highs/ index.html, CNN, November 17, 2006.

6. It may occur to some readers to wonder why, if being by nature very happy is a liability, there are any very happy people; why does my glow-in-the-dark friend exist? From the standpoint of evolutionary theory, the answer is that how successful a particular human design is depends in part on how common

it is. What we would expect, and what we observe in many areas, is not a single design for every human but a range. Tall people are better at, among other things, picking high-growing fruit. If there are few tall people there will be a lot of unpicked fruit high up, making height an advantage. If there are lots of tall people that advantage is no longer available to balance the disadvantages of height. Similarly for personality. If almost everyone is cautious, there will be attractive opportunities to be grabbed by the few who are brave. I will leave it to the reader to work out the advantages to being naturally happy in a world where everyone else is naturally glum.

7. Quoted at http://www.trebach.com/drugwar/ChemicallyEnhanced.html; Savulescu, Foddy, and Clayton is at http://bjsm.bmj.com/cgi/content/extract/38/6/666.

8. For a fairly detailed discussion, see Mehlman, Benger, and Wright, 2005.

9. Another answer that has been offered is that present athletes are competing against past athletes, trying to break their records. The past athletes did not have access to steroids, so steroid use by present athletes is unfair competition. Past athletes also did not have sports equipment reinforced by carbon fibers, modern training and diet regimens, and a variety of other things that present athletes have – but perhaps this is the one advantage we hope to be able to control.

10. U.S. military studies found that soldiers can stay awake and function alertly for 40 hours, get 8 hours of sleep, and then stay awake for 40 more, all without the impaired judgment of old-fashioned uppers. http://www.modafinil.com/article/soldiers.html. There is also evidence that the drug boosts mental abilities in other ways: http://www.futurepundit.com/archives/000534.html.

11. http://www.modafinil.com/article/soldiers.html from *The Ottawa Citizen*, October 11, 2003.

12. Ridley, 1999, p. 162.

13. From C. Robin Timmons and Leonard W. Hamilton, *Drugs, Brains, and Behavior*, at: http://www.rci.rutgers.edu/~lwh/drugs/chap02.htm, largely based on Timmons and Hamilton, 1990.

14. Spencer, McClintock, Sellergren, Bullivant, Jacob, and Mennella, JA, 2004. See also http://pheromones.com/professional.html.

15. "Drink Safe Technology" is a package of testing strips for date rape drugs.

16. Fisher, 2004, especially chapter 4.

17. Fisher, 2004, p. 89.

18. Fisher, 2004, pp. 89–92.

Chapter 17

1. For an intriguing fictional picture of a species where the old are no longer fertile but are utterly devoted to the welfare of their descendants, see Niven, 1973, and other books of his set in the same universe.

2. I do not know who first made this point, but it goes back at least to Drexler, 1987.

3. Medawar, 1946. For simplicity, I am ignoring here the distinction between lethal dominants and lethal recessives.
4. For a current project along these lines, DeGrey's Strategies for Engineered Negligible Senescence, see http://sens.org/.
5. *Consumer Reports*, January, 1992, p. 12. Some more recent studies have failed to detect any benefit from antioxidant supplements, however, and the question is still open.
6. Suppose everyone lives forever; how fast does population go up? Starting with what was a stable population of 10 billion, if each couple has 2 children and then stops we get about 15 billion in 30 years, 25 billion in a century; the growth pattern ends up linear. If every couple has 2 children every 40 years, on the other hand, we end up with an exponential growth pattern at 2.5% per year, giving about 21 billion in 30 years, 118 billion in a century, and over a trillion in two centuries.
7. In 1998, for example, of 401 incumbent congressional representatives who sought reelection, 395 won – a success rate of better than 98%. That somewhat exaggerates the advantage, since an incumbent who is confident of losing may decide not to run – but in that year there were a total of only 435 incumbents and presumably some of them decided to retire for other reasons.
8. Perhaps most famously stated by Sherlock Holmes, "A man should keep his little brain attic stocked with all the furniture that he is likely to need, and the rest he can put away in the lumber room of his library, where he can get it if he wants it." http://www.quoteworld.org/author.php?thetext=Sir%20Arthur%20Conan%20Doyle.
9. Elizabeth Moon was a 1st Lieutenant with the U.S. Marine Corps before she retired to write science fiction and fantasy. For a more famous example, consider Conrad, first a sailor and later a novelist.
10. This discussion ignores a variety of complications, such as the effect of such a pattern of saving and consumption on the market interest rate, which would carry us well beyond the limits of this book. See Robin Hanson's intriguing essay at http://www.primitivism.com/uploads-dawn.htm.
11. Arguably, "rehabilitation" may become much easier as a result of other technologies – VR immersion to show the criminal how the crime looked from the victim's point of view or using advanced biology or nanotechnology to revise the criminal's personality. Both pose the possibility of other and less defensible uses.
12. "Believing cryonics could reanimate somebody who has been frozen is like believing you can turn hamburger back into a cow." (Cryobiologist Arthur Rowe, quoted in "Frozen Future," *National Review*, July 9, 2002.) A webbed FAQ supporting cryonics points out in response that there are some vertebrates that can survive freezing but none that can survive grinding: http://www.faqs.org/faqs/cryonics-faq/part4/. Current procedures for cryonic suspension attempt to minimize the problem of damage from ice crystals by replacing body fluids with what is, in effect, antifreeze. A further

step, currently available for head-only suspension, is to vitrify rather than freeze the body's water – turning it solid without letting it crystallize.

13. For an intelligent discussion by a proponent of cryonics, see http://www.merkle.com/cryo/.

Chapter 18

1. Feynman, 1960. Later quotes in the chapter are from the same source.
2. This is a slight overstatement, since some DNA apparently carries no useful information.
3. Readers interested in the subject should probably start with Drexler, 1987. It is at http://www.foresight.org/EOC/index.html.
4. My thanks to Robert Freitas and Eric Drexler for useful comments on this chapter.
5. Feynman, in his 1959 speech, discussed building small tools, using them to build smaller tools, and so on all the way down. The same idea appears in Robert Heinlein's story *Waldo* (Heinlein, 1950).
6. For a more detailed discussion, see Freitas (1999, section 8.5.1), at http://www.nanomedicine.com.
7. Freitas, 1998, at http://www.foresight.org/Nanomedicine/Respirocytes.html.
8. Dawkins, 1986.
9. A solution I proposed, in a somewhat different context, in Friedman, 1973, chapter 25.
10. A problem with an early version of such a technology, minus the nanotech element, was brought to public attention by the 2004 S-class Mercedes. It used a fingerprint scanner for identification, which led to at least one owner losing a finger to carjackers: http://www.assaabloyfuturelab.com/FutureLab/Templates/Page2Cols__266.aspx.
11. Orwell 1949, part III, Chapter III.
12. Drexler's Foresight Institute has proposed a set of guidelines for avoiding some of the risks of nanotechnology: http://www.foresight.org/.
13. http://www.pbs.org/wgbh/pages/frontline/shows/plague/sverdlovsk/; http://www.nbc-med.org/SiteContent/MedRef/OnlineRef/CaseStudies/cssverdlovsk.html.
14. For a much more detailed analysis of the gray goo problem – aka ecophagy – see Freitas, 2000, at http://www.foresight.org/NanoRev/Ecophagy.html.
15. Both design and purpose are, of course, metaphorical, since evolution is not a conscious actor. But the implication of biological evolution – organisms designed as they would be by a designer whose objective was reproductive success – is the same as if they were deliberate.

Chapter 19

1. Silver, 1998.
2. Hollander, 1988.

3. For an early discussion of some of these issues, see Freitas, 1985. More recently, the courts have held that a computer can't practice law in Texas; http://www.rfreitas.com/Astro/LegalRightsOfRobots.htm.

4. Ian Banks' *Culture* novels provide a science fictional account of a society with people rather like us who are, in effect, the pets of vastly superior artificial intelligences.

Chapter 20

1. http://www.cbsnews.com/stories/2002/06/13/earlyshow/contributors/ tracysmith/main512169.shtml, http://www.halfbakery.com/idea/Arcade_ 20Treadmill. Perhaps more interesting is the Nintendo Wii, a video game whose controller is designed to let your onscreen avatar mirror your real-world actions – at least to the extent of following the movement of your hand. Sony's EyeToy achieved a similar effect by using a camera to watch your motions and tell the PlayStation 2 it was attached to what you were doing.

2. An experiment in which monkeys with brain implants were trained to move a robot arm with their thoughts is described at http://www.cbsnews.com/ stories/2003/10/13/tech/main577757.shtml. A simpler approach that has now been used for several patients with prosthetic arms surgically transfers nerve endings from shoulder to chest, so that nerve signals that would normally control the missing arm instead cause a twitch in the chest, which signals the prosthetic arm. http://www.washingtonpost.com/wp-dyn/content/article/ 2006/09/13/AR2006091302271_pf.html, http://www.danishtechnology.dk/ robot/20163,3.

3. "Raffles and Mrs. Blandish," in Orwell, 1968, pp. 212–224, at http://www. george-orwell.org/Raffles_and_Miss_Blandish/0.html.

4. Tod Kendall, "Pornography, Rape, and the Internet," currently at http://www. law.stanford.edu/display/images/dynamic/events_media/Kendall%20cover% 20+%20paper.pdf. The author provides substantially more evidence for his conclusion than my brief summary.

5. Some readers may be reminded of the world described in Lewis, 1946. For some reason he called it "Hell."

6. Nozick, 1974, pp. 42–45.

7. Castronovo, 2006, provides an interesting, although by now slightly out of date, discussion of massively multiplayer online games. For a description of gold farming as of June 2007, see http://www.nytimes.com/2007/06/17/ magazine/17lootfarmers-t.html?ex=1339732800&en=1676d344608cb590 &ei=5090&partner=rssuserland&emc=rss. For interesting comment by Steven Levitt, see http://freakonomics.blogs.nytimes.com/2007/06/19/gold-farmers-on-the-web/.

8. A fictional version of such a world, the Metaverse, is presented in Neil Stephenson's 1992 ingenious, entertaining, and not very serious science fiction novel

Snow Crash. An earlier version appears in Vernor Vinge's 1987 novelette *True Names*, mentioned back in Chapter 3 as perhaps the earliest description of the importance of online anonymity.

9. Nozick, 1974, chapter 10.

Chapter 21

1. Anderson, 1962.
2. This quote, and others in the chapter, are from Clarke, 1981, at http://www.spaceref.com/news/viewnews.html?id=844.
3. While it sounds like wild-eyed speculation, the idea of using buckytubes to support a space elevator was seriously proposed by Richard Smalley of Rice University, who was awarded the 1996 Nobel Prize in chemistry for his discovery of fullerenes, the family of carbon molecules to which buckytubes belong. Images of a variety of fullerenes can be found at http://cnst.rice.edu/pics.html. There is an optimistic article about using carbon nanotubes to build a space elevator, perhaps as soon as 2017, at http://www.sciencenews.org/20021005/bob9.asp.
4. The possibility of mining a planet's rotational energy suggests an interesting science fictional idea: An interstellar expedition discovers a planetary system none of whose planets are rotating, because the inhabitants used up all of their rotational energy – at which point their interplanetary civilization, based on transport using that energy, collapsed.
5. 1950 DA.
6. In this section I am to some degree violating my rule of only discussing the next few decades. While we might launch our first interplanetary spaceship that soon, it is very unlikely that we will reach another star before my self-imposed timer has run out.

Chapter 22

1. The numbers are based on calculations by R. J. Rummel at http://www.hawaii.edu/powerkills/welcome.html and http://www.freedomsnest.com/rumrud.html.
2. One could argue that the Chinese civil service system – exams open to all, with the high scorers awarded positions in the civil service that carried with them status and income in a polygenous society – was such a system of selective breeding. I do not know of any evidence that it was intended to be.
3. Read, 1958. At http://www.fee.org/pdf/books/I,%20Pencil%202006.pdf.
4. For a more detailed presentation of these ideas see Friedman, 2001, chapters 3 and 4.
5. An old estimate from Viscusi, 1991.
6. Friedman, 2000, p. 30. Also see Buchanan and Tullock, 1962, Mueller, 2003, and other works in the public choice literature.

7. The IPCC site is http://www.ipcc.ch/. The 2007 report is at http://www. ipcc.ch/ipccreports/ar4-wg2.htm. The upper end of the range of estimated sea level rise in the 2001 report was 80 cm. The 2007 report gives a variety of scenarios, predicting rises ranging from 0.18 to 0.59 meters while refusing to describe any of them as a maximum, and mentioning the possibility of much larger rises over periods of thousands of years and the inability to be certain that those will not occur over mere centuries. For a critique of the view of global warming as a massive catastrophe that must be stopped, see http://www.cato.org/pub_display.php?pub_id=9125. More drastic scenarios have been proposed that could lead to much larger increases in world sea levels, however, including some involving the collapse of the Antarctic ice sheet. See, for instance: http://www.abc.net.au/7.30/content/2007/s1870955.htm.

8. Friedman, 1972, at http://www.daviddfriedman.com/Academic/Laissez-Faire_In_Popn/L_F_in_Population.html.

9. For details of how markets allocate across time, see Friedman, 1996, chapter 12, or Friedman, 1986, chapter 12, at http://www.daviddfriedman.com/Academic/Price_Theory/PThy_Chapter_12/PThy_Chapter_12.html.

10. I sketch my views, and provide links to additional information, at http://daviddfriedman.blogspot.com/2007/02/global-warming-nanotech-and-who-to.html. "The latest results from the Geophysical Fluid Dynamics Laboratory (Knutson and Tuleya, *Journal of Climate*, 2004) suggest that by around 2080, hurricanes may have winds and rainfall about 5% more intense than today. It has been proposed that even this tiny change may be an exaggeration as to what may happen by the end of the 21st Century." (Chris Landsea, one of the authors of an earlier IPCC report, in his webbed explanation of why he publicly resigned from the IPCC in protest over politically motivated misstatements by the lead author of the section to which he had been asked to contribute.) http://sciencepolicy.colorado.edu/prometheus/archives/science_policy_general/000318chris_landsea_leaves.html.

Bibliography

al-Baari, Fath. *Sahih al-Bukhari*, 9th c. (The quote is from a translation webbed at http://members.tripod.com/safia71/pictures.htm.)

Anderson, Poul. 1962. *The Makeshift Rocket*, New York: Ace.

Ariosto, Ludovico. 1998. *Orlando Furioso.* Guido Waldman, tr. Oxford: Oxford University Press.

Baker, R. R., and Bellis, M. A. 1992. "Human Sperm Competition: Infidelity, the Female Orgasm and Kamikaze Sperm." Paper delivered to the Fourth Annual Meeting of the Human Behavior and Evolution Society, Albuquerque, NM, July 22–26, 1992.

Baker, R. R., and Bellis, M. A. 1994. *Human Sperm Competition: Copulation, Masturbation and Infidelity.* London: Chapman & Hall.

Barkow, Jerome H., Cosmides, Leda, and Tooby, John. 1992. *The Adapted Mind: Evolutionary Psychology and the Generation of Culture.* Oxford: Oxford University Press.

Benson, Bruce. 1989. "The Spontaneous Evolution of Commercial Law," *Southern Economic Journal,* Vol. 55, No. 3, pp. 644–661.

Benson, B. L. 1998. "Evolution of Commercial Law." In P. Newman, (ed.). *The New Palgrave Dictionary of Economics and the Law,* London: Macmillan Press.

Benson, B. L. 1998. "Law Merchant," In P. Newman, (ed.). *The New Palgrave Dictionary of Economics and the Law,* London: Macmillan Press.

Blackstone, William. 1979. *Commentaries on the Laws of England,* first ed. 1765–1769, Facsimile from University of Chicago Press.

Bodde, Dirk and Morris, Clarence. 1973. *Law in Imperial China.* Philadelphia: University of Pennsylvania Press.

Bredart, Serge and French, Robert M. 1999. "Do Babies Resemble Their Fathers More Than Their Mothers? A Failure to Replicate Chrstenfeld & Hill (1995)." *Evolution and Human Behavior,* Vol. 20, No. 3, pp. 129–135.

Buchanan, James and Tullock, Gordon. 1962. *The Calculus of Consent.* Ann Arbor: University of Michigan Press.

Buckley, William F. 2000. *Let Us Talk of Many Things: The Collected Speeches with New Commentary by the Author.* Forum. pp. xxii–xxiii. Rocklin: Prima Lifestyles.

Buss, David M. 2000. *The Dangerous Passion: Why Jealousy Is as Necessary as Love and Sex.* London: Bloomsbury Publishing.

Buss, David M. 2004. *Evolutionary Psychology: The New Science of the Mind.* Boston: Pearson.

Casanova, Giacomo. 1971. *History of My Life,* Willard R. Trask, tr. New York: Harcourt Brace and World.

Castronovo, Edward. 2006. *Synthetic Worlds.* Chicago: University of Chicago Press.

Christenfeld, N. and Hill, E. 1995. "Whose Baby Are You?" *Nature,* Vol. 378, p. 669.

Clarke, Arthur. 1981. "The Space Elevator: 'Thought Experiment', or Key to the Universe." In *Advances in Earth Oriented Applied Space Technologies,* Vol. 1. London: Pergamon Press.

Daly, Martin and Wilson, Margo. 1988. *Homicide.* New York: Aldine de Gruyter.

Daly, Martin and Wilson, Margo. 1992. "The Man Who Mistook His Wife for a Chattel." In *The Adapted Mind,* pp. 292–297.

Davies, Stephen. 2002. "The Private Provision of Police during the Eighteenth and Nineteenth Centuries," in *The Voluntary City: Choice, Community, and Civil Society,* ed. David T. Beito, Peter Gordon, and Alexander Tabarrok. Ann Arbor: University of Michigan Press.

Dawkins, Richard. 1986. *The Blind Watchmaker: Why the Evidence of Evolution Reveals a Universe without Design.* New York: Norton.

Diamond, Jared. 1987. "The Worst Mistake in the History of the Human Race," *Discover Magazine,* May, pp. 64–66.

Drexler, Eric. 1987. *Engines of Creation: The Coming Era of Nanotechnology.* New York: Anchor.

Faille, Christopher. 2007. "Trading on Reputation: Stateless Justice in the Medieval Mediterranean." *Reason Magazine,* January, pp. 66–69.

Feynman, Richard. 1960. "There's Plenty of Room at the Bottom," Engineering and Science (California Institute of Technology), February, pp. 22–36. Reprinted in B.C. Crandall and James Lewis, eds., *Nanotechnology: Research and Perspectives,* MIT Press, 1992, pp. 347–36.

Fisher, Helen. 2004. *Why We Love: The Nature and Chemistry of Romantic Love.* New York: Owl Books.

Flinn, Mark. 1988. "Parent–Offspring Interactions in a Caribbean Village: Daughter Guarding." In *Human Reproductive Behaviour: A Darwinian Perspective,* eds. L. Betzig, M. Borgerhoff Mulder, and P. Turke, pp. 189–200. Cambridge: Cambridge University Press.

Foldvary, Fred E., and Klein, Daniel B. eds. 2003. *The Half-Life of Policy Rationales: How New Technology Affects Old Policy Issues.* New York: NYU Press.

Freeman, Derek. 1983. *Margaret Mead and Samoa: The Making and Unmaking of an Anthropological Myth.* Cambridge: Harvard University Press.

Freitas, Robert. 1985. "Can the Wheels of Justice Turn for Our Friends in the Mechanical Kingdom? Don't Laugh. . . . " *Student Lawyer,* 13(January), pp. 54–56.

Freitas, Robert. 1999. *Nanomedicine, Vol. I: Basic Capabilities.* Austin: Landes Bioscience.

Freitas, Robert A. Jr. 1998. "Exploratory Design in Medical Nanotechnology: A Mechanical Artificial Red Cell," *Artificial Cells, Blood Substitutes, and Immobilization Biotechnology*, 26 (4), pp. 411–430.

Freitas, Robert A. Jr. 2000. "Some Limits to Global Ecophagy by Biovorous Nanoreplicators, with Public Policy Recommendations," Foresight Institute, April.

Friedman, D. 1972. "Laissez-Faire in Population: The Least Bad Solution," New York: Population Council. (Occasional Paper).

Friedman, D. 1973. *The Machinery of Freedom: Guide to a Radical Capitalism*. New York: Harper and Row.

Friedman, D. 1979. "Private Creation and Enforcement of Law – A Historical Case." *Journal of Legal Studies* Vol. 8, No. 2 (March), pp. 399–415.

Friedman, D. 1986. *Price Theory: An Intermediate Text*. Cincinnati: Southwestern.

Friedman, D. 1994. "A Positive Account of Property Rights," *Social Philosophy and Policy*, Vol. 11, No. 2 (Summer), pp. 1–16.

Friedman, D. 1995. "Making Sense of English Law Enforcement in the Eighteenth Century," *The University of Chicago Law School Roundtable* (Spring/Summer), pp. 475–505.

Friedman, D. 1996. *Hidden Order: The Economics of Everyday Life*. New York: Collins.

Friedman, D. 2000. "Privacy and Technology." In *The Right to Privacy*, ed. Ellen Frankel Paul, Fred D. Miller, Jr., and Jeffrey Paul. Cambridge: Cambridge University Press.

Friedman, D. 2001. *Law's Order: What Economics Has to Do with Law and Why It Matters*. Princeton: Princeton University Press.

Friedman, D. 2005. "From Imperial China to Cyberspace: Contracting without the State," *Journal of Law, Economics, and Policy* 1, pp. 349–370.

Gass, S. I. and Garille, S. 2001. "Stigler's Diet Problem Revisited." *Operations Research*, Vol. 49, No. 1, pp. 1–13.

Greif, Avner. 2006. *Institutions and the Path to the Modern Economy: Lessons from Medieval Trade*. New York: Cambridge University Press.

Hanson, Robin. 1994. "Can Wiretaps Remain Cost Effective?" *Communications of the ACM*, December.

Heinlein, Robert. 1948. *Beyond This Horizon*. Reading: Fantasy Press.

Heinlein, Robert. 1950. *Waldo and Magic, Inc*. Garden City: Doubleday.

Heinlein, Robert. 1966. *The Moon Is a Harsh Mistress*. New York: Putnam.

Hirschleifer, J. 1971. "The Private and Social Value of Information and the Reward to Inventive Activity." *American Economic Review*, Vol. 61, No. 3, pp. 562–574.

Hollander, Lee M. tr. 1988. *Saga of the Jomsviking*. Austin: University of Texas Press.

Klein, Daniel B. ed. 1997. *Reputation: Studies in the Voluntary Elicitation of Good Conduct*, Ann Arbor: University of Michigan Press.

Knoll, Andrew H. 2004. *Life on a Young Planet: The First Three Billion Years of Evolution on Earth*. Princeton: Princeton University Press.

Levin, Ira. 1991. *The Boys from Brazil*. New York: Bantam.

Lewis, C. S. 1946. *The Great Divorce*. New York: Macmillan.

Mann, Charles C. 2005. *1491: New Revelations of the Americas before Columbus*, New York: Knopf.

McNeill, William H. 1978. *Plagues and Peoples.* New York: Anchor.

Meadows, Donella H., Meadows, Dennis L., Randers, Jørgen, and Behrens, William W. III. 1972. *Limits to Growth.* New York: Signet.

Medawar, P. B. 1946. "Old Age and Natural Death." *Modern Quarterly* 1, pp. 30–56.

Mehlman, Maxell J., Benger, Elizabeth, and Wright, Matthew M. 2005. "Doping in Sports and the Use of State Power," *Saint Louis University Law Journal,* Vol. 50, No. 1, Fall, pp. 15–73.

Mencken, H. L. 1900. *In Defense of Women.* New York: Knopf.

Mueller, Dennis C. 2003. *Public Choice III.* Cambridge: Cambridge University Press.

Niven, Larry. 1969. *The Shape of Space.* New York: Ballantine.

Niven, Larry. 1973. *Protector.* New York: Ballantine.

Nozick, Robert. 1974. *Anarchy, State, and Utopia.* New York: Basic Books.

Oldstone, Michael B. A. 1998. *Viruses, Plagues, and History.* Oxford: Oxford University Press.

Orwell, George. 1949. *Nineteen Eighty-Four.* New York: Harcourt Brace.

Orwell, Sonia and Angus, Ian eds. 1968. *The Collected Essays, Journalism and Letters of George Orwell.* Volume III. New York: Harcourt Brace Jovanovich.

Parker, Don B. 1983. *Fighting Computer Crime.* New York: Scribner.

Pinker, Steven. 2002. *The Blank Slate: The Modern Denial of Human Nature.* New York: Viking.

Posner, Richard. 1978. "An Economic Theory of Privacy," *Regulation,* May/June, pp. 19–26.

Posner, Richard. 1978. "The Right of Privacy," *Georgia Law Review,* Vol. 12, No. 3 (Spring), pp. 393–428.

Read, Leonard. 1958. "I, Pencil: My Family Tree as Told to Leonard Read." *The Freeman,* Vol. 8, No. 12, pp. 32–37.

Ridley, Matt. 1999. *Genome . . . The Autobiography of a Species in 23 Chapters.* New York: HarperCollins.

Ridley, Matt. 1995. *The Red Queen: Sex and the Evolution of Human Nature.* New York: Penguin.

Rosen, Winifred and Weil, Andrew T. 2004. *From Chocolate to Morphine: Everything You Need to Know about Mind-Altering Drugs.* Boston: Houghton Mifflin.

Savulescu, J., Foddy, B., and Clayton, M. 2004. "Why We Should Allow Performance Enhancing Drugs in Sport." *British Journal of Sports Medicine,* Vol. 38, No. 6, pp. 666–670.

Sayers, Dorothy. 1947. *Unpopular Opinions.* New York: Harcourt Brace.

Scheck, Barry, Neufeld, Peter, and Dwyer, Jim. 2000. *Actual Innocence: Five Days to Execution, and Other Dispatches from the Wrongly Convicted.* New York: Doubleday.

Schneier, Bruce. 1994. *Applied Cryptography: Protocols, Algorithms, and Source Code in C.* Hoboken: Wiley.

Schulman, J. Neil. 1983. *The Rainbow Cadenza.* New York: Simon & Schuster.

Silver, Lee M. 1998. *Remaking Eden.* London: Weidenfeld & Nicholson.

Spencer, N. A., McClintock, M. K., Sellergren, S. A., Bullivant, S., Jacob. S., and Mennella, J. A. 2004. "Social Chemosignals from Breastfeeding Women Increase Sexual Motivation," *Hormones and Behavior,* Vol. 46, No. 3, pp. 362–370.

Stephenson, Neil. 1992. *Snow Crash.* New York: Bantam.

Sterling, Bruce. 1992. *The Hacker Crackdown: Law and Disorder on the Electronic Frontier.* New York: Bantam.

Sterling, Bruce. 1997. *Holy Fire.* New York: Bantam.

Stiegler, Marc. 1999. *Earthweb.* Riverdale: Baen.

Stigler, G. 1945. "The Cost of Subsistence," *Journal of Farm Economics,* Vol. 25, No. 2, pp. 303–314.

Stout, Rex. 1948. *"And Be a Villain."* New York: Viking.

Timmons, C. Robin and Hamilton, Leonard W. 1990. *Principles of Behavioral Pharmacology.* Upper Saddle River: Prentice Hall.

Vinge, Vernor. 1987. *True Names . . . and Other Dangers.* Riverdale: Baen.

Viscusi, W. Kip. 1991. *Reforming Products Liability.* Cambridge: Harvard University Press.

White, Lawrence H. 1995. *Free Banking in Britain: Theory, Experience and Debate, 1800–1845.* London: Institute for Economic Affairs.

Williamson, Oliver E. 1983. *Markets and Hierarchies: Analysis and Antitrust Implications.* New York: Free Press.

Wright, Robert. 1994. *The Moral Animal: Evolutionary Psychology and Everyday Life.* New York: Vintage.

Index